Big Change, Best Path

Successfully managing organizational change with wisdom, analytics and insight

Warren Parry

accenturestrategy

KoganPage

LONDON   PHILADELPHIA   NEW DELHI

*To my teachers and to Terhi, Anttoni and Kristo
from whom I have learned so much*

First published in Great Britain and the United States in 2015 by Kogan Page Limited

2nd Floor, 45 Gee Street
London EC1V 3RS
United Kingdom
www.koganpage.com

1518 Walnut Street, Suite 1100
Philadelphia PA 19102
USA

4737/23 Ansari Road
Daryaganj
New Delhi 110002
India

Warren Parry asserts his moral right to be identified as the author of this book.
Copyright © Accenture, 2015

The right of Warren Parry to be identified as the author of this work has been asserted by him in accordance with the Copyright, Designs and Patents Act 1988.

ISBN   978 0 7494 6942 9
E-ISBN   978 0 7494 6943 6

British Library Cataloguing-in-Publication Data

A CIP record for this book is available from the British Library.

Library of Congress Cataloging-in-Publication Data

Parry, Warren, author.
  Big change, best path : successfully managing organizational change with wisdom, analytics and insight / Warren Parry.
    pages cm
  ISBN 978-0-7494-6942-9 (paperback) – ISBN 978-0-7494-6943-6 (ebk)   1. Organizational change–Management.   I. Title.
  HD58.8.P3627 2015
  658.4′063–dc23

                                                                    2015031270

Typeset by Graphicraft Limited, Hong Kong
Print production managed by Jellyfish
Printed and bound by CPI Group (UK) Ltd, Croydon CR0 4YY

CONTENTS

07   *On Track*: Win the war for resources and move out of the middle ground   143

08   *In the Dark*: Mobilize around the vision   165

09   *Sleepy in Success*: Get back in the game   191

10   *Building Momentum*: When good is not good enough to jump to the next level   219

11   *On the Run*: Keep it together when the goal is rapid growth   245

For additional resources, please visit **www.accenture.com/changetracking**

Learn about the Change Map at **www.accenture.com/changemap**

FOREWORD

We live in times of great uncertainty and an ever-increasing pace of change. The inexorable advance of technology and the digital revolution, continued globalization alongside geo-political uncertainty, changing demographics and even the expectations and attitudes of younger consumers and employees are all making their impact felt.

As a result, the importance of agility, adaptability and innovation have risen to the top of the agenda for businesses everywhere. Charles Darwin's understanding of evolution – the need to adapt to survive – has never been more pertinent to the context of business. However, being able to understand the need for organizational change is one thing; the real priority now is the ability to execute change, and to be able to create and sustain this ability on an ongoing basis. The days when organizations had the time and luxury to 'unfreeze' and 'refreeze' before dealing with the next change programme are clearly over.

The problem, though, is that our ability to effectively manage big change in organizations is patchy at best. Many change initiatives fail to deliver on their objectives, falling significantly short or failing altogether. They run over budget, miss their performance goals or are unable to sustain improvements over the longer term.

Understanding organizational change has long been a focus for business leaders and academics, reaching way back to FW Taylor in the early 1900s, the father of scientific management and probably the world's first management consultant. Yet despite all the methods, tools, models and writing on the subject, why is it then that so many businesses still struggle so much with managing organizational change?

A critical issue has been the lack of empirical evidence and real analytical insight on how change really works in organizations, large and small. Because of that, the tendency has been to apply the traditional methods of programme management and change management in a one-size-fits-all, often one-dimensional view of an organization. And so executives and managers have stuck to long-established models of change, such as the change commitment curve, or mantras of communication, creating 'change champions' and training people.

Savvy business leaders know that one-size-fits-all approaches are limited because everyone in the organization will have a different perception of a change initiative. Top management may believe that all the changes are aligning to the strategy and that progress is being made. Middle managers, however, might be struggling, constantly putting out fires and unable to keep up with all the changes. Meanwhile, the people and teams that are most directly affected by new systems and changing job roles might be feeling completely overwhelmed and threatened. Stress at these levels of an organization is among the highest, often accompanied by lower engagement.

Clearly myriad variables are involved in organizational change. Management needs to pull numerous levers, but in what sequence and with how much force? What's needed are more data, additional insights and a common language to be able to express where people are and how they are feeling, and then to know which actions to take for each group of employees to align with the overall change.

Enter Warren Parry. Over more than fifteen years of research, he and his team have created the most comprehensive dataset on what happens during the process of change. To date, they have collected data from more than 750,000 individual respondents, across hundreds of change programmes in more than 150 organizations across all sectors and sizes. And now, under the ownership of Accenture, with its scale and reach, this dataset continues to grow. From it, they have gained fascinating insights into how people across organizations understand and respond to change, what makes a difference and what doesn't. They are now even able to predict change outcomes by identifying the dynamics occurring within an organization.

I first worked with Warren over 10 years ago, and I could see that the methods, tools, visualization techniques and insights he generated would provide a new, much deeper understanding of the dynamics of change. The models of change, the drivers of change and the ways of understanding outcomes were drawn from numerous sources, but then refined over many years from the actual data and patterns of change that were starting to emerge.

Given the huge dataset, one of the most significant challenges has been to uncover meaning from the information. Because there are many variables involved, traditional regression analyses would be too limiting and would impose hypotheses on the data, when it was really important to be able to approach the data with an open mind – let the data tell the story. As such, Warren and his team adopted emergent statistical pattern-recognition approaches, in particular, a technique called self-organizing maps (SOMs).

This was a first in the field of business and management, requiring some groundbreaking work in visualization. Outputs from statistical analyses are typically unintelligible for anyone not versed in the techniques, and that is particularly true for SOMs. Being able to visualize the many insights has been critical to advancing the research and its practical applications. The map analogy used throughout this book, and the ability to turn statistical data outputs into a 3D map-like image with the sense of the journey and the many different routes towards the top of the mountain, has been an incredibly powerful heuristic. It allows people to quickly understand the constructs, the insights and the position that different groups will find themselves on during a journey of change. Indeed, the database itself is gathered from what Warren has always referred to as the 'wisdom of the travellers', that is, the people themselves who were involved in or experiencing change journeys.

One of the first and most important insights from the research has been to help answer the question empirically about the actual rates of change success. According to the data, somewhere between one in three or four of all groups implementing change initiatives improve their performance; about the same number stay the same; around one in five shuffle sideways and then return back to where they were; and a little over one in four get worse. These results provide a slightly more optimistic view of failure rates than much of the research to date, but that may in part be due to the self-selected group of organizations that are motivated to undertake the systematic tracking of change in the first place.

As the change database has grown over time, consistent patterns and behaviours of change in organizations large and small became evident across all kinds of industries. The notion of 'capital cities' as the most frequented regions of the map emerged as a way of explaining how different starting or landing points exist on the change map. These hugely reinforce the idea that change is not one journey; instead it's travel through many co-existent states. Thus different parts of the organization, various teams and even individuals can be affected by and perceive changes in quite different ways. It then follows that effective organization change management will thus require different actions and interventions depending on where people are.

The data clearly show this, as there are well-trodden paths between the different capital cities that are driven by different combinations of interventions. Not all the paths lead upwards to higher performance, so the power of the analysis and the insights from the research are to provide not only a view as to where the different parts of an organization are at any point in time, but also to be able to define and predict what will be the best combination of interventions to move each group – and therefore the change programme – in the right direction. The different capital cities, and the different routes and paths are all explained in detail through the different chapters of this book.

In the end, though, the most important insights are what management interventions work and what are the dominant factors in successful change programmes. As it turns out, some of the most common and long-held beliefs of organization change management don't stand up to scrutiny when examined in the cold light of this kind of extensive data and sophisticated analytics. The research, for example, makes clear that change programmes themselves are not the primary cause of organizational dysfunctions; they merely expose those dysfunctions. In other words, trying to implement a major change programme at an organization that lacks adequate leadership, employee alignment around a reasonably coherent vision, trust in management and so on will likely be setting up the initiative to fail. To use another analogy, we need to start with the chicken and not always focus solely on the egg.

Another myth about change that the research fundamentally challenges is the idea that there is always an initial performance dip because of people's inertia and resistance to change (the so-called commitment curve). But when trusting relationships are in place, performance tends to improve across all stages of a change programme as employees willingly commit to the initiative up front before they really know exactly where they're headed. In essence, successful change is as much an emotional as an intellectual process and people don't need to know everything in advance. This insight really resonates with me, as its clear that this long held view that people are always resistant to change can't be true, and we need to adopt a more positive model of thinking and work harder to engage people effectively.

Of all the myriad factors that determine the success or failure of change programmes, trust in leadership is one of the most important. In the end, we can communicate all we like, encourage, cajole or spend considerably on training, but if trust in leaders is not there then any successful outcome becomes highly uncertain. This is an extremely important lesson that leaders in all walks of life have been needing to confront much more in recent years. The global financial crisis that began in 2007 massively damaged trust in a vital part of the economy, and there have been far too many abuses of trust across all walks of life, from politics to sports. Business leaders now talk regularly about restoring trust with customers, shareholders and, albeit less frequently, with their own organizations and employees. The process has to start with a clarity of vision and direction, with an aligned sense of purpose, and then with authenticity and integrity in actions and behaviours. All these attributes can be seen clearly from the research highlighted throughout this book. Ideally, employees should be in a state in which they trust both the senior leadership and their own managers and are therefore prepared to support change with a motto along the lines of, 'Fine, let's get on with it. Just tell me what I need to know or where we are going along the way'.

This book is rich in content, both in its insights and ideas. It provides invaluable information for business leaders, for change management consultants and practitioners and for professionals in HR and other functions like finance who might also have a strong interest in the successful progress of change. This book has been the culmination of many years of research built around a clear vision of how analytics can help us find our way, all of which could not have been possible without the passion, foresight and relentless commitment of Warren Parry. He has created something unique and valuable for all of us who are seeking to understand how to make organizations better, to manage the constancy of change and to create agility and adaptability. This book challenges many of our long-held beliefs, and it needed to. Meanwhile, the base of data continues to grow, and we will continue to learn. At last we are able to put some science together with the art of organizational change. The goal is to help generate a higher level of success – something that would be worth billions of dollars if we are to believe the statistics – and to bring a much sharper focus to the practice of organization change management.

Peter Cheese
Chief Executive
Chartered Institute of Personnel and Development (CIPD)

ACKNOWLEDGEMENTS

This book is the result of the efforts of many people across a long period of time. I would like to thank them for their generous support, for the insights shared throughout the process and for the tremendous effort in developing and refining the ideas to finally put them down in book form. My deepest gratitude goes to my research colleagues, who conducted the research that lies at the heart of this book and with whom I have had the privilege of working for over 15 years; and to the Accenture Strategy book-writing team, who have been with me every step of the way for the last 15 months to write down the research insights and produce the book in its final form.

Research colleagues

I am indebted to Paul Carey, Dr Doug Shaw, Dr Stephen Fraser, Cameron Peake and Jonathan Spittle for their commitment and passion to discover what really drives change in organizations. It has truly been a remarkable journey; testing, shaping and validating the research insights with our clients.

Paul's depth and breadth of knowledge in the field of organizational behaviour change has been a guiding light since our first meeting in 1996. His rigorous approach to statistical analysis has shaped our research agenda and forms the cornerstone of this book. Doug joined our team in the early days to independently validate our change model while he worked for the Commonwealth Scientific and Industrial Research Organisation (CSIRO) (in November 2003). He has remained a trusted adviser, guiding our approach and methodology development, bringing critical thinking along with practical judgement to the most difficult analytical problems we faced along the way. I came to the world of research from a background in architecture, fine arts, psychology and business. I am indebted to Paul and Doug for acting as my mentors, patiently responding to my endless questioning. Discovering the power of pattern recognition through the use of change maps was one of the most important 'step jumps' in our research. Stephen Fraser from CSIRO made that jump possible by his far-sighted application of self-organizing maps (SOM) to our change database. Cameron Peake also enabled that jump by his creative use of analytics to visualize algorithms, making simple what was extremely complex. Cameron remains at the forefront of the research today in Accenture, leading our analytics team in the development of digital applications. Jonathan Spittle, who worked alongside me in Change Track Research since our earliest days, tested the ideas and insights we discovered with clients. Leading hundreds of discussions on client results and providing sharp feedback meant our research was deeply grounded in realities that managers faced every day as they sought to bring about change in their organizations.

I also wish to thank many others who contributed to the research effort, in particular Dr Christina Kirsch, who worked for many years with me to deepen and share our research findings in an academic context; and to Dr Simon Poon and Paul Lui from the University of Sydney, who undertook further work to independently validate our findings.

It is also important to recognize that funding and a whole host of other resources were needed to sustain this level of research effort. To quantify the amount of effort involved, we already had undertaken more than 5,000 research and development (R&D) days when we joined Accenture in 2013. Since then, within Accenture we have been able to carry out much more research. And, in addition, I wish to express my thanks to CSIRO for supporting our research and to the Australian government for recognizing our innovative work through the awarding of R&D grants in 2008, 2010 and 2011.

Putting in place the legal agreements needed to collect and store data and to manage intellectual property has been essential to our work. I express my thanks for the invaluable contribution from our lawyer Mark Davidson, and my admiration of the skills of Charles Berman, our patent attorney who was able to conceptualize and capture our ideas in writing when even we were struggling to define what those ideas were in the early stages. Moreover, I am thankful for the administrative and logistical support provided by many staffers who worked for and with Change Track Research – Johanna Baker, Vanessa Shearman, Peter Campbell, Bill Henderson, David Wong, Simon Stephens, Rick Mare and his team.

Book-writing team

Turning research insights into a book was a huge undertaking that would not have been possible without the dedicated efforts of Karen Wolf, Tim Gobran and Cameron Peake from Accenture Strategy; and Paul Carey, Doug Shaw, Alden Hayashi and Elizabeth Moller. The effort, passion and determination of this team over the last 15 months to refine the insights and concepts and present them both in text and graphics have been nothing short of remarkable, and I express my deep gratitude.

Karen's ability to 'sort the wheat from the chaff' meant that we kept a razor-sharp focus on communicating the key messages in what could have easily become an overwhelming amount of information. Tim's deep knowledge of organizational change practices helped ensure that our insights were turned into practical actions that empower leaders and managers of change, and he skilfully kept our project team on track with necessary deadlines. Elizabeth attended to the many details that were needed to bring the work across the finish line. Paul, Doug and Cameron were involved every step of the way and I am thankful for their efforts in drafting and reviewing manuscripts and, where needed, they helped validate the research findings as we progressed through the chapters. Alden's considerable skills in writing (and rewriting) brought together the manuscript, ensuring that readers could more easily understand the complex ideas that we were presenting.

While the book team attended the overall design and the smallest details, I am indebted to a number of critical readers who invested many hours in reading drafts and providing feedback about what needed to be improved. Their frankness and helpful insight are much appreciated. I would like to thank Randy Wandmacher from Accenture for his valuable insights from his extensive background in organizational change. Many thanks also to my colleague and friend Sam Pearson for reading drafts and for willingly sharing his experience and wisdom, having been a global change manager himself. In addition, I am appreciative of Greg Oaten's feedback, bringing practical advice in managing change in difficult organizational environments.

My thanks also go to the highly professional team at Kogan Page. Helen Kogan endorsed the book from day one and Melody Dawes and her team have offered valuable feedback and kept us on track as we managed all the assorted details of publishing.

All that said, any remaining weakness in the story line or lack of accuracy in the facts or interpretation remain mine, and mine alone.

Support for the research vision and this book

I also want to express deep thanks to those who helped me sustain the vision for the book from the time of its earliest infancy to where it is now. It is remarkable to see how the smallest of ideas can grow and develop if the right support and encouragement are provided.

Robert Peake, John Ashby, Dr Dexter Dunphy and Dr Bruce Hobbs were early supporters who recognized the need for sophisticated analytics. I am indebted to them for their belief in my ideas and for their continued encouragement to keep researching, developing the ideas and writing them down. Margareta Lonnberg's encouragement played a critical role when I moved from a focus on leadership development into the wider context of organizational change.

Accenture has been the earliest adopter of an insight-driven approach to change, largely due to the foresight of Peter Cheese and Aimie Chapple. They recognized the importance of measuring change in organizations, and I am indebted to them for their encouragement to expand the scope of the research and take the development of the methodology to the next level. Peter's enthusiastic support over the last 10 years has left his mark on this book. During many times when it was difficult to see the forest from the trees, his sharp perceptions and deep understanding of what it really takes to manage people are what made the difference.

In 2005, after having invested a considerable amount of time, money and effort in the research but feeling very much 'in the dark', I questioned whether or not I had gone down the wrong path. Comments from Dr Bob Thomas at the Accenture Institute for High Performance helped sustain my efforts. After listening to me for 20 minutes he said, 'You are two years ahead of us and anyone else', helping me realize I was not crazy to pursue this path and recognize the importance of colleagues who shared the same vision.

The core Accenture Change Tracking team that I work with has provided daily inspiration. In addition to others I have already mentioned, I would like to thank Nicholas Whittall, Elizabeth Wagner, Sameer Mathur, Jane Buttsworth, Andy James and all those in the Accenture Interactive team led by Dr Stephen Kirkby.

There are many others at Accenture who have opened doors and shared invaluable lessons from a wider global community: Trevor Gruzin, David Smith, Walter Gossage, Yaarit Silverstone, Himanshu Tambe, David Andrews and Paul O'Keeffe, to name a few. My many thanks also to all the consultants with whom I have worked over the years. Their feedback has helped to add to the body of knowledge and to validate research findings across all levels of the organization and across a very diverse range of industries and cultures. From inside and outside Accenture, numerous clients, scholars, strategists and consultants have generously given their time, experience and expertise.

I also save my deepest thanks for those clients that have enabled us to gain a more profound understanding of what it means to manage change at scale in large complex initiatives. I am indebted to the numerous leaders and managers in many organizations who have had the courage and sheer persistence to more successfully manage change. Without their willingness and the willingness of the many thousands of staffers who have taken the time to share their personal journeys through our surveys, our research would not have been possible. I hope this book is a testament to the collective wisdom expressed by all of those travellers we have met along the way, and I hope that we have done justice to the stories and journeys that they shared with us.

Family and friends

Let me finally give a special set of thanks to recognize the support provided by my family and friends who enthusiastically believed in me and this book. I can't thank them enough.

The patient support and emotional encouragement from my wife, Terhi Hakola, enabled me to write this book. As a creative person herself – a doctor and artist who knows what it takes to heal people and to give birth to new ideas – she provided the support that helped me to persevere through the many struggles to bring this book to the light of day. Lastly, growing up in a world where my two boys, Anttoni and Kristo, simply accept many changes in society that I have struggled to come to terms with, I have found that their willingness to share their views and challenge my assumptions has repeatedly brought fresh perspectives, for which I am very grateful.

Warren Parry

Publisher's acknowledgements

For the chapter epigraphs, thanks to:

Megginson, LC (1963). From 'Lessons from Europe for American Business', *Southwestern Social Science Quarterly* 44 (1): 3–13. Brotton, J (2012). From A HISTORY OF THE WORLD IN 12 MAPS by Jerry Brotton, copyright © 2012 by Jerry Brotton. Used by permission of Viking Books, an imprint of Penguin Publishing Group, a division of Penguin Random House LLC; A HISTORY OF THE WORLD IN 12 MAPS by Jerry Brotton, copyright © 2013 by Jerry Brotton, London, page 6. Reproduced by permission of Penguin Books Ltd. Levine, A (2014). From *On the Edge: The Art of High-Impact Leadership* by Alison Levine. Copyright © 2014 by Alison Levine.

Used by permission of Business Plus, an imprint of Grand Central Publishing. Moore, T (2004). 'Introduction – The Dark Night' from DARK NIGHTS OF THE SOUL by Thomas Moore, copyright © 2004 by Thomas Moore. Used by permission of Gotham Books, an imprint of Penguin Publishing Group, a division of Penguin Random House LLC; also used by permission of Little, Brown Book Group Ltd. Hawking, S (1993). Excerpt(s) from BLACK HOLES AND BABY UNIVERSES AND OTHER ESSAYS: AND OTHER ESSAYS by Stephen Hawking, copyright © 1993 by Stephen W Hawking. Used by permission of Bantam Books, an imprint of Random House, a division of Penguin Random House LLC. All rights reserved. Any third party use of this material, outside of this publication, is prohibited. Interested parties must apply directly to Penguin Random House LLC for permission; also used by permission of Writers House. Hillary, E. Used by permission of the Sir Edmund Hillary estate, **www.edhillary.com**. Sun Tzu. From *The Art of War*, translated by Thomas Cleary, © 1988, 1991 by Thomas Cleary. Reprinted by arrangement with The Permissions Company, Inc, on behalf of Shambhala Publications Inc, Boston, MA. **www.shambhala.com**. Kerpner, J (2004) 'When the killer whale came panicked herrings in fishnet', *Aftonbladet*, 8 January 2004. Krakauer, J (1996). Excerpt(s) from INTO THE WILD by Jon Krakauer, copyright © 1996 by Jon Krakauer. Used by permission of Villard Books, an imprint of Random House, a division of Penguin Random House LLC. All rights reserved. Any third party use of this material, outside of this publication, is prohibited. Interested parties must apply directly to Penguin Random House LLC for permission. Also used by permission of Pan Macmillan copyright © Jon Krakauer, 1998. Sartre, JP (1947). Situations I, Jean-Paul Sartre © Editions Gallimard, Paris, 1947. English quote: Critical Essays, Jean-Paul Sartre © Seagull Books, 2010. Frankl, VE. 'Man's Search for Meaning' by Viktor E Frankl. Copyright © 1959, 1962, 1984, 1992 by Viktor E Frankl. Reprinted by permission of Beacon Press, Boston; *MAN'S SEARCH FOR MEANING* by Viktor E Frankl, Published by Rider, Reprinted by permission of The Random House Group Limited; also used by permission of the Viktor Frankl estate. Confucius. *Analects of Confucius*, 475BC–220AD.

Changing how we change

" *It is not the strongest of the species that survives, nor the most intelligent, but the one most responsive to change.*

LEON C MEGGINSON, PARAPHRASED FROM CHARLES DARWIN

The successful execution of high-impact change programmes – new business strategies, post-merger integrations, systems implementations and so on – has become increasingly crucial to the long-term competitiveness of organizations. Not surprisingly, managing change is now among the top priorities for most chief executive officers (CEOs). With great technological advancements, the critical issues ahead of us won't be technological challenges but people issues.

In Asia, there is a saying that accurately captures the essence of change: 'Out of great confusion comes bliss, certainty and progress'. Everyone who has managed organizational change initiatives has more than likely experienced confusion. Even when goals are clear, literally hundreds of obstacles can impede progress and not all of them are under a person's control. There can be competing corporate priorities, conflicting deadlines, project scope creep, insufficient resources, inadequate staff training – and the list goes on. But as the saying goes, bliss, certainty and progress can arise from such great confusion. How, though, does that happen? What are the steps that leaders need to take, particularly when they are implementing change initiatives involving hundreds, if not thousands, of people?

We have written this book to share insights from our research and practice with clients across the world. Our goal is to clear the confusion about organizational change; to find answers to the questions that trouble leaders, managers and staffers (and the consultants who assist them); and to provide a framework and system for helping organizations to navigate successfully through change. Our approach has been to collect data from hundreds of thousands of 'travellers' – individuals who have undertaken all kinds of change journeys. We didn't start by inventing another theory but chose to gain insights from the perceptions and reactions of real people undergoing real change. In our work, we have used sophisticated analytics to reveal the patterns of change in order to build maps and the navigation systems to help organizations to stay on track. We found that, across organizations, countries, cultures and different types of change, there is remarkable consistency and even predictability in how people and organizations navigate change. In this book, we show how these insights can significantly improve the success rates of organizational change initiatives at a time when such knowledge is most needed, as businesses head into an era of greater change and uncertainty.

Returning to the expression 'Out of great confusion comes bliss, certainty and progress', our research has found that 'bliss' in terms of organizational high performance is elusive. For groups, business units and organizations that make it to the top, only about one-third are able to remain there. Unfortunately, complacency and, ironically, the lack of further change taking place are the typical causes of the downfall. But what about 'certainty' in a rapidly changing world? The insights we found, and our framework for navigating change, provide certainty in terms of cause and effect. Through our research we have identified the 10 key drivers of performance in change initiatives. Excelling in each of those leads to success; gross deficiencies in any will result in mediocre outcomes or even failure. With respect to 'progress', our approach will help *any* organization to improve its performance in implementing change. From the start, our goal was not to study only those organizations that had successfully implemented change initiatives so that we could hold them up as exemplary models for others to emulate. Instead, our goal was to enable people to get better at managing change no matter what their current capability and, to that end, we have studied all kinds of change journeys – 'the good, the bad and the ugly'. These included not only groups and organizations that have gone from average to excellent, but also those that have made the transition from poor to mediocre. We also looked at those initiatives that have gone from the highest levels of performance and crashed down to the worst – because, when it comes to change, studying failure reveals as much as studying success.

Lastly, returning to 'confusion', we uncovered some interesting insights from our research. Many leaders strive to clear up confusion as soon as possible. Indeed, great confusion is typically viewed as an enemy that must be vanquished quickly. But confusion can actually be a valuable part of managing change. In this book, we show how leaders can completely transform people's experiences, often taking negative emotions such as fear and frustration and turning them into positive outcomes. The trick is to view confusion as 'work in progress' – a time for people to synthesize at a deep emotional level the values of the old ways along with the new. In fact, well-managed confusion can be a stepping stone for building employee engagement. As such, it is a 'free' resource, waiting to be converted into positive energy and constructive activities.

In a broad sense, that is how progress is made. In the past, the conventional wisdom has been that confusion is bad and that successful change is an orderly, linear process that is entirely manageable. But organizations that have tried to apply such approaches have often failed, leaving many to believe that change is inherently messy, chaotic and perhaps even random. Our research, however, has found that the truth lies between those two contrary perspectives. Change is indeed a manageable process but it doesn't always travel in a straight line. Change is a journey that more often than not takes circuitous routes, sometimes backtracking and often becoming stuck. That said, all change initiatives do tend to follow very predictable pathways, whether through actions that lead to failure or those that move people towards success. This book is about how organizations can implement change initiatives more effectively by skilfully navigating those predictable – but often hidden – pathways. In short, this book is about a paradigm shift in the way that organizations need to think about and manage change.

A shift in thinking is sorely needed. Organizations are now facing a fundamental challenge that will increasingly determine their ability to compete in the future. Change will go well beyond just discrete, individual projects and will instead require the enterprise-wide capability to manage continuous initiatives – a competence that must become fundamental to the way that organizations do business. Without that capability, executives will have difficulty managing the myriad geopolitical and macroeconomic risks, disruptive technologies, changes in customer behaviours and threats from new business models. In such a highly competitive, unpredictable environment, agility has become increasingly important, for example, to implement new business strategies to exploit market opportunities. Agility will enable executives to react quickly and efficiently to the ever-changing business landscape, where new threats can emerge with little warning, leaving many organizations scrambling to respond.

Our research: capturing the experiences of 750,000 travellers

Our research began with two simple questions that our clients often asked: 'How can we tell if our change programme is on track to high performance? And if it's not on track, what corrective actions should we take?' From the start our goal has been to turn insight into action, and our approach to answering these questions was to collect data from as many people as possible who had undergone different change initiatives. As such, we studied 250 change programmes over a 15-year period, including acquisitions, mergers, restructurings, technology implementations, cost reductions, turnarounds, downsizings, culture changes, growth initiatives, new business models and so on. Some of these were organization-wide transformations; others were initiatives with specific objectives, such as reducing costs or improving customer service.

These change programmes took place at more than 150 organizations in 50 industries and 25 countries. Over one-quarter of these organizations were in the Fortune Global 500. In addition, both small- and medium-sized organizations were also well represented. About one-third of them earned at least US$15 billion in annual revenues; 45 per cent earned from $1 billion to $10 billion annually; and about one-fifth earned less than $1 billion annually. At these organizations, we surveyed more than 750,000 employees, all of whom were involved in change programmes. These individuals were across hierarchical levels, from front-line staffers to all three major levels of leadership: corporate executives, business unit or divisional leaders, and team leaders. Our reason for doing this was simple: anyone travelling to another country for the first time would benefit greatly from the knowledge of others who have journeyed there before. Given that change is a journey, the most obvious way to gain valuable knowledge is to ask previous travellers about their change experiences. Did they have sufficient resources for the trip? Were their loads too heavy? Were they travelling too fast? How well did their leaders communicate? How clear were people's roles? What did they feel? We asked questions such as these across many dimensions, including business performance and the success of the change programme.

To build our database, we surveyed those individuals at predefined intervals, such as every four to six months, or before and after a system went live. Altogether the information consisted of more than 30 million data points representing the continuous perceptions and observations about various change initiatives at those different organizations. The database is thus a record of the experiences and perceptions of those who have implemented change, as well as those who have been on the receiving end of change. In essence, it is the collective wisdom of people who have undergone change initiatives – a collective wisdom that is far beyond the knowledge of even the most experienced change managers.

A unique database of wisdom and insight

Our database is unique in several ways. First, it contains information about the conditions of a change initiative – the type, amount, pace and stage of change. Numerous past articles have stressed the speed, complexity and uncertainty of change, its acceleration as time goes by and the adaptability needed to deal with it, especially under the digital and social media revolution. One conventional wisdom is that a considerable amount of change over a relatively short span of time will be too disruptive for organizations to absorb, but is that really true? To date, very little evidence has been presented. Our database allows us to answer such questions about the amount, pace and type of change – questions that lie at the heart of organizational agility. As it turns out, we found that the optimal pace of change is slightly faster than what the participants consider 'okay' (on a scale of too slow, okay, and too fast), and in most organizations there is no evidence to suggest that the pace should be slowed down. In fact, **the organizations that have the most change taking place at a fast pace are the ones that achieve the most benefits realization from change – and improve their performance the most across times of change.**

Moreover, the database also includes information about the benefits achieved from an initiative as well as the business outcomes, such as improved customer service and better cost management. This is in addition to a number of other variables, such as the amount of resources available, the skills of those involved, the strength of leadership and so on. It is important to note that we have all that information in the same dataset, enabling us to examine and model how all those variables were interacting with each other – an analysis that required billions of calculations. To our knowledge, there is no equivalent organizational change database of this size and scale, incorporating so many different factors.

Thanks to that dataset, we could test our assumptions and see how they compared against the data. We confronted our own mental maps and models along the way, often being surprised that change did not occur in the way that we thought it could or should be happening. We could also determine the key factors that lead to success or failure, from the earliest stages of a change journey to its completion, and from the most off-track results to the most desirable. Our goal, however, wasn't merely to explain why some change initiatives succeeded while others failed. We also wanted to develop a system that could detect the early warning signs that an initiative was headed for trouble, so that people could take corrective actions before small issues had become large problems. After all, it is relatively easy to look back and say what should have been done. The real challenge in managing change is to know when and where action is needed while change is happening – or even before it happens.

Moving beyond myths

From the onset of our research, our philosophy has been to let the data do the talking. As such, we did not hesitate to discard old models and frameworks that simply failed to stack up against the accumulated wisdom of the hundreds of thousands of travellers we surveyed. In fact, our research has led to a number of insights that have helped to debunk many long-held myths that change leaders and practitioners have relied on – but that have not yielded results. Throughout this book, we discuss those insights and summarize them at the end of each chapter. Below, we list the top 12 take-aways from our research, some of which we have already mentioned. These insights deal with the nature, navigation and interventions of change.

What is the nature of organizational change?

Myth: *change is a straightforward process that moves from A to B to C and so on, from the beginning of an initiative to its end.*

Our research: *change is a non-linear process with no beginning and no end.*

A fundamental mistake that organizations make is to apply straight-line change models – project timetables, critical-path methods and so on – that tend to assume that change occurs in a linear, straightforward fashion. But change occurs through the actions of people, and our research has shown that initiatives rarely proceed in an organized, linear way. Many programmes take circuitous routes, sometimes backtracking and often becoming stuck for months, if not years. The problem here is that organizations have been using tools that are not built for the way that change actually occurs – in essence, people have had to adapt to their tools instead of the other way around. That said, change initiatives do tend to follow certain predictable pathways, whether through actions that lead to failure or those that move groups towards success, and our maps and framework capture that predictability.

Myth: *too much change too fast is destructive.*

Our research: *the highest-performing groups have the most amount of change taking place at a very fast pace.*

The highest-performing groups tend to thrive from an increased amount and pace of change. They almost dare the organization to throw more change at them. Developing this 'fitness for change' is similar to athletes at the beginning of training. The more they train, the more they build up their conditioning and the more exertion they can undertake without any drop in performance.

Myth: *change causes organizations to go off track.*

Our research: *change does not cause organizational dysfunction; it merely exposes it.*

When we examined those groups that dropped from higher levels of performance to the lowest levels, we found that at least 85 per cent already had major underlying issues before the change programme came along. People might blame the initiative for their problems, but the data shows that a dysfunctional culture and behaviour – for example, a lack of trust in leadership – were ingrained in the organization prior to the implementation of change.

How best to navigate change?

Myth: *change solutions can be boiled down to a handful of simple rules.*

Our research: *successful change requires a complex, coordinated strategy of multiple actions sustained across time.*

Change management is among the most complex organizational processes. It took us 33 billion calculations to derive our change map. Although executives don't like to hear this, they must accept complexity as an integral part of change initiatives. Indeed, successful change requires multiple actions sustained across time.

Myth: *change is driven from the top down and is resisted by middle management.*

Our research: *effective change leadership radiates out from the centre, starting first with leaders and their teams who want to change, then joining with likeminded others, and eventually reaching every corner of the organization.*

Our research clearly shows that the role of the business unit leader, who often sits unnoticed between corporate and team leadership, is the one that plays the most significant role in effectively implementing change, delivering business benefits and ensuring that ongoing business performance remains high.

Myth: *business performance always takes a dip before improving.*

Our research: *business performance generally increases throughout a change programme.*

In many models that describe the stages of change, the assumption is that, in the beginning of an initiative, inertia and resistance need to be overcome – and business performance dips accordingly. But this is not the case. The highest-performing groups improve business performance consistently across all stages of change.

Myth: *people must suffer through the 'valley of despair' as a normal part of change.*

Our research: *people do not necessarily have to experience negative feelings as part of the change process, although such emotions can in certain cases be beneficial if they are understood and well managed.*

The notion of a 'valley of despair' is based on the work by the noted psychiatrist Elisabeth Kübler-Ross (Kübler-Ross, 1973), who described the five phases of grief that people go through when faced with death or loss: denial, anger, bargaining, depression and then acceptance. We found, however, that in high-performing groups, positive feelings remained high throughout all stages of the change programme.

Myth: *to come to terms with change, people must first have an intellectual understanding of it then an emotional agreement.*

Our research: *in high-performing groups, the reverse is true – emotional agreement precedes the intellectual understanding.*

The 'commitment curve' is one of the building blocks of change management (Conner, 1993). According to this, people must first be aware and then understand the vision and direction of a change programme before buying into it and committing themselves. But our research shows that, although that progression is true for low-performing groups, it is actually reversed for high performers, particularly in the early stages of change. For high-performing groups, trust in leadership was so high that people were willing to commit to a change programme before fully understanding it.

What interventions to use?

Myth: *all change can be managed effectively by applying universal best practices.*

Our research: *a one-size-fits-all approach to change will generally fail.*

Organizations often manage change by focusing on a few obvious factors – for instance, holding people accountable – that seem to have produced results in the past. But there is no such thing as a single list of actions or interventions, a single sequence of events or a single method that will apply in all situations, or even at different stages of the same initiative. Our research has uncovered a number of different regions (including the nine capital cities) each containing individuals and groups with similar characteristics, including performance levels, conditions of change, behaviours, dynamics and challenges. A set of actions that might be effective in one region could easily be counterproductive in another.

Myth: *organizations will achieve the best results by focusing on communication, training, team leadership and accountability.*

Our research: *other factors, often hidden from view and difficult to define, have a greater impact on the outcomes of a change initiative.*

Of course, communication, training, team leadership and holding people accountable are all important elements in bringing about change, but they play only relatively minor roles in benefits realization and improving business performance. For benefits realization, vision and direction – building understanding and gaining agreement – is by far the most important factor, three to four times as important as any other intervention. To drive improvements in business performance, the most important factors are business leadership, and systems and processes along with passion and drive.

Myth: *charismatic and empathetic leaders build organizational trust through the quality of their one-to-one relationships.*

Our research: *one-on-one trusted relationships with and among leaders are necessary but not sufficient. To drive change forward, organizations also need a system of trust aligned at multiple levels of leadership – a 'trust grid'.*

High-performing groups build a 'trust grid', where each level of leadership is dependent on the other levels, and the trust holds together in an interrelated series of actions. In combination, these actions develop staffers' confidence that leadership knows what it is doing, is responsive to their needs, and is ready and willing to provide support to help every person to bring about change. The synergistic effect of collective leadership action goes well beyond what is possible from a single level of leadership acting in isolation from the others or in one-to-one relationships.

Myth: *focusing on emotions does not lead to business outcomes, so it is better to ignore them and just get on with the tasks at hand.*

Our research: *both positive and negative emotions can have a huge impact on the benefits that are ultimately realized.*

The role of negative and positive feelings should not be underestimated. In terms of benefits realization, an abnormally high level of fear and frustration can result in a decline by more than 20 per cent in the benefits realized, while a high level of passion and drive can lead to an increase of 50 per cent. These differences can easily translate to millions of pounds to the bottom line when considering what is at stake in large change programmes.

Defining high performance

As we analysed the data, we realized early on that we needed to define exactly what is meant by a 'successful' change programme that achieves 'high performance'. Interestingly, previous studies tended to look at change initiatives by focusing on whether they had achieved the intended benefits, such as a reduction in operating costs or an improvement in customer service. But in our ongoing research we found that achieving those benefits often came at a price, sometimes leaving an organization less competitive over the long run. The stress and strain of a major initiative might, for example, leave staffers exhausted and cynical, resulting in the departure of many talented employees. As such, we adopted a much broader definition of 'high-performance change' to include four criteria:

- **Realizes benefits from the change**: this includes completing a project or programme on time and on budget, and realizing the benefits outlined in the business case.

- **Improves business performance across the course of the change**: daily business performance should not decline during a change initiative; instead it should improve, as measured by key metrics such as customer service levels, employee productivity and operating costs.

- **Builds people's capabilities to manage change**: while change is taking place, critical capabilities need to be developed to achieve and sustain high performance. These include skills and staffing, leadership, teamwork, systems and processes, and so on.

- **Leaves the organization in good shape to undertake further change:**
  even if benefits are achieved and performance is improved, change is
  a failure if people are left exhausted and unable to undertake further
  change – for example, if negative feelings remain high or key
  employees have left because of a lack of trust in leadership.

We found that achieving all four of these objectives lies at the heart of
successful change. Although organizations might start a change programme
with weaknesses (for example, a deficiency in team leadership), those that
are successful build capability in these areas *while* change is taking place.
The groups and organizations that make it to the highest levels of performance in change programmes build strengths across the board. Thus, any
definition of success must include the long-term consequences of any action,
such as the ability for the group or organization to continue to achieve its
objectives long after the particular activity is over. To our knowledge, no other
approach to organizational change takes into account such a comprehensive view when assessing the success or failure of various initiatives.

Crunching the data and testing the results

Using the above definition of high performance, we could then analyse the
data using a number of sophisticated techniques, both linear and non-linear.
These steps and our research methodology are described in greater detail in
Chapter 2. It is important to note that this research was not conducted in
isolation of the challenges of real organizational change. We have worked
with numerous change leaders who were under intense pressure to deliver
results. We were part of their change process, and our ability to identify
issues and predict outcomes mattered enormously. If we did not accurately
map the issues they were dealing with, or if we sent them in the wrong direction, then we certainly heard about it. Literally thousands of conversations
across all levels of organizations took place in parallel with our research, at
times friendly and at times hostile to our presence.

We sometimes jokingly referred to our analysis and results as 'an excuse'
to have difficult discussions about the real issues of organizational change.
In the business world, the reality is that people generally need hard data to
talk about softer and more intangible issues. Throughout our research, we
never lost sight that our purpose was to accurately identify important issues
and have the conversations required to better manage change. This has
personally been both exciting and challenging. We were able to bring science
to what is commonly considered the 'art' of organizational change, and the
challenges we faced required us to find new and innovative ways of solving
real-world problems.

A map and predictable pathways for change

To manage change, today's executives typically use project plans, schedules, budgets and employee/customer surveys. These tools might help indicate the current situation and direction at certain points in time – for example, whether a project is on schedule and on budget, and whether people's current perceptions are positive or negative – but they don't warn of upcoming obstacles or other problems. They also don't predict outcomes, and they don't offer any guidance on how to get back on track when a project falters. In fact, leaders often don't learn that they are off track until minor issues have festered into major problems, and even then they have little information about which interventions to apply. The fundamental flaw with such approaches is that they are reactive, which tends to reinforce the mistaken assumption that change is inherently unpredictable, chaotic and possibly even random. But if there is anything that our research has shown, it is that change follows mostly predictable patterns, and those patterns are captured in our system.

From the beginning, our purpose in collecting data was not merely to enable us to evaluate an initiative after it has occurred. Our larger goal was to provide ongoing, timely feedback that could help manage the seemingly unruly dynamics of the change process itself by providing the right guidance for fine-tuning any interventions. This, we believe, represents a fundamental shift in perspective, from a reactive to proactive mindset. Interestingly, organizational change is often described as a journey, yet accurate maps showing the complex interactions between people, change, resources and performance have not been available for groups to plot getting from one location to another. Lack of such maps, for common use by all stakeholders, has been a major cause of misalignment and wasted effort in change projects.

Using the data we collected, we built multidimensional change maps, comparing data across teams, organizations and change programmes (see Figure 1.1 – the main change map – and see too the full-colour version of this map on page 20). These maps represent the various patterns we identified through an extensive analysis of the data. Specifically, we found that groups undergoing change initiatives tend to fall into different clusters – represented by different regions on our map, from very low to high performance – with similar characteristics, behaviours, dynamics and challenges. Unlike other tools such as budgets and project schedules that are linear and one-dimensional, our maps capture the multidimensional complexity of

FIGURE 1.1 Change map showing the different regions of change

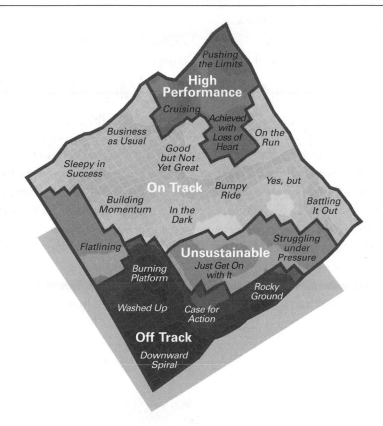

change initiatives. As we describe in Chapter 2, the maps are drawn in two-dimensional space but they encompass 44 different dimensions, representing a step difference from how change programmes have been viewed in the past.

Our maps and overall framework help outline the relationship between performance, change processes and various organizational characteristics that affect performance and the success of change programmes. These range from the available resources, the stage of change and strength of leadership, to the feelings of individual participants in the change initiative. It is important to note that our system measures the benefits being delivered from a change programme, the strength of key drivers and the impact on business performance *while* change is taking place. In other words, our system provides leaders, managers and teams with the information they need to keep their programmes on track, and this includes early warnings about future obstacles as well as prescriptive advice to handle current problems.

Where the action is: nine capital cities

To be useful, a system for organizational change must present information in a way that expresses a situation unambiguously to leaders, managers and staff (who all need to make decisions from different perspectives) and shows the best course of action. What makes the GPS system in a car powerful isn't really the underlying satellite and computer technology – it is the user interface that displays a map and provides simple instructions about what to do next. Furthermore, for that system to be even more valuable, it would enable consumers to look ahead and alter their course to adjust for traffic jams, bad weather, road construction and other adverse conditions. That describes the system we have developed, but instead of helping drivers to get from point A to B, we enable organizations to better navigate their change initiatives – because others have travelled those paths before.

Our change maps have regions that indicate areas of similar performance, characteristics and dynamics. In one such region, named *Case for Action*, located near the bottom of the capital cities map (see Figure 1.2 – see too the full-colour version of this map on page 21) with low performance, the

FIGURE 1.2   Map of the nine 'capital cities' regions

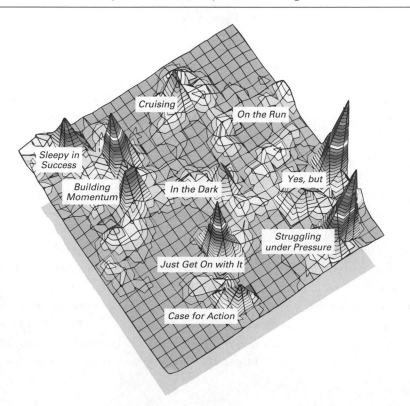

levels of fear and frustration run so high that they impede teams from making any progress. Even adding more staffing and other resources will be futile until management can address those negative emotions, and our data suggests various ways to accomplish that.

That is, our maps not only contain descriptions of the various regions; they also include information about the different pathways leading in and out of those areas. These results are based on more than 30,000 paths taken by different teams, business units, divisions and entire organizations, and we can describe those journeys and tie them directly to the different decisions that people made to move from one location to another. For example, for those in the region *Case for Action*, we know that the most common pathway is to a region of higher performance named *Just Get On with It*. And to navigate that transition, our research tells us that people must concentrate on small wins, setting achievable targets to improve accountability, teamwork, and passion and drive, all while focusing on better team leadership to lower everyone's level of fear and frustration. In fact, if the team leader cannot lower people's fears and frustrations, the group is likely to remain stuck in *Case for Action* for quite some time, no matter what else they try. These and other prescriptive pathways are described in detail in Chapters 3 through 11.

Furthermore, we have discovered that most groups undergoing change tend to reside in one of nine different regions. We use the term 'capital cities' to refer to those regions, which include both *Case for Action* and *Just Get On with It*. In fact, we found that about 75 per cent of all groups that we measured tend to end up in the nine capital cities. As such, it behoves organizations to master the dynamics of those nine regions. Develop the skills to recognize and unlock those nine patterns, and your organization can master change initiatives in an uncertain and unpredictable world.

The change imperative

The long-term competitiveness – if not survival – of organizations will increasingly depend on their ability to manage change, specifically, whether they have developed agility as a core capability. Indeed, one recent study (The Global Agenda, 2014) reported that the most significant challenge that CEOs face when implementing investments in digital business initiatives (such as cloud computing, data analytics, and social and mobile technologies) was, by some margin, the difficulties encountered in managing change. This was well above other challenges, such as skills shortages, insufficient funding and poor cross-functional cooperation.

Yet if we look at the track record of organizational change to date (see box 'The evolution of organizational change'), the results have been mediocre at best. Various studies have investigated the failure rates of major change efforts, and the results have been sobering, indicating that as many as three out of four such initiatives fail to deliver on their objectives. The price of such failures can be staggering, not just in terms of costly overruns, blown budgets and other direct hits to the bottom line – it is also the ancillary costs of the stress and pain that people experience when getting 'bumped and bruised' if change initiatives go awry.

The evolution of organizational change

Organizations invest considerable resources to implement change, but a huge disconnect exists between the complexity they are dealing with and the sophistication of the tools they use. Indeed, although we live in a world of algorithms and breathtaking scientific advancements, we continue to rely on tools out of the Stone Age to track and navigate change. To understand our current predicament, some historical context is needed.

In the world of engineers, counting, quantifying and classifying are a routine part of their jobs, and the saying that 'You can't manage what you can't measure' is a fundamental truth. In the field of change management, measurement methods and tools have generally reflected the predominant paradigm of their respective era, with advances often prompted by the evolution of technology, coupled with the increasing sophistication of the statistical models and mathematical algorithms used to analyse data. Over the years, four major frameworks for understanding organizational change have been espoused, tested and applied. Each has reflected a different era and paradigm of thought, and each has suffered characteristic 'blind spots'.

In the era of scientific management, people conducted the first scientific studies of the detail of human work and work process flow, introducing the concepts of work standardization and quality control that still resonate today. The measures and methodologies used were simple by today's standards: time-and-motion studies, observations, task-based structural analysis and comparisons of pre-/post-measurements of productivity or output.

In the next era of human relations, the focus shifted more towards the human aspect of change, and theories of motivation became more sophisticated, moving beyond extrinsic motivators such as salary to intrinsic ones: the work itself and the autonomy of the employee. As such, organizations collected data about the attitudes and feelings of people through various mechanisms, such as employee surveys investigating motivation and satisfaction. Feelings were taken into account as 'morale' or 'employee attitudes', which we now understand as 'engagement'. Employee engagement, however, was later found to be just a small piece of the overall puzzle.

The next era – sociotechnical systems – aimed for a balance between the two previous eras, focusing on the complex interactions between and joint optimization of technological and social subsystems. High importance was placed on employee involvement and participation, and the interaction between people, systems and processes and the development of skills became the real job of change. Organizations were described as 'open learning systems' that would evolve but eventually settle into a steady state, which proved to be a flawed assumption. Vision and direction became the focus of the leader's attention, but the measurement of change as a continuous process of ongoing adaptation was difficult, and storytelling became popular as a means to access the complex realities of change.

Finally, in the current era of complex adaptive systems, the goal is to implement change in a more holistic way, making it easier to achieve and more sustainable over the long run. Here, implementing an initiative means managing multiple, overlapping systems – such as rapidly fluctuating international financial markets, global supply chains and social media – in which various changes are taking place simultaneously. Change is now seen as a continuous process of adaptation to constantly changing external conditions, and the approach to managing change has shifted from one where employees are consulted in a process that is dominated by an external 'change expert' to one where the change practitioner is skilled in process facilitation, helping stakeholders to see the 'cause and effect' of their actions. Also, there is more focus on actively shaping the process of change itself and using insights from sophisticated measurement systems and techniques, which become critical success factors.

The fundamental problem has been that, even as change has evolved towards complex adaptive systems, we continue to use tools and approaches from earlier eras. And that explains the sorry state of change management today, in which project overruns, delays and derailments have become all too prevalent. In short, we have been implementing change in a complex, multidimensional world without the proper guidance to navigate through such programmes. Our framework seeks to address that shortcoming, and we believe that our insight-driven approach to change represents a fundamental shift in the way that organizations think about and manage organizational change.

This poor track record of organizational change continues despite – or perhaps because of – the overwhelming volume of information written about the topic. A huge part of the problem is that many of those books, articles and white papers have been based less on hard empirical evidence and more on misconceptions, faulty assumptions and a misplaced faith in certain 'best' practices such as 'communicate, communicate, communicate', 'push hard on costs' and 'increase engagement'. As such, leaders who have struggled to identify the underlying drivers of change have been looking in the wrong places to find the solutions to their problems.

All this does not bode well for the future. If anything, businesses in the coming years will be experiencing more change, moving at an even faster pace. For one thing, digital technologies will continue to dramatically transform industries. In *The Second Machine Age* (2014) Erik Brynjolfsson and Andrew McAfee point to a future of unprecedented disruptive change as a result of technological advancements: 'Rapid and accelerating digitization is likely to bring economic rather than environmental disruption, stemming from the fact that as computers get more powerful, organizations have less need for some kinds of workers. Technology progress is going to leave behind some people, perhaps a lot of people, as it races ahead'. According to Brynjolfsson and McAfee, the critical issues ahead of us will not be technological challenges but people issues, for example, figuring out how to unleash the power of human creativity and ingenuity. And if we have not managed change well to date, how are we going to do so in the future, with even greater amounts of change?

In short, we have reached a crossroads, and there has never been a more important time to find new and more effective ways to manage organizational change. We simply won't realize the benefits of emerging technologies, offering new hope for our work and lives, if we keep going as we have been. No less than a step change is required.

We believe that our new framework for managing change provides that leap. The approach described in this book is not based on past assumptions or conventional wisdoms but on the synthesis of the experiences of hundreds of thousands who have undergone change programmes. Moreover, our insights and our navigation system can provide that collective knowledge in real time to those in the midst of implementing change. In that regard, our approach is not unlike that of TripAdvisor, which delivers up-to-date information to consumers so that they themselves can make better decisions about their journeys, including any corrections and adjustments along the way. Similarly, our system provides change leaders with access to data – in our case, the insights from others who have undergone change initiatives –

so that they can better plan and guide their own journeys. In other words, our goal from the start was to put a system in the hands of non-experts, that is, normal everyday leaders who must navigate change programmes in real time.

So, where do we go from here? In the next chapter, we discuss our basic research in greater detail and describe the development of a model and maps that enable organizations to track their change progress and formulate interventions. That system provides information on pathways that will allow organizations the confidence to know that, if they take certain actions, they will arrive at particular destinations. The remainder of the book is structured around the dynamics of the capital cities (and their associated zones) – nine locations where the vast majority of people undergoing change will tend to reside. Some of these cities are comfortable and vibrant. Others provide temporary residence in difficult conditions for those who would rather not be there. Still others are like frontier towns in the Wild West, where risks are high and surprises often unpleasant. These regions and their characteristics are highlighted in Chapters 3 through 11, one for each capital city. (Note: throughout the book we use numerous examples of specific organizations to illustrate key points. To protect the confidentiality of our clients, we may at times alter identifying details of their companies. Also, some examples may represent a composite of organizations from our research with similar experiences.)

Before moving on, we need to refer back to a myth we cited earlier. Change management is among the most complex processes, and yet managers often want a simple basic plan for success. 'Tell me the two or three things that I need to do', is something we frequently hear. But that is a woefully misguided request. People dealing with change programmes must accept complexity because of the inherent nature of such initiatives. But, as we shall see, complexity does not necessarily mean incomprehensibility, and our change maps are the first step in uncovering the patterns that will help make the complex more accessible.

MAP 1 Change map showing the different regions of change –
find out where your change programme positions on the
map at **www.accenture.com/changemap**

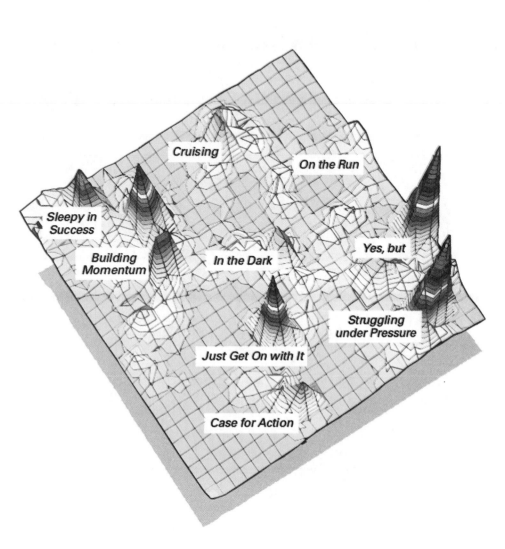

MAP 2 Map of the nine 'capital cities' regions

Understanding change through maps

> *Where would we be without maps?*
> *The obvious answer is, of course, 'lost'.* **JERRY BROTTON**

A global company undertaking a major US$100 million implementation of a new IT work-scheduling system found that its change initiative was in trouble. Three months after the 'go-live' stage, the system had been installed but wasn't fully functional. It was experiencing 1,000 manual overrides per day when the industry standard is 120, and frustration was mounting among the 380 people involved in the implementation. With the initiative already $3.8 million over budget, executives were struggling to get the initiative back on track.

Ironically, everything seemed to be going smoothly earlier. The company had followed the conventional wisdom of change initiatives, focusing on employee training and communication. After a readiness survey had shown sufficient scores in both of these areas, senior leadership felt comfortable enough about the programme that they cut the change-management budget, saving $280,000. After the system went live, though, problems quickly surfaced and the business was eventually forced to add employees even though the initiative was designed to reduce staff numbers. As morale continued to plunge, executives were in a quandary with little guidance to make important decisions. A huge part of the problem was that they lacked the kind of hard data they needed to get at the root causes of why the programme had faltered. 'Everyone was blaming the IT solution for the problems. Conventional wisdom said to use business metrics and customer data to drive improvement. [But] what data did I have on that? Lots of anecdotal perceptions but no real facts that I could work with', recalled a manager for the company.

Consultants, academics and various experts have written countless volumes about organizational change. Yet despite this seeming wealth of information, organizations continue to struggle with implementing change. The problem is that, for all the books, articles and white papers written on the topic, very little has been based on empirical evidence and analytics, and the frameworks presented have lacked practical value. As such, managers have simply not been able to understand change – its complex interactions of multiple variables – in ways that allow them to drive towards more successful outcomes.

In Chapter 1 we discussed how we have tackled the problem from the ground up, first by building a large dataset of hundreds of thousands of people who have undergone change initiatives. In this chapter, we describe the techniques used to analyse the data to derive a model of change that directly links performance outcomes with various factors, including 10 important drivers. Using that model, we were able to identify patterns of change initiatives and visualize those results through the use of maps.

This research has taught us three invaluable things about change:

- A piecemeal approach to change rarely works; instead, successful change programmes require a coordinated package of highly focused actions sequenced throughout the various stages of the initiative, all underpinned by a sustained commitment from management.

- We found that the vast majority of change programme participants, individuals and groups, tend to fall into one of nine clusters, each containing individuals and groups with similar characteristics, including performance levels, conditions of change, behaviours, dynamics and challenges.

- We discovered that even though change journeys might sometimes appear to proceed in chaotic and random ways, they are actually quite predictable – and largely dependent on the decisions made by leaders and managers.

The research: distilling the wisdom of 750,000 travellers

As discussed in Chapter 1, we studied 250 change initiatives at 150 global corporations, ultimately canvassing more than 750,000 employees. Our survey consisted of more than 3,000 queries that we later narrowed down to 44 core questions. Numerous studies (for example, see Frost, 1996) have shown that the people most knowledgeable about the goings-on within an organization are typically those closest to the action – whether it is managers responsible for costs and budgets, or employees on the front line of customer service. Their understanding of a situation is usually more accurate than that of others further removed, such as outside consultants and external experts.

Using that data, we could then analyse the complex interactions between the variables studied and follow those interactions from the earliest stages of a change initiative to its completion, and from the worst performance to the best, or vice versa. Through that kind of analysis we could then determine the key drivers that lead to success. That is exactly the kind of information that was lacking in the US$100 million IT initiative for the company in our example above. As that manager lamented, he lacked the necessary facts to help guide his decision-making.

Finding patterns in the data: using sophisticated quantitative techniques

Analysing the data was a complex, intensive process. Our goal was to determine the key factors of success, the things that worked well. To identify those drivers, we utilized sophisticated quantitative analyses. Specifically, we applied exploratory factor analysis to describe the relationships among the myriad observed variables in terms of a much lower number of unobserved factors. We also used confirmatory factor analysis to build reliability in the factor model, and we deployed the following:

- correlation analysis – to measure the degree of linear association between one variable and another (eg X–Y plots);

- regression analysis – to quantify the relationship between a variable of interest and one or more other variables;

- regression trees – to handle non-linearity, interactions between variables, non-normality, and differences in variability in different parts of the data space;

- structural equation modelling (SEM) – to establish causality (and not merely correlation) between certain variables.

The model: linking performance outcomes to change conditions, processes and drivers

Using the results from our quantitative analyses, we were able to build a model of organizational change processes, including the factors that need to be measured and managed (see Figure 2.1). We developed this model so that

FIGURE 2.1   The change model

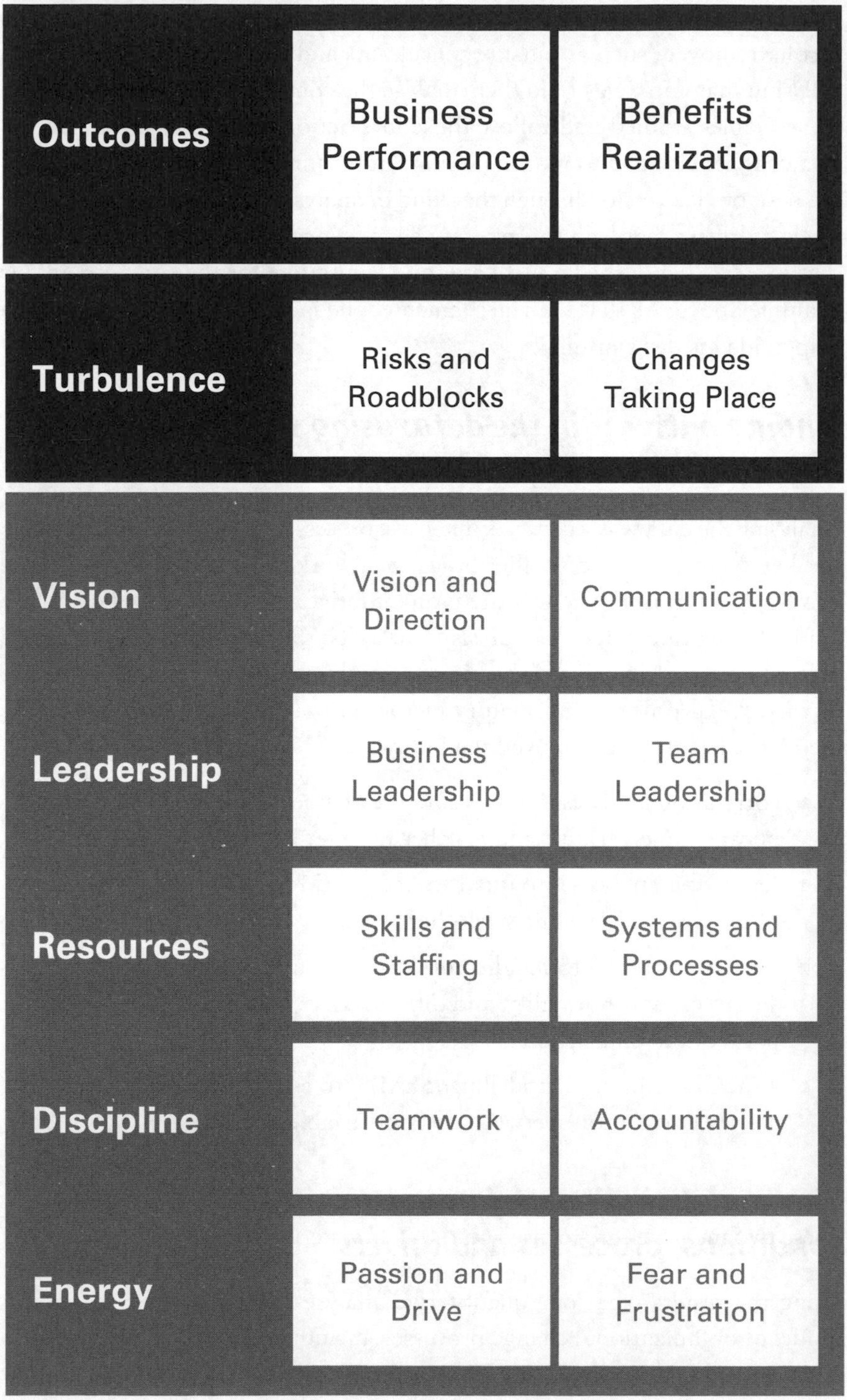

Outcomes	Business Performance	Benefits Realization
Turbulence	Risks and Roadblocks	Changes Taking Place
Vision	Vision and Direction	Communication
Leadership	Business Leadership	Team Leadership
Resources	Skills and Staffing	Systems and Processes
Discipline	Teamwork	Accountability
Energy	Passion and Drive	Fear and Frustration

organizations could answer the following question: 'Is our change programme on track to high performance?' In other words, the goal was not to conduct post-mortems of failed change initiatives. The goal was to provide leaders, managers and teams with a framework to deal more effectively with change in order to keep any programme from falling by the wayside. In particular, we wanted to enable people to know when, where and how to take the corrective actions required to get themselves back on track, as well as the steps necessary to stay there.

The change model outlines the relationship between performance outcomes, turbulence (the conditions under which change takes place) and the 10 specific drivers that affect performance. These range from the available resources and strength of leadership, to the feelings of individual participants in the change effort. All these quantities can be measured and assessed while change is occurring in order to determine any actions that should be taken.

Performance outcomes: business performance and benefits realization

At the top of Figure 2.1 are two performance outcomes:

1 **Benefits realization:** are the benefits listed in the business case for the change initiative being realized in practice? Benefits realization measures the extent to which planned functionality and/or capability either has been or will be achieved. The benefits of the change vary from one organization to the next, and are typically outlined in the business case driving the change programme.

2 **Business performance:** is the organizational performance increasing in daily operations as indicated by the key metrics of effectiveness, customer service and cost management while the initiative is being implemented? The need to maintain customer service levels and manage costs in the business does not diminish because change is taking place. In fact, if costs sky-rocket or customer service declines while change is being implemented, we would regard this as a failure to properly manage change.

These two measures are focused on the first two criteria for high-performance change as discussed in Chapter 1, and they have been shown in a number of research studies to be very good 'lead' indicators of a company's objective performance across time.

Turbulence: taking into account the conditions under which change takes place

Although managerial actions and the ways in which people respond can greatly affect the outcome of a change initiative, they themselves are moderated by other factors – in much the same way as the conditions of a road, the shape of the terrain and the weather can influence the ease (or difficulty) with which a vehicle reaches its destination. We use the term 'turbulence' to denote such conditions under which change takes place, which can be grouped into two categories: 1) the changes taking place (specifically, the type, amount, stage and pace of change); 2) the risks and roadblocks (the barriers that prevent benefits from being delivered).

It is important to note that the type, amount and pace of change are largely controllable by top management, with teams and even business leaders having little or no control over these variables. But, with knowledge about them, managers can adjust their strategy accordingly in order to work within the given constraints. Our research has shown that groups that understand what they can and cannot change and then work creatively with their resources are far more likely to be successful.

Changes taking place: the amount, pace and stage of change

The characteristics of the change process itself – namely, the amount, pace and stage of change – can greatly affect an initiative. The *amount* of change can range from minimal to moderate to overwhelming, depending on four factors:

- internal restructuring – whether the amount of reorganization and top management changes are disruptive;
- new ways of working – whether new behaviours are required due to changes in culture, values and attitude;
- changing size and shape – whether the organization, division or business unit is altering its size and shape due to mergers, joint ventures or partnerships;
- overall growth – whether the growth that is occurring is substantial, such as through the introduction of new products or entry into new geographies.

Another key characteristic of the change process is the *pace* of change. How quickly must the changes progress? To measure this variable, we use a seven-point scale, but for those involved in a change initiative the pace can more generally be divided into three categories: 1) too slow; 2) okay; 3) too fast. Lastly, the *stage* of change must also be considered, that is, whether an initiative is just commencing, about to finish, or somewhere in between. Again, we use a seven-point scale to measure this variable, but it can generally be divided into three broad categories: the early, middle and late stages of a change programme.

Risks and roadblocks: obstacles to change

Risks and roadblocks are often related directly to one of the 10 drivers (discussed in the following section) but they can also be very specific to a particular initiative. For example, the 'silo' mentality of an organization might be a major roadblock if it impedes different divisions from sharing information and working together on a corporate-wide reorganization. We ask about the extent to which each of the risks and roadblocks identified prevent the full benefits of the change programme from being achieved.

The 10 managerial drivers of change

At the heart of our model are 10 key drivers of performance outcomes. These are notable for being under at least partial control of the change participants. They represent important areas in which actions can be identified that enable people to make a difference in the outcome of a change programme. And therein lies the problem with many change initiatives that focus on just one or two drivers. On the $100 million IT initiative at the global company cited above, executives assumed that they could concentrate mainly on communication and training, but as it turned out there were other important factors at play. The following are descriptions of the 10 drivers we identified, each of which has the potential to obstruct a change initiative if not properly managed:

1 **Vision and direction** is a measure of whether the idea and plan behind the change initiative resonate with those involved. This driver has four main components: whether people understand the organization's vision for the future; whether they agree with the organization's future direction; whether they have confidence and trust in the

executive team; and whether they recognize the need to do things differently.

2 **Communication** is a measure of whether people are getting the information they need regarding the change initiative. Further, is that information being received through face-to-face interactions with their immediate manager versus written form? By analysing the communication scores with respect to other survey questions (regarding, for example, business performance), we can determine the effectiveness and quality of those different channels.

3 **Business leadership** is a measure of how effectively the business is being led and managed by those at the business unit, business area or division levels. As a prerequisite for success, do those leaders have the capacity to learn fast and make changes in tactics on the fly? And do they have the leadership agility to be successful under the pressure and fast-moving action required by the changes taking place? Business leadership is divided into two separate elements. The first is the ability to implement: how well is the change process being managed, and is remedial action taken quickly and efficiently to address identified problems? The second is management commitment: do the business area managers actively demonstrate support and commitment for the change? Do they provide the appropriate levels of time and resources needed to ensure the process is successful? Has their leadership won the confidence and trust of their teams?

4 **Team leadership** is a measure of whether the direct supervisor has the skills to manage people and their performance, and it is also about whether team members feel valued. Does the supervisor build and mobilize people's commitment? Does he or she support and coach people to develop their potential? Does he or she instill confidence and trust in the team members? Does he or she utilize their full talents and capabilities, and recognize and reward them for their contributions?

5 **Systems and processes** is a measure of whether the main resources that are available to the change programme are adequate for its successful implementation. Even with optimal team spirit, strong leaders, good internal communication and employee engagement, a programme will not achieve high performance if people lack the equipment or systems and processes needed to achieve the stated goals.

6 **Skills and staffing** is a measure of whether teams have sufficient staffing, with the right people in the right roles. Specifically, do those individuals have the talent or ability to master the skills and knowledge that are required to carry out their roles effectively?

7 **Teamwork** is a measure of whether people can work together effectively to achieve the intended outcomes. It incorporates whether people feel part of the team and are actively involved in initiating, planning and implementing change. It also assesses whether teamwork is a natural way of operating for them.

8 **Accountability** is a measure of three things: whether an individual's roles and responsibilities are clear; whether the team has clear performance objectives and measurable outcomes; and whether people on the team are held responsible for achieving their objectives.

9 **Passion and drive** is a measure of whether people are motivated by positive feelings to achieve results and to invest more of their time and energy. Passion is about the excitement and enthusiasm of the team, while drive is about people's enthusiasm for their work and for each other.

10 **Fear and frustration** is a measure of people's negative feelings and reactions, which can include fear, frustration, anger, confusion, impatience and a sense of loss as a change initiative moves through different stages. A small level of such emotions can actually be productive, prompting people towards action, but too much can distort communications, make people bitter and resentful, and result in them wanting to quit. As such, this measure also considers whether team members intend to leave, and whether rumours have become rampant as a result of the organization allowing an information vacuum to develop, with negative feelings distorting any communications.

Benchmarking: showing what actions are needed

The data for a particular group can be shown graphically so that people can see if they are above or below the norm, and how far away they are from achieving the level required to sustain high performance. Figure 2.2 displays the results for the change programme at the company discussed earlier in the chapter. In the driver profiles, the line in the centre indicates the norm from

FIGURE 2.2   Sample driver profile

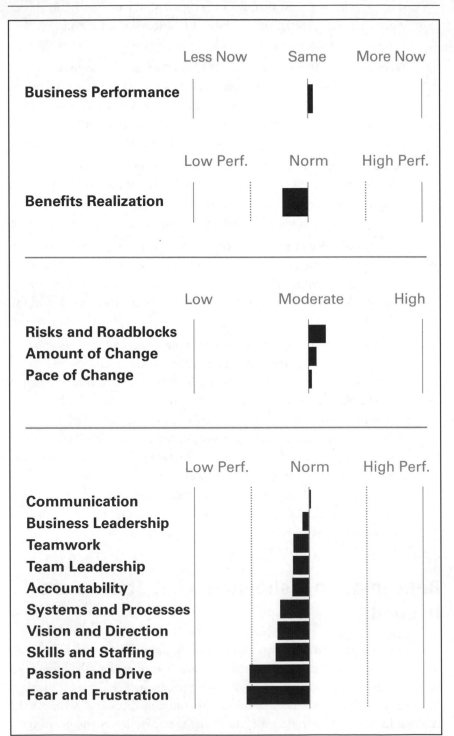

our database. The midpoint mark on the right indicates the level required to achieve improvement in business performance in the top 10 per cent, and the midpoint mark on the left equates to a decline in business performance to the bottom 10 per cent. For this particular company, business performance has shown a slight improvement.

Reviewing this driver profile further, we see that benefits realization is below the norm for this company. The factors related to turbulence – risks and roadblocks, amount of change and pace of change – are all slightly higher than moderate. Note that, in order to simplify the driver profiles, we do not include the stage of change, one of the factors of turbulence. The 10 drivers are then shown from best performing to worst performing. In this case, each driver is either at or below the norm, with communication being the best-performing driver, and fear and frustration being the worst. Note that the way to read fear and frustration in the driver profile is that low performance for this driver is to the left of the norm, indicating high levels of fear and frustration.

These results, taken three months after the 'go-live' stage, clearly indicate why the change initiative had run into trouble. Although the level of communication seems fine, what the company hadn't realized was that accountability was low, especially at the top-management level. Moreover, the level of passion and drive was extremely low. As it turns out, both of those drivers are keys to good cost management. The lesson here is that looking at one variable – for example, just the worst-performing driver, which in this case is fear and frustration – in isolation can be very misleading. It would be like measuring only someone's blood pressure to ascertain that person's overall health when, instead, doctors need to look across the entire body to make a proper diagnosis.

It is important to emphasize that the driver data in the profiles (as shown in Figure 2.2) are tied directly to both improvements in business performance and benefits realization. This is often not the case with traditional surveys that measure culture, communication or engagement and then show the results as average data, leaving leaders to interpret and guess for themselves about what is really driving performance. So, for example, busy managers might be told they need to increase communication, yet although they might agree with that directive, they might not really follow through because they do not see it as a priority. That is, they don't recognize how the directive connects with achieving the performance outcomes that they are being held accountable for. In contrast, our data specifies the level of communication that is needed to drive improvement, and that information helps build a more compelling case for people to follow through on the recommended actions.

Looking deeper: what truly drives performance?

The survey results for the $100 million IT implementation in the example company helped identify the problem areas for that particular company. Analysing the results for *all* groups in our research helped answer a much larger question: what truly drives performance? Figure 2.3 shows how the 10 drivers are related to improvements in business performance. We conducted a regression analysis, confirmed by Structural Equation Modelling (SEM) to determine the strength and significance of each driver compared to the variable being assessed, in this case business performance. Note that business leadership, systems and process, vision and direction, and passion and drive are the main drivers, while fear and frustration have a negative effect (meaning that higher levels will decrease performance). Team leadership has little or no direct impact on business performance, but has strong secondary impacts on drivers that influence business performance, such as fear and frustration.

FIGURE 2.3   Drivers of improvement in business performance

FIGURE 2.4   Drivers of benefits realization

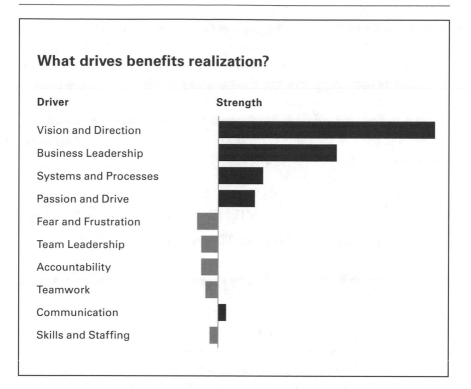

Figure 2.3 and Figure 2.4, which shows the drivers of benefits realization, help debunk a popular myth about change, and they explain why so many initiatives go off track. Communication, training (skills and staffing) and accountability have been the traditional cornerstones of many change programmes: they are concrete and tangible factors that can easily attract funding and are relatively simple to measure and convenient to manage. As such, leaders often focus on these few 'favourite' factors that they believe have produced results in the past. In actuality, though, those drivers have relatively little impact on improving business performance and achieving the benefits of change. Instead, the real drivers are vision and direction, business leadership, systems and processes, and passion and drive. (Note that for the drivers from team leadership downwards, these factors have small significance to benefits realization and any negative correlations can be attributed to 'noise' due to the very large effects of the highly significant drivers.)

Unfortunately, some of the high-impact drivers – such as passion and drive, and vision and direction – are less definable and more intangible. Moreover, they are not typically measured and managed in organizations.

In fact, more often than not, organizations assume that those factors will take care of themselves. Yet it is the hidden drivers that have the most impact on high-performance change, and that is why many initiatives fail to achieve their objectives – simply because they focus on only a fraction of the important factors that need to be managed. That, certainly, was a key issue that the global company experienced in managing its $100 million IT initiative. Executives there assumed that, because the levels of communication and training were sufficient, everything would proceed smoothly through to completion. As that company learned, though, achieving high-performance change requires much more than just managing one or two factors.

From data to maps: visualizing the complex interactions of different variables

Driver profiles indicate where potential problems might occur, but organizations need to be careful when considering that information. Adjusting just one driver – for example, increasing the staffing on a programme – can often fail to improve performance and might even be counterproductive. What organizations need is a more comprehensive system that takes into account all the different, complex interactions between the numerous pertinent variables. Furthermore, we have found that change rarely follows a simple, straightforward path. Instead, it is a non-linear journey with multiple pathways that groups can take. As such, maps are needed to capture and integrate all the complex information we have collected so that it can be presented in a clear, understandable framework. Ideally, such navigational tools would provide an effective early warning system, enabling organizations to spot potential issues and resolve them before they become large problems. They would also clearly indicate the actions required to stay on a path to high performance, such that organizations can make wise decisions about what resources to apply, where to deploy them and when to make those moves. All this would then take the guesswork out of change.

Developing such maps required advanced analytical methods. As we discussed in Chapter 1, we applied a self-organizing map (SOM) technique to identify natural groupings of our survey respondents. These clusters were then plotted with nearby locations to indicate groups with similar properties. The resulting map of the clusters represents a multidimensional, consolidated view representing *all* of the major coordinates of change. On the map, each point on the landscape is a unique combination of strengths and weaknesses (see Figure 1.1 – the change map on page 9 or the colour version of this map on page 20). Regions at the top are in an area of high performance; those at the bottom are in locations of very low performance.

Maps on 44 different dimensions

The driver profiles discussed earlier provide accurate data about a single group's current position. The change map helps place that position within the context of *all* change journeys undertaken by different teams, business units and organizations. Further, the maps contain much more information than just that indicated by the two-dimensional renderings shown in this book. In actuality, the change map has 44 different dimensions linked with the 44 core questions of our survey. In Figure 2.5 we plot the map in three-dimensions, with the vertical axis indicating fear and frustration (on the left-hand figure) and passion and drive (on the right). Note that, as one might expect, fear and frustration tend to be lowest in regions of high performance, and highest in regions of low performance (and the reverse is true for passion and drive),

FIGURE 2.5   Three-dimensional maps of fear and frustration, and passion and drive

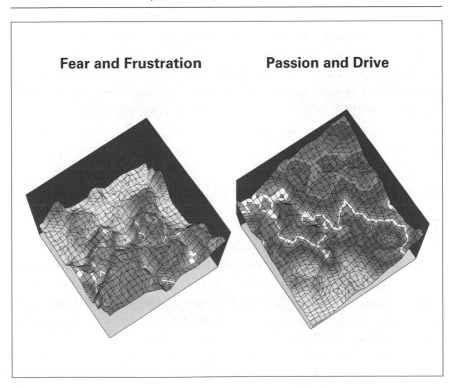

Fear and Frustration   **Passion and Drive**

but within that general topography there are numerous valleys and hills, indicating local minima and maxima. Our survey data can be displayed with respect to any of the 44 dimensions. In other words, underneath the surface of our change map are 44 three-dimensional layers of data, all similar to the ones shown in Figure 2.5.

We often use the two-dimensional map to talk about the different areas of change, but the three-dimensional views help illustrate the steep hills and valleys where small changes can lead to large improvements or drops. That is, the differences from one position on the map to another are not always incremental or step by step. Recognizing this terrain is critical in understanding the powerful nature of some specific interventions. For example, the terrain with respect to fear and frustration tends to be steep, where people can move from a very high level of fear and frustration to a very low level rather quickly because the process is non-linear – it is more like a tipping point.

The change map is based on more than 30 million data points from the more than 750,000 people we surveyed regarding their change initiatives. When a group is positioned on the map, it is situated with respect to all other groups, divisions, business units and organizations that have also undergone change initiatives. That location can easily change, according to the circumstances. For example, a company undergoing a restructuring might find itself at the bottom of the map even though it had been at the top during a previous reorganization just the year before. Moreover, our change map is universal. That is, there are not different maps for different change programmes. Just as with any map of the world, any person or group would be located somewhere on our change map and be able to find the way to anywhere else. Moreover, people can compare their routes with those of other travellers.

Four zones and 20 regions: classifying the topology of change

As mentioned earlier, we used a SOM technique to identify natural clusters in the data. Through that process, which required 33 billion calculations, we found that the different clusters fell into four zones on the change map – *High Performance*, *On Track*, *Unsustainable* and *Off Track*. *High Performance* contains the top 10 per cent of groups from our database in terms of business performance and, as we will see in Chapter 3, it is difficult to stay at this peak level. *On Track* means that performance is improving and groups positioned here are above the norm on overall driver strength.

For the many groups that reside in this zone, performance is acceptable but by no means great. *Unsustainable* means that performance is improving or around the same, but driver strength is below the norm. Examples include groups that come out of restructurings by focusing on cost management while failing to build sufficient capability to go to the next level. This is why we call it 'unsustainable'. *Off Track* means that performance is declining, and groups located in this zone have less than the norm in driver strength. For the $100 million IT initiative that we discussed at the start of this chapter, we found that many groups were in *Unsustainable* and *Off Track*, indicating the presence of underlying issues that would eventually become big problems.

Each of the four zones contains different regions (a total of 20 across the change map), representing the different ways in which groups typically react to change, the amount of change being experienced, the characteristics of the work environment, and so on. We have named those areas in ways that highlight their respective strengths or weaknesses. *In the Dark*, for example, is a region where most aspects of change capability are above the norm, but vision and direction are lacking and the level of management commitment is relatively low.

Emotion can be a particularly abstract concept in management, but our change map helps ensure that it is never ignored. In the region *Just Get On with It*, for example, leaders focus on tasks; they drive accountability; they build systems; and they deliver training. But they don't pay enough attention to emotions, as people feel undervalued and uninvolved, with high levels of frustration. The map makes clear that, unless leaders in this region address the emotional needs of their teams, change will stop dead in its tracks.

Nine 'capital cities': where do most change groups reside?

When we looked at the frequency of where groups were located on the change map, we found a very uneven distribution. Of the 20 different regions, **the vast majority of groups – around 75 per cent – tended to reside in what we call 'capital cities' (see Figure 2.6 or the colour version of this map on page 21). These nine locations have the highest population densities, and each of them represents distinct dynamics with recurring patterns of behaviour.**

Each of the four zones – *High Performance*, *On Track*, *Unsustainable* and *Off Track* – has at least one capital city. For example, most people in *High Performance* reside in *Cruising*, and hence that region is denoted a capital

FIGURE 2.6   Map of the nine 'capital cities' regions

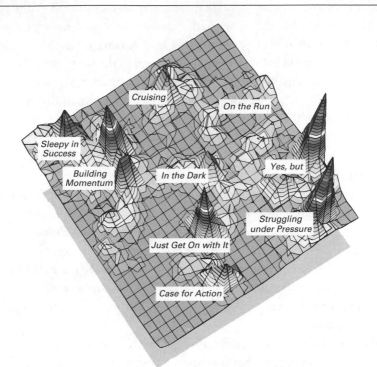

city. The main reason that groups tend to reside in capital cities is because they are unable to resolve the common difficulties and challenges they face. In the capital city *Case for Action*, for example, negative emotions are rampant, with workers feeling helpless, undervalued and cynical about change. If people could move on from the capital cities they would, but instead many become stuck.

The advantages of maps: visualizing complex information

From the earliest times in recorded history, maps have aided navigation – they have helped people to describe the world around them, to communicate this information to others, and to organize further ways of traversing and exploring unfamiliar terrain. Maps are representations of reality that serve to package the essence of the data gathered, to compress that information into meaningful symbols, and to show comparisons between the current location and other possible destinations.

Similarly, our change maps capture the relationships among ranges of variables, while simultaneously showing the different possible pathways from any given location. Instead of old-fashioned graphs laboriously charting one aspect of change at a time, our change maps display a wealth of information: where different parts of an organization are with respect to each other and in relation to where they have been, as well as the direction in which they should be heading. The information is set across a landscape that also shows other organizations' experiences of change, so that people can quickly see where change is on track and where it is not.

Moreover, most traditional measurement tools, such as climate and culture surveys, examine factors and provide relative scores that have an assumed but unproven relationship with improved business performance. And no consideration is given to the stage or complexity of the change process. Our change map has an empirical basis that ties the 10 drivers to business performance, and it inherently takes into account the various stages and complexities of different change initiatives. As mentioned earlier, each position on the map is defined by answers to the 44 core questions of our survey, and thus the map actually contains 44 three-dimensional layers of data. In other words, each location on the map captures a specific dynamic of change represented by a unique combination of different variables. As such, moving from one position to another on the map requires more than just a change in one factor – for example, an increase in the level of communication. Instead, any movement takes a larger change in dynamics – an increase in communications along with a greater agreement to the vision, deeper trust in leadership, improved teamwork and so on.

Also, leaders of large-scale programmes do not typically have just one team but multiple teams that they need to track. Because the change map is universal, leaders can see in a single view how their different teams are doing in relation to each other and with respect to the end goal. In some cases, for example, the map can show when a management team is in a completely different part of the change map than the rest of the organization, or if the IT team is lagging behind the sales group. In addition, the map can help identify the reasons for such disconnects. Figure 2.7 shows the change map for the $100 million IT initiative that we discussed at the start of this chapter. Note that the management team for that change programme was actually in *On Track*, while other groups were in *Unsustainable*. Not surprisingly, further analysis revealed that the level of vision and direction for managers was high, while the level of fear and frustration was low. For team members, the reverse was true.

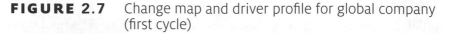

FIGURE 2.7   Change map and driver profile for global company (first cycle)

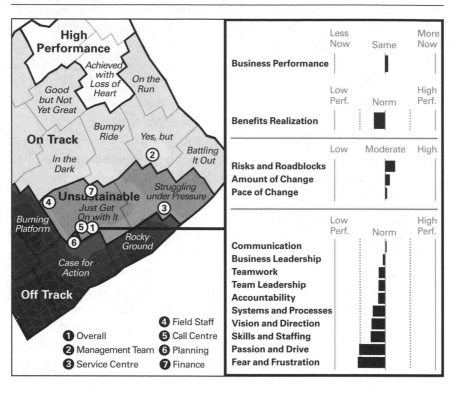

Therefore, using the change map, organizations can focus their interventions on the areas that will have the most impact towards achieving the desired outcomes. To do that, though, they first need to be aware of the common pathways leading into and out of the various regions on the change map.

Common pathways: getting from one region to another

Just as groups tend to reside in certain locations (the capital cities), they also tend to follow the same trails on their change journeys. By analysing our database we were able to identify those common pathways, some leading to higher performance and others travelling downwards. By understanding those patterns of movement, organizations can better manage their change initiatives. That is, **instead of thinking of change as a series of unknown and potentially chaotic events, organizations should now view it as a process**

FIGURE 2.8 Pathways example for *Just Get On with It* region

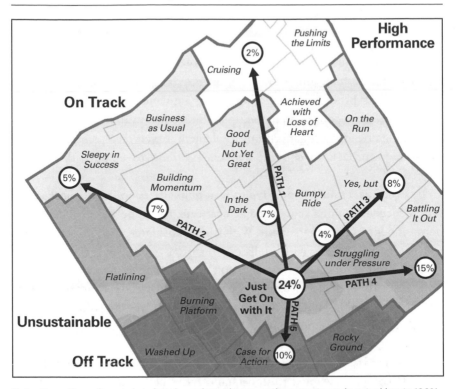

Note: Our pathway figures show just the major pathways, so the percentages do not add up to 100%.

marked by consistency and predictability *depending* on the decisions they make.

Consider groups that reside in *Just Get On with It*. Figure 2.8 shows the common paths taken by previous travellers out of this region. Note that some of these lead to further deterioration or travelling within the same zone of performance, while others lead to significant improvements. Identifying these common pathways was one of the most exciting discoveries from our research.

Not only were we able to identify those common pathways, we were also able to determine the specific actions behind each of those journeys. Again, this was based on all of the data we collected on the thousands of groups that we studied. For instance, to leave *Just Get On with It* for an area of higher performance, we know that team leaders must do three specific things: lower the level of fear, clarify the vision and strengthen people's commitment to the change initiative. Behind that, they must have the competence and capacity to carry out these tasks, preferably with the support of at least the next level of management.

A coordinated package: highly focused actions sequenced across time

In medieval times, people using a giant catapult to attack a castle knew that hurling one boulder wouldn't suffice. Breaching the thick stone walls required many hits, and from a number of angles. Breaking down the barriers that prevent organizations from implementing change requires the same kind of coordinated, multiple attacks from different perspectives. Unfortunately, many organizations implement a piecemeal, single-variable-at-a-time approach to change, frequently failing to achieve the desired objectives.

Indeed, **successful change typically requires a coordinated package of highly focused actions sequenced across time, all supported by a sustained commitment from management.** We have encapsulated such information in our navigation system, which tells organizations what needs to be done to move a group from its current location on the change map to an optimal path towards high performance. Change initiatives are characterized by numerous variables interacting together, and our system allows users to visualize those interactions and the ways in which they can be adjusted to improve performance.

After the $100 million IT system (in the company example above) went live, the company wanted to understand what had gone wrong. Through our analysis, we found that staffers were frustrated with the new system's software problems, a slow rollout of upgrades and inaccuracies in the database. In fact, people simply did not trust the new, fully automated, rule-based system – this, combined with a lack of role clarity, led to an excessively high number of manual overrides. Also, staff training had concentrated on *how* to use the system and not on its role in the business. Moreover, the survey results had identified various weaknesses in the drivers, including an abnormally low level of accountability.

Based on those findings, a strategy was devised for getting the IT initiative back on track. To increase the confidence of those using the system, the technical issues were addressed and staffers received additional training that focused on *why* the system was needed as well as on how it would be affecting their workflow. Also, teams were given greater autonomy, for instance, in managing budgets with clear targets for which they were then held accountable. These and other measures led to substantial improvements with respect to a number of drivers. After six months of intensive work to address the various issues, fear and frustration had decreased considerably, teamwork had improved dramatically, and the level of vision and direction was up by around 50 per cent. All this translated directly to the bottom line. The company was able to bring the initiative back on budget, and it more than halved its transactional costs from $14 to $6, all while achieving slightly better customer-service metrics. The end result: the company saved $5 million on its operational budget of $28 million.

Obviously, it is not always possible for individuals to influence factors outside their control, such as the amount of change taking place, the level of resources and the training they receive. But by using the collective wisdom of hundreds of thousands of change travellers, our approach enables people to work more creatively within the known constraints. Having established where they are on the map, they can develop an action plan of the multiple interventions required to get a group's driver scores from where they are to where they need to be in order to reach a region of higher performance. And, as they implement those interventions, they can then track their progress – the driver scores along with measures of business performance and benefit realization – so that they can clearly see the impact of those actions. This then enables them to revise and refine their action plan as needed.

Of course, any change process will inevitably lead to tensions between the old and the new, but our maps and navigation system help bring those issues to the forefront so that they can be discussed openly. It is through such difficult conversations that progress is typically made. In the case of that company's $100 million IT initiative, after we conducted a survey of the 380 people involved in that change programme we could then help the company to identify the key issues. Armed with that hard data, executives then held an intensive series of 45 team meetings, through all company levels, to discuss the various actions needed to get the initiative back on track. Thanks to that process, trust was restored, and people began to take ownership of the outcomes so that, ultimately, old patterns of poor performance could be broken. Since this approach to change happened in a way that engaged people and built their strength, the organization was left ready to respond to further change. And there is another benefit to using maps: in our experience, maps not only enable travellers on a journey to plot their routes, they also provide visual and spatial information that can help boost morale, particularly as people begin to near their destinations. 'We're almost there!' can be a powerful rallying cry to help the weary make it over the finish line.

The typical change journey: non-linear but predictable

Change journeys do not typically go from origin to destination in a linear, straightforward fashion. They often take detours, get stuck at some

FIGURE 2.9   Change map and driver profile for global company
(first and second cycles)

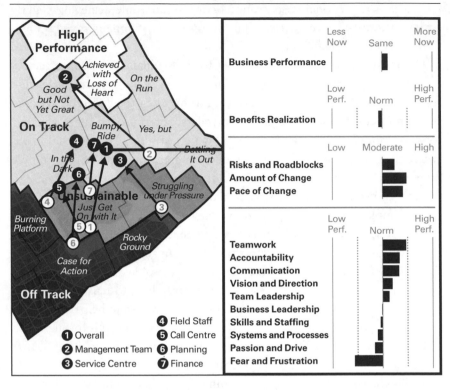

locations, double back and go through intermediate steps. Indeed, **very few groups can move from the lower regions of the change map to the highest possible levels of performance in just one step**. That said, we should emphasize again that, **although change may not be a linear process, our research definitely shows that it is neither chaotic nor random. Instead, change is highly predictable and entirely dependent on the decisions that people make.** Figure 2.9 shows the movement of different groups in that $100 million IT initiative, before and after the company had implemented the interventions we discussed earlier.

Overall, the change programme moved from the *Unsustainable* to the *On Track* zone, with the management team making the most improvement. On our change map, that amount of movement might not look all that impressive – and, to be sure, the initiative had a way to go before reaching the *High Performance* zone. As we noted earlier, though, even that seemingly small improvement helped save the company $5 million on its operational budget of $28 million.

Mastering the nine dynamics of change

For many organizations, implementing change initiatives can be a confusing, overwhelming process, but that is only because they lack an effective framework. Our research has identified nine capital cities on our change map, where most groups tend to reside as they undergo change. The good news is that when the dynamics of those cities are mastered, an organization will basically have the capabilities to manage any challenge with change, from groups with very low performance to those with extremely high, as well as everything in between. In other words, master those nine dynamics and you become a master of change. To get change to work for you instead of against you, leaders and managers need to understand the underlying characteristics, dynamics and challenges of those nine capital cities.

The remainder of this book is focused on those capital cities. In Chapters 3 through 11, we describe the strengths and weaknesses of each city, the critical issues that require attention, and the typical complications, including the reasons why it is difficult to escape certain regions. In addition, we show the traffic on the common routes from those cities to other locations, and we describe what decisions will lead to which pathways. We start with change programmes that are achieving the very best performance (Chapter 3) and then move to the very worst (Chapter 4) and everything in between (Chapters 5 through 11). At the end of each chapter, we provide a summary checklist of the main points and key research findings so that readers can jump from one chapter to another, depending on the issues in their organization.

SUMMARY FOR CHAPTER 2: KEY INSIGHTS

● Our research has taught us three invaluable things about change:

- A piecemeal approach to change rarely works; instead, successful change programmes require a coordinated package of highly focused actions sequenced throughout the various stages of the initiative, all underpinned by a sustained commitment from management.

- The vast majority of change programme participants and groups (about 75 per cent) tend to fall into one of nine clusters, which we call 'capital cities', each containing individuals and groups with similar characteristics, including performance levels, conditions of change, behaviours, dynamics and

▶

challenges. They get stuck because they are unable to resolve the common difficulties and challenges they face.

– Even though change journeys might sometimes appear to proceed in chaotic and random ways, they are actually quite predictable – and largely dependent on the decisions that leaders and managers make.

● To effectively navigate change, leaders need to understand that the relationship between what happens with people – how they react and respond to change – and the impact on business outcomes is not simple and it is not linear.

● The change model shows the relationship among performance outcomes, turbulence (the conditions under which change takes place) and the 10 specific drivers that affect performance. These range from the available resources and strength of leadership, to the feelings of individual participants in the change effort.

● Communication, training (skills and staffing) and accountability have been the traditional cornerstones of many change programmes. But, in truth, those drivers have relatively little impact on improving business performance and achieving the benefits of change.

● Business leadership, systems and processes, vision and direction, and passion and drive are the main drivers of business performance, while fear and frustration has a negative effect (meaning that higher levels of this will decrease performance).

● The real drivers of benefits realization are vision and direction, and business leadership – followed by systems and processes, and passion and drive.

● Change maps that capture and integrate the complex information collected on change programmes take the guesswork out of change. Change maps help organizations to find their way, acting as an early warning system to the problems about to beset an initiative, while modelling scenarios proactively to find the best path forward.

03

High Performance
Reaching the highest levels of performance

> *Never let failure discourage you. Every time you get to the base of a mountain (literal or metaphorical), you're presented with a new opportunity to challenge yourself, to push your limits beyond what you thought possible, to learn from climbers on the trail ahead of you, and to take in some amazing views.* **ALISON LEVINE**

Six years ago, a subsidiary of a multinational financial services company was in serious trouble. It was losing millions of dollars a year and needed to embark on a major transformation just to survive, with all aspects of the business being examined and reviewed. Across the full six-year period of that continuous change initiative, over 50 per cent of the staff turned over – their numbers were reduced by 15 per cent in a global downsizing that was non-negotiable; the company went through three changes of CEO; and only a fraction of the senior executives remained. Ultimately, though, the effort paid off. Now the organization has become profitable for the first time in years, enabling it to pay the biggest dividend in its 40-year history. By almost any measure, the major change initiative was a resounding success.

Unfortunately, such success stories are more commonly the exception than the rule. According to our research, only 10 per cent of groups that undertake change initiatives eventually arrive in the *High Performance* zone. Moreover, getting to organizational 'heaven' does not happen by accident. Nearly all of the groups that do so come from regions in the *On Track* zone. In fact, only a small percentage of groups ever make it to *High Performance* directly from the *Off Track* or *Unsustainable* zones. This supports the notion that change navigation involves a series of steps – one, two or even more steps to move from the lower regions of the change map to the highest possible levels of performance.

In the *High Performance* zone, benefits realization and business performance are at their peak levels. Moreover, a high amount of change is taking place at a fast pace and all of the drivers are at or close to high-performance levels. One of the most interesting things about this zone of top performance is that it is not a single state but instead consists of three separate regions: *Pushing the Limits*, *Achieved with Loss of Heart* and *Cruising* (the latter being a capital city). Each of these areas has its distinct set of dynamics and challenges. For *Pushing the Limits*, the major challenge is to continue performing at the edge of what is possible. In *Achieved with Loss of Heart*, people struggle with having delivered benefits for their organizations, but are left questioning 'What's in it for me?' For groups in *Cruising*, everyone must resist the temptation of sitting in the comfort zone of being successful and becoming overly complacent. Any failure to address these issues adequately can lead to a group quickly tumbling out of *High Performance*. Before we discuss those specific challenges, though, let's take a closer look at how people are able to reach the top of the change map in the first place.

Getting to *High Performance*

When CEOs recount war stories of their past change programmes, they often omit many of the twists and turns so that the dilemmas they faced and the wrong choices they took are all but forgotten. Lessons learned are typically oversimplified – for example, 'communication and teamwork were the keys to our success' – thus making them difficult to apply in other settings. The difference for us is that we followed and measured the progress of the above-mentioned global financial services company as it navigated through its change initiative, so success and failure were tracked at every step of the way. For six years, the changing behaviour and responses of the entire organization of 1,000 staff were monitored at 12 measurement points, each roughly six months apart. By analysing that data, we could identify the decisions they made at each stage in time and track the consequences of those choices.

So, what is needed to make the leap to *High Performance*? The answer, according to data of the financial services firm above, as well as that of all the other groups that managed to reach the top, is seemingly simple in theory yet very difficult to accomplish in practice: a 25–45 per cent average increase across all drivers is needed in order to move from *On Track* into *High Performance*. That is, **getting to *High Performance* requires more than improving on a single or even a few dimensions. What is needed is high driver strength across all 10 change drivers**. In other words, no single action will magically rocket an organization or group to *High Performance*. Rather, multiple actions are needed, sustained across long periods of time.

In the *On Track* zone, organizations are able to realize on average 79 per cent of their change benefits. If they seek to increase that to the 92 per cent achieved in *High Performance*, they will need to expend considerable additional effort. Vision needs to be embraced across all levels in the organization, translating into increases in the amount of change, especially with respect to the new way of working. The pace of change also increases, going from 'okay' to 'just faster than okay', which is the optimal level. Among the critical actions that will distinguish those that make the transition from those that don't are the following: the business leader's commitment to embracing the change, increased communication, involvement in a well-managed change programme, higher levels of trust in senior leaders, quick remedial action to identified problems and improved levels of customer service. Simply taking out costs will not suffice.

For the global financial services firm cited above, during the heart of its final push to reach the top the company increased the level of its business and team leadership each by close to 40 per cent, building strong alignment across all levels of leadership. In addition, the level of communication increased by 64 per cent, while fear and frustration dropped by 43 per cent. Not surprisingly, workplace morale also experienced an upswing. As one employee remarked, 'Things are definitely changing here and the pace of change is, in itself, increasing... This is positive, necessary and exciting – one gets to feel one is part of something worthwhile and meaningful. We can be proud of where we are and where we're going!' As another employee put it, 'I love what I am doing and would continue to do [it] without any second thought!' Interestingly, when we analysed all the text comments in our database, the word 'love' only starts to be used in a consistent manner for groups that have moved into *High Performance*: 'I love my job', 'I love working with my colleagues', 'I love working for this company' and so on.

High Performance insights

As mentioned earlier, *High Performance* is where groups are at the peak levels of performance and benefits realization. Moreover, all of the 10 drivers are well above the norm, especially teamwork, accountability, and vision and direction; and fear and frustration is at low levels. In our study of groups and organizations that were able to reach *High Performance*, we uncovered two important insights about the zone: 1) high-performing groups thrive on change; 2) reaching the top is one thing, remaining there is quite another.

FIGURE 3.1   Change map and driver profile for the
High Performance zone

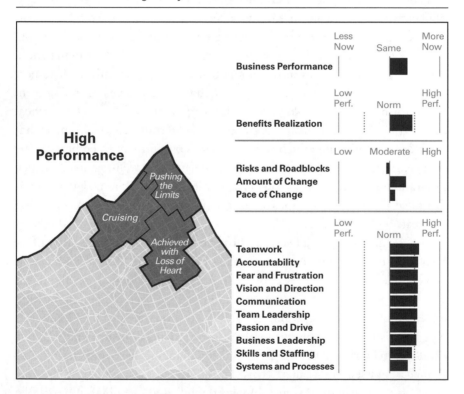

Insight 1: high-performing groups thrive on change

Achieving high performance is not for the faint of heart, given that it requires groups to take on large amounts of change at a fast pace. As discussed in Chapter 1, a common misconception is that too much change, or change that is too fast, is bad for organizations. But our research shows that high-performing groups generally thrive on change, both in terms of the amount and pace. That was certainly the case at the global financial services firm cited above, which experienced tremendous upheaval over a six-year period, with a staff turnover of over 50 per cent and a new CEO every two years on average.

Insight 2: reaching the top is one thing, remaining there is quite another

In our research, we found that about two-thirds of groups that make it to the top for the first time are not able to stay there. The absence of further change taking place is one of the main reasons why, and another reason is the loss of driver strength. Groups that seek to remain in *High Performance* must continually improve their business performance or risk slipping to a region of lower performance. This means continual increases in business effectiveness, customer service, cost management and so on. In today's fast-moving business world this means not just being good once, but continually improving in order to remain at the top. It's one thing for a project or programme to reach *High Performance*, it's quite another for leaders to build the capability for continuous change – namely, agility – into their organization as a whole. Indeed, successful change requires that daily activities need to continually improve while change takes place, for example, as the systems and processes that underpin them are undergoing transition. Organizations need to maintain customer service levels and ensure that their ability to manage costs in the business does not diminish because change is occurring. In fact, if costs get out of control or customer service declines while change is being implemented, we would regard this as a failure to properly manage change, and this is one of the common reasons why groups can spiral down from *High Performance*.

The challenges of *High Performance*

In the past, investments in IT infrastructure have often been held up as the driver for organizations to move into *High Performance* and maintain a leading edge in the market. Our results, however, show that although resources and infrastructure are important, they are not the most crucial factors. In fact, on the profile for the *High Performance* zone (see Figure 3.1), the two least important drivers are skills and staffing, and systems and processes. In contrast, the most important drivers are teamwork and accountability. Moreover, the importance of great leadership and management – to keep teams functioning at this level and build the necessary critical mass to stay there – cannot be underestimated. There is no question that all of the recognized business skills, including strategic planning, decision-making, project management and all aspects of people management, are standard prerequisites for any organization in *High Performance*. But this is not where the extra edge comes from. Supporting and sustaining high levels of change capability is the key, and a leader's mastery of the psychological dimensions of those processes plays a critical role.

Our research has repeatedly shown that leaders' actions – or inactions – are guided by their mindsets. For example, if their mindset is focused on achieving programme outcomes rather than on building organizational change capabilities, then they will take different actions and achieve very different results. In nearly all instances where groups fall out of *High Performance*, leaders have been caught off-guard, not paying attention to what needs to be done before it happens and not taking steps to build strong capabilities before additional change takes place. **It is important to note that organizational falls from *High Performance* are typically preceded by collapses in some or all of the 10 key drivers, and could therefore have been anticipated.**

What this is saying is that traditional leadership skills are only half of the equation that is needed for success. Leaders in charge of organizational change are often stretched to the limits. As well as managing day-to-day operations and planning for the organization's future, they must restructure, reorganize and keep the heads and hearts of the organization aligned by dealing with people's reactions to change. To do that, they need the right mental attitude and emotional (psychological) processes that enable them to persevere through the various challenges that will inevitably come their way. Moreover, it is not just a matter of the right mindset. Leaders managing organizational change must also possess considerable internal strength, courage and determination to continue forging forward even when the path ahead looks bleak.

With that in mind, let's now take a closer look at the specific challenges of *High Performance*. Of the three regions in the zone, only *Cruising* is a capital city so we will spend more time discussing it. First, though, we take a look at the two other regions: *Pushing the Limits* and *Achieved with Loss of Heart*.

Pushing the Limits

Not many reach the rarefied atmosphere of *Pushing the Limits*, which is at the very peak of the change map. These exceptional groups are full of excitement and drive. Trust in leadership is exceptionally high, teams are crystal clear about their performance objectives and measurable outcomes, and people feel highly valued and are very satisfied with their jobs. Everyone is on the same page. To reach the *Pushing the Limits* region, teams must be close-knit, exhibiting a high level of trust between individuals.

For teams that aspire to reach this region, the importance of account-ability, in the true meaning of the word – highly disciplined teamwork with clarity of role and purpose and clear objectives – cannot be underestimated. It involves a clear intention and sustained effort across long periods of time. Consider the rollout of a major IT programme across a retail and consumer goods company: in the early phases of the rollout, senior managers and their teams worked hard to gain cooperation across the business; they had not underestimated the challenge of gaining business buy-in and keeping their promises, and the programme made it to *Pushing the Limits*. Our data shows that vision is important in *Pushing the Limits* but it comes second to accountability.

Other characteristics of the *Pushing the Limits* region are that distress and anger are very low, and people are not thinking of leaving. Fear, though, is higher than normal. Although not at an overwhelming level, fear sits in the background because the amount of change that is occurring is high, particularly as the group achieves higher growth. Faced with the unknown, it is natural that people's anxieties might rise. But the fear level is kept in check because the trust in business unit leaders and organizational leaders is extremely high. Sometimes small 'touchpoints' with executives can have a huge impact in helping to stabilize fears. In addition, the data also unequivocally show that leadership plays a *supporting* role by providing the resources, such as work-group processes and systems, required to sustain a high level of performance and by creating an environment in which teams can strive to do their best.

Making it to the top might be quite an achievement, but the air is thin there and it takes considerable energy to keep pushing for continuous improvement. Once at the summit, the view may be spectacular and vast but there is nowhere else to go but down. There are many forces – both internal and external to the organization – that can come into play and affect whether a group remains at the top. Depending on the organizational culture, others could resent the group for doing so well and resources could become increasingly difficult to attain; the group itself might become arrogant or overly confident, leaving it vulnerable to changing conditions; or the leaders of such groups become bored or distracted, particularly if they tend to be entrepreneurial leaders.

Performing on the edge

To understand the challenge of continuously *Pushing the Limits*, consider John Bertrand, the Australian yachtsman who was the winning skipper of the *Australia II* in the 1983 America's Cup. With that victory, Bertrand ended the US 132-year reign of dominance. How did he reach the rarefied atmosphere of *High Performance*? The right mindset certainly helped. 'Every night before I went to sleep', he recalled, 'I shut myself away and lived in my own mind the feeling of being out in front, in the quiet, in the midst of the tension. And as I dreamed my separate dreams, it became easier'. Bertrand relentlessly trained his crew – building trust and discipline so that they could confidently sail to a win when the opportunity arrived: 'I told them that... when the moment comes, we will do what great teams always do... We are going to sail our boat as it has *never* been sailed before. Nothing is going to stop us' (Bertrand and Robinson, 1985: 210).

After winning the America's Cup, the temptation might have been to become complacent. Indeed, many businesses reach the top only to fall back because they cannot defend that space and handle the uncertainty of competing on the edge. Not Bertrand, though. Several years after his stunning victory, his new boat broke in two in a new quest for the cup. Although disappointed, he was hardly crushed by the setback. 'We're talking about life on the edge. People focus on the boat breaking, but that's the reality of living on the edge', he explained. 'Even though our boat broke and sank, that's the game we were playing. If we weren't on edge, we weren't going to be competitive.' Indeed, **many athletes (and organizations) fall from the elite ranks because they become too risk averse. Instead of striving to be the best, they play not to lose**.

Of course, living on the edge would be foolish without the proper preparation, and Bertrand made sure that his team was always ready for competition. As he reminded his crew before the critical 1983 race, 'All we have to do is to reproduce our winning form. Nothing different. Just the moves we know will be successful... No one is asking anything more of you than what you have already produced a thousand times before' (Bertrand and Robinson, 1985). Also, to warn his crew against doing anything rash – going beyond their limitations and looking for the one magical manoeuvre that would give them a decisive advantage – Bertrand succinctly said, 'it never works'. This is the same message that we have found about reaching the top. What gets people there and keeps them there are the simple basics: highly focused teamwork, the discipline of accountability, passion and drive, and – as Bertrand ably demonstrated – excellent team leadership.

Achieved with Loss of Heart

The majority of groups that arrive in *Achieved with Loss of Heart* do so from the *On Track* regions of *On the Run*, *Bumpy Ride* and *Yes, but*. A defining characteristic of people who make it to this region is that they arrive feeling bumped and bruised. They have strived to reach the top, and for their organizations they have delivered the necessary outcomes, only to fall short of their personal goals. Reaching *High Performance* in the third year of a shared services implementation was a positive outcome for one company in our study, as employees had worked hard to move up from the lower regions of *On Track*. When the firm arrived in *Achieved with Loss of Heart*, though, it was visible that the change had taken a toll. People were tired and some of the leaders and members in their teams had had difficulty in their work–life balance. In reality, performance in this region is at much the same level as in *Cruising*, but the environment is markedly different. Inhabitants of *Achieved with Loss of Heart* have lost out personally even as they have delivered benefits for their organizations. How exactly, though, does that disappointment tend to play itself out?

In *Achieved with Loss of Heart*, people are high achievers who have set ambitious targets and have accomplished much. Their determination is great, with very high levels of teamwork and accountability. Vision and direction are clear, and team leadership is strong. People see where they are going and they know what to do to get there. Yet although distress, anger and fear are low, the promise of reward has not exactly worked out as expected, breeding discontentment.

The name of the region – *Achieved with Loss of Heart* – says it all: people have delivered on outcomes for the organization yet at a potentially high cost to themselves. As a result, individuals can be left feeling undervalued and possibly even bitter and angry. In some cases, staff might become cynical, especially if the organization has failed to recognize their contributions. Moreover, making it to the *High Performance* zone can easily result in burnout, particularly if employees have neglected their work–life balance. The hard truth is that groups might not have received the support they needed to get to the highest levels of performance. In our research, people cited a lack of resources, systems and processes, and skills and staffing as their biggest challenges for this region, more so than in surrounding areas. Other challenges, to a slightly lesser degree, included people's feelings that they were not being adequately rewarded and recognized, and that their talents were not being fully utilized. The underlying feeling is, 'What's in it for me?' and 'Why can't we have the resources we need to get the job done?'

Failing to meet the expectations of one's aspirations can be extremely harmful in unexpected ways. Some people withdraw, intentionally avoiding co-workers, or they seek jobs that are not as demanding. Even though a group still has confidence in its immediate boss, members feel that the senior leadership is out of touch with what they need.

In such an environment, rumours often abound, causing tension among the various groups in the organization. To relieve stress, workers resort to sarcastic humour or adopt wry attitudes, or they resort to blaming and undermining others. But if group members can manage to stay close, they focus on developing an effective strategy, dispelling rumours and working together to improve mutual recognition and the group's morale. When members start feeling better about themselves, they begin pushing for what they need in terms of resources. This path, however, is not common – only 8 per cent of groups move from here into the *Cruising* region, and even fewer make it to *Pushing the Limits*.

Instead, 70 per cent drop down the change map. Indeed, the far more typical path is for the entire group to become disaffected, which is disastrous because many of these people are such high performers. When that happens, members begin to explore individual rather than team agendas in order to resolve their own dissatisfactions. Relationships with management deteriorate and communications break down. For their part, leaders easily become frustrated, knowing that morale is wavering. From the comments we have collected, we see that increasing the sense of urgency also creates anxiety, which is helpful if it pushes everyone to action but can instead be counterproductive if it immobilizes people.

This situation can be likened to a group climbing to just under the summit of a mountain, where hikers stand on a slope exposed to avalanches. It is a precarious state, with people, including the highest performers, questioning whether they should stay or not. If good employees do leave, that makes the situation all the more difficult for the morale and working environment of those who remain. That is why so many groups have difficulty maintaining their position in *Achieved with Loss of Heart*, let alone moving higher on the change map. In fact, only 18 per cent of groups stay in this region; most groups either move on or fall down.

Arriving bumped and bruised

According to conventional wisdom, people will often quit their jobs when they find themselves disengaged from their work. But **in *Achieved with Loss** *of Heart*, **good employees don't leave because they are disengaged, they leave precisely because they are *very* engaged with their work. They are fully engaged, but not feeling valued.** After devoting themselves wholeheartedly to a cause, high performers can easily become burnt out and question the rationale behind their efforts: 'What's the point, after all?'

So it is not surprising that people might want to leave. But these workers are the very individuals that management wants to retain. Our research has shown that they often hold key positions, and when they leave they take business, important clients and key expertise with them. All too often, organizations only become aware of the problem when it is too late to persuade their best people from moving on. At that point, even a skilled leader needs considerable time and resources in order to repair the damage.

John Bertrand recognized that competent team members would sometimes lose focus under pressure – it is just what happens. But rather than exposing an individual in the team and making it their personal failure, he had the team practice 'failure routines' in advance. These became just a part of what the team did in its normal course of action – the safety net of the team making it easier for an individual to lose focus and then quickly bounce back. This also helps individuals to feel valued when the going gets tough, as the team rallies around the failure.

To prevent the defection of good employees, business unit and team leaders must engage the senior executives at higher levels of the organization. It is important that those top decision-makers recognize the need to provide adequate resources, yet they are often too out of touch. Sometimes senior executives might be too busy with their own self-interests of engaging in organizational politics, fighting turf battles rather than developing their people. As such, organizations should encourage business unit and team leaders to become more independent and assertive, with a mandate to convincingly argue their case for resources with top management. The more those leaders are able to pose the lack of resources as a challenge to people's creativity and ingenuity, the more likely groups will be to receive the necessary resources. Also, within teams, instead of focusing on individual agendas, people should be encouraged to align around common goals. Team-building exercises, constructive confrontation meetings and coaching can all be invaluable to help establish that type of environment.

Moreover, because people in *Achieved with Loss of Heart* tend to feel unrecognized, unrewarded and unfulfilled, leaders need to take the time to display empathy and nurture employees' talents and potential. Although it is not always possible to influence factors such as the amount of change taking place, the level of resources available and so on, ample evidence exists that groups can make great strides in improving their situations through open and honest discussions. (We explore this topic in our description of the *Yes, but* region in Chapter 7.) Specifically, groups that understand what they can – and cannot – change and that feel recognized for who they are and for what they bring to the table can become energized, working creatively within their constraints and with their given resources to achieve very successful outcomes.

Cruising, a capital city

We now visit *Cruising*. In discussing this capital city of the *High Performance* zone, we will describe the particular features of the landscape, what people experience in dwelling here, how they organize and, when things take a turn for the worse, what influences the changes in this region.

Groups in *Cruising* are performing remarkably well, with both benefits realization and business performance at the very highest levels (see Figure 3.2). In other words, this is where results are truly being delivered from the change programme. Groups here are typified by low amounts of fear and frustration, with a moderate amount of change taking place and low to moderate risk as well as minimal stress. In *Pushing the Limits* and *Achieved with Loss of Heart* (the regions adjacent to *Cruising*), much higher amounts of change are occurring, creating more turbulence and higher levels of negative feelings. But in *Cruising*, life is good and positive emotions are high, with teams being both cohesive and productive.

In *Cruising*, generally speaking, energy is abundant, with passion and drive, and communication, among the highest-scoring drivers. Workplace loyalty is also high, and teammates feel valued for their contributions. This is the place where people want to be. (Unfortunately, only 7 per cent of groups get to experience this region.) Workers are literally cruising on their confidence. They are clear on their roles and responsibilities, and their performance objectives are clear and measurable.

Moreover, workers have high confidence in their immediate managers, and leaders are generally perceived well. In fact, the level of trust and confidence in organizational, business unit and team leadership is extremely high. This indicates that people feel a sense of alignment, cooperation and even synergy between different levels in the organization. The primary role of leadership teams in *Cruising* is to provide support and guidance for other groups. As we will see in subsequent chapters, the main issue for managers in this region is not what is going on with their own groups, but how their groups can help others who are struggling in more difficult regions.

FIGURE 3.2   Change map and driver profile for *Cruising* region

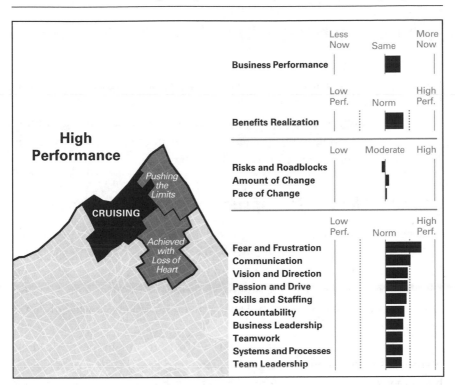

The driver profile for *Cruising* shows just three areas that need attention: team leadership, systems and processes, and teamwork (see Figure 3.2). As discussed earlier, team leadership and teamwork are the very drivers that groups need to improve in order to move into *Pushing the Limits*. In most cases, however, leaders don't bother to focus on them, because they might have other fires to fight outside the group and, truth be told, most groups are content just to be in *Cruising*. After all, things are going well and people feel no real need to change.

Indeed, our research shows that only 3 per cent of groups in *Cruising* make it to *Pushing the Limits*. Examining the data provides insight into why that is the case. As it turns out, groups that want to move between those two regions must achieve a greater than 30 per cent improvement in team and business leadership, teamwork and accountability. Also, an increasing amount of change will help – and not hinder – progress. It is as if groups need to rally and tell themselves, 'Let's go for broke and literally push ourselves to the very limits of what we can achieve.' But is it truly worth the effort? The answer is not clear-cut: groups that successfully make the transition will achieve a significant but moderate 10 per cent improvement in business performance and benefits realization.

Thus the challenge for most groups in *Cruising* is not to move up but to maintain their current position – something that only 34 per cent of groups are able to do. Again, examining the data from the driver profile yields some insights as to why that is so. Groups in *Cruising* have slightly lower scores with respect to 1) systems and processes, and 2) teamwork. This starts to signal that failing to provide the resources needed to sustain high performance, and neglecting to nurture teams that are at the heart of change, can potentially become big issues further down the road.

Sitting in the comfort of success and complacency

A large area of concern in *Cruising* is that groups tend to be challenged by the comfort that comes with success. After change has kept a group going for a considerable amount of time, suddenly there is a lack of adrenaline from the change initiative. A common syndrome is for people to be lulled into a sense of false complacency, leaving them unprepared for handling the next round of problems.

We should warn here that the name '*Cruising*' might be misleading. '*Cruising*' should not imply anyone lounging on a beach chair with a martini but rather sitting in a jet fighter at 30,000 feet. If people take their eyes off the situation, they can spin out of control very quickly. Indeed, the danger here is that people – especially leaders – might become complacent, with success blinding them to emerging issues. As Bill Gates, the former CEO of Microsoft, once said, 'Success is a lousy teacher. It seduces smart people into thinking they can't lose' (Gates, 1995). Moreover, if leaders become too detached from their groups, they could easily become out of touch with other parts of the organization. Although *Cruising* might be the place of comfort in the *High Performance* zone, the harsh reality is that **around 66 per cent of groups that are in this region for the first time do not make it back a second time**.

The bottom line is that, unlike all the other capital cities, the challenge in *Cruising* is not to manage change in order to get somewhere else. Instead, the challenge is to stay in the same location, and that requires sustaining high performance, which can be very difficult to do. In some respects, **groups in *Cruising* need to become *change resilient*, and the crucial challenge is to plan against potential failure when the temptation is instead to bask in success**.

Carol Dweck, a psychology professor at Stanford University, has looked at the difference between two different types of mindsets: one that considers success to be the result of the talent of the individuals at the top (fixed mindset), and another that takes success as something to be earned (growth mindset) (Dweck, 2006). For the first mindset, people tend to feel that nothing more needs to be done once they have achieved success. The thinking is that, 'We're at the top because we're so gifted'. For the second mindset, reaching the top merely provides opportunities to use that success as a platform for further learning, and that is the type of perspective that helps teams to sustain their success.

Leaders need to keep in mind that they reached *High Performance* in the first place not by magic or good luck, but because they built strong driver capability in their groups. To stay there and thrive, this same capability needs to be nurtured and actively supported and sustained. So, instead of becoming complacent and taking change capabilities for granted, leaders need to redouble their efforts and anticipate changes, such as a drop in accountability, while there is still time to address any emerging issues before they become larger problems. In particular, they should consider the possibility that, after having strived to change their groups in one direction – for example, by focusing on improving teamwork – they might then encounter an unanticipated challenge that comes from an entirely different direction – for instance, a decrease in the resources available or a lack of growth, which is a real risk in *Cruising*. As such, leaders need to ask themselves and their groups the following: if the change initiative were to fail at this point, where would the problem likely come from?

Of course that question is hypothetical, and a group or organization might not encounter any of the potential difficulties raised. But those issues – however far-fetched they might seem – will provide information on possible risks that a group might choose to address proactively, rather than waiting for problems to manifest, requiring people to react defensively. Leaders should remember the extreme difficulty of trying to find a creative solution to a pressing problem when the consequences for failure are dire. Much easier is when they are looking for ways to ward off a potential issue when there is room to manoeuvre and resources are still available.

Indeed, generating a future based on how a team might fail and developing strategies to manage those scenarios before they happen is just as important – if not more so – as the process of using people's imagination to envision a positive future. Either way, the key is to remain open-minded about the future in order to be better prepared for any changes on the horizon. 'If an organization is narrow in the images that it directs toward its own actions, then when it examines what it has said, it will see only bland displays', notes Karl Weick, the organizational theorist. '[But] an organization that continually sees itself in novel images, images that are permeated with diverse skills and sensitivities, thereby is equipped to deal with altered surroundings when they appear' (Weick, 1979).

Common pathways exiting *Cruising*

We have described the characteristics of the capital city *Cruising* and its challenges. We have analysed the paths that groups take when moving out of *Cruising*. This information offers clear indications of where problems can arise and, armed with such knowledge, proactive leaders can then implement measures to change-proof their organizations. Based on our findings, 34 per cent of groups remain in *Cruising*, and those that leave this region move in one of five main directions (see Figure 3.3). We will discuss each of those pathways, highlighting some case examples in more depth. (Note: the examples in this section represent a composite of organizations from our research with similar experiences of change.)

FIGURE 3.3   Common pathways exiting *Cruising*

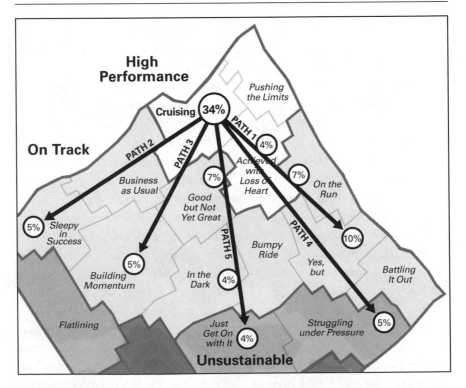

Path 1: *moving to* Achieved with Loss of Heart, On the Run *and* Yes, but

Twenty-one per cent of groups move down this path. For example, a midsize accountancy firm, initially in *Cruising*, merged with a competitor. Initially, the new and bigger firm had more leverage to attract clients and saw some benefits. However, after the first year, as deeper integration took place, the changes needed to merge successfully had begun to 'bite'. The amount and pace of change had increased but resources had deteriorated, partly due to issues adopting a single IT system. The sheer effort to integrate the firms caught them off-guard. The accountability and communication necessary to reprioritize activities dropped. As passion and drive waned, benefits dropped and an alarming decline in customer service occurred. The problem was that the building blocks of good management were neglected. Good staff felt unrecognized and started to leave as conflicts went unresolved. The directors used cost management as the main means to keep control, but got less and less in return.

Path 2: *moving to* Sleepy in Success

On this path 5 per cent of groups move to *Sleepy in Success*, where change has moved off the agenda and 'okay' performance is considered good enough. For example, an industrial cleaning company had grown through acquisitions but now was consolidating. Overly ambitious shareholder return targets brought pressures, and staff numbers were reduced, ageing equipment was not replaced and supply deliveries were delayed. But no one seemed to care. Top leaders lost focus, and teams simply slid into complacency without realizing what was happening. On this path, it is as if people are running on autopilot. When thing are going well, neglecting to nurture good team leaders comes at a cost.

Path 3: *moving to* Building Momentum

Five per cent of groups head down this path. In the industrial cleaning company, cracks started to appear as newly hired business leaders – who had joined to be part of something great – began to question where the organization was going, and some of them decided to leave. Growth and other types of change dropped, and a gap opened between top management's vision and the leaders running daily business. Teams were not rewarded and recognized, either because leaders mistakenly assumed that all was well, or because they were too distracted to notice. People still understood the purpose of the change and felt involved. But their energy had nowhere to go and their leaders were not focusing their efforts. The key was to keep close alignment among leaders and nurture talents when things were going well.

Path 4: *moving to* Struggling under Pressure

On this path 5 per cent of groups plummet to *Struggling under Pressure*. Returning to the merged accountancy firm discussed in Path 1, administration and finance teams found it difficult to cope with the drop in growth and increase in restructuring. Risks and roadblocks increased. Management lost focus on teamwork and accountability. Their teams still had the resources needed to make change happen, but they couldn't juggle conflicting priorities effectively. Trust in leadership at all levels declined; benefits and performance plunged; and the balance of emotional energy quickly shifted to the negative. A narrower focus replaced the broad strategic perspective of *Cruising*, as leaders concentrated on day-to-day operational issues.

Path 5: *moving to* Good but Not Yet Great, In the Dark *and* Just Get On with It

The fastest way to fall from *Cruising* is to reduce the amount of change taking place, paired with a loss of vision and confidence in senior leaders. For example, in a chemical company a dramatic drop in growth and new ways of working – the lifeblood of *Cruising* – became their downfall. This was not the teams' fault; top management had misread the situation and were not able to reformulate their vision. Risks and roadblocks increased, and awareness of the need for change declined, as though people couldn't grasp the reality in front of them. Fifteen per cent of groups follow this path, which heads down to *Just Get On with It*. The lesson here is that, even after organizations reach the top, they still need to keep a watchful eye and resolve the tensions around change. Leaders should be prepared for all scenarios, the 'good, the bad and the ugly'.

Getting to the top – and staying there

When planning for potential failures, leaders should be aware that the formula used to achieve success may not be the same as that required to sustain it. In fact, the very competencies that lead to success – drive, determination and fast decision-making, for example – can become counterproductive, especially when executives allow arrogance and impatience to affect their management style. Consequently, leaders may need to consider reinventing themselves. This could mean building relationships with those outside the group, even when doing so might go against the grain of team solidarity. When a group has been successful and even admired within the organization, leaders should consider using the group's success to encourage the development of other groups, particularly those that are potentially influential in obtaining important expertise or resources. To accomplish that, leaders should consider consulting with those who can think strategically and carry out effective relationship management. Also, they should push the organization to reward and recognize the efforts and achievement of their group members. As discussed earlier, when an organization is unresponsive to a group's success, people may become disillusioned and begin to consider leaving.

In this chapter, we have discussed the *High Performance* zone and have looked at its three distinct regions, including the capital city *Cruising*. Next, in Chapter 4, we turn to the very depths of performance and investigate those groups in which very little goes right. In other words, having described the blissful 'heaven' of those change programmes that achieve high performance, we now focus on the tortuous 'hell' of those initiatives that crash and burn.

SUMMARY FOR CHAPTER 3: KEY INSIGHTS

- Organizations that realize the greatest benefits from change and the highest levels of performance also have the greatest amounts of change taking place at a fast pace. To reach this level and remain in *High Performance*, groups need high driver strength across all 10 change drivers, not just improvements on a single or even a few dimensions.

- Only 10 per cent of groups that undertake change make it to the *High Performance* zone – and this means not just being good once but continuously improving customer service levels, effectiveness and the ability to manage cost and resources.

- Travellers in *High Performance* use the word 'love' – such as 'I love my job' and 'I love working with my colleagues' – more than in other zones.

▶

- Highly focused teamwork, accountability, passion and drive, and excellent team leadership are what get people to the top and keep them there.

- The top level of performance is not a single state but instead consists of three separate regions:

  – In *Pushing the Limits*, at the very peak of the change map, the major challenge is to perform at the edge of what is possible, look into the unknown and create a new future.

  – In *Cruising*, people must resist the temptation of sitting in the comfort zone of being successful and becoming overly complacent.

  – In *Achieved with Loss of Heart*, people struggle with having reached their organization's goals but being left 'burnt out', undervalued and under-recognized.

- Getting to the peak of performance is one thing; staying there is quite another. Only about one-third of groups that make it to the top for the first time are able to remain there.

- When groups fall out of *High Performance*, leaders have been caught off-guard, not paying attention to building strong capabilities before they are hit with unexpected change. This is one of the biggest risks to groups in *Cruising*, which are vulnerable as they bask in success.

- Small human 'touchpoints' help to stabilize the inevitable fears that arise in *High Performance* and they nurture the high trust levels needed to stay there.

Off Track
When everything falls apart

04

> *You probably know more about the depths of your soul from the periods of pain and confusion than from times of comfort. Darkness and turmoil stimulate the imagination in a certain way. They allow you to see things you might ordinarily overlook.* **THOMAS MOORE**

Employees felt powerless as the internal reorganization was implemented. Because two business units were being combined at the global company, many were afraid that their jobs would be eliminated. As employee fear and frustration ran high, trust in senior management plummeted, worker morale hit rock bottom and the reorganization stalled. It was a shock for the executives involved to learn, just four months into the change initiative, that the programme had come to a halt. What happened?

On paper, the reorganization in the above example had made perfect sense. In practice, however, the initiative was anything but successful. Clearly there was a huge disconnect between the intention for well-managed change and the reality on the ground. Was this an isolated case? Hardly. Of all the groups in our database, 10 per cent are in the *Off Track* zone. Of those, nearly half tend to get stuck there. As such, it behoves organizations to learn about the characteristics and dynamics of this zone in order to better understand how to break out of the patterns of poor performance.

In Chapter 3 we described change programmes that had arrived in organizational 'heaven', delivering exceptional performance. In this chapter, we discuss the other end of the performance spectrum: the management 'hell' of the *Off Track* zone, where change programmes go seriously wrong, failing to deliver benefits, and where team performance across all levels of the organization has hit rock bottom. We share our research findings about the different dynamics of this zone, including how people react in such difficult circumstances and how leaders respond. We then focus our discussion on *Case for Action*, the capital city of the *Off Track* zone, and explain the actions shown by our research to work best in getting change programmes back on track.

Off Track dynamics and misconceptions

For groups in *Off Track*, business performance is declining, and all of the key drivers of change are well below the norm (see Figure 4.1). In particular, the change benefits are not being delivered and people have little confidence that the initiative will improve business performance in the future.

For many managers and employees, the characteristics and dynamics of *Off Track* will sound all too familiar. In general, groups have less support and resources than those in other zones, and people feel that they lack what is needed to do their jobs. As such, they become angry at the way they are being treated, and many view the change initiative as merely an excuse to downsize staff, freeze pay and downgrade worker benefits. Eventually, employees begin to resent management, blaming senior leadership for perceived mistakes such as expanding overseas too quickly or betting on the wrong technology in an emerging market. Oftentimes, relationships with customers become frayed, leading to additional stress to those employees who must deal with clients on a daily basis.

All this leads to old scripts and everybody's worst nightmares being rerun in the present: 'the senior leadership is interested only in profits', 'this always happens to us' and 'I told them this wouldn't work'. Cynicism sets in; the momentum for change plummets; and staffers begin to blame colleagues for their own poor performance. Conflicts are widened to engulf other groups – an atmosphere of 'us versus them'. The senior leadership might talk about the organization being more cohesive, but that doesn't happen at the operating level as cooperation between different departments is sorely lacking. To exacerbate matters, people receive little useful information about the

FIGURE 4.1   Change map and driver profile for *Off Track* zone

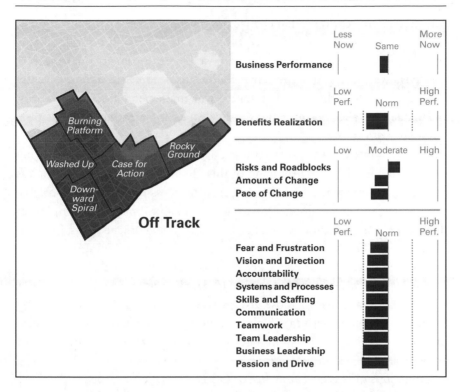

changes taking place. Instead, most of the information they obtain is from the rumour mill.

'Joke' is the most commonly used word to describe what is happening when a change programme goes *Off Track*. 'This change initiative is a joke', 'This company is a joke', 'My work is a joke' and 'Management is a joke' become all too familiar complaints. We discovered this when we analysed more than 100,000 text-written comments from the people we surveyed. In contrast, the most common word for people in the *High Performance* zone is 'love', as in, 'I love my job' and 'I love working with the people in my group'.

In essence, when a change programme goes *Off Track* people feel as if they have reached rock bottom. They find themselves on the receiving end of change they didn't want, change they don't like and change over which they feel they have little or no control. Before we begin to delve deeper into the underlying dynamics of the *Off Track* zone, we need to discuss two major misconceptions about change initiatives: 1) change causes groups to go off track; 2) too much change, too fast, is bad.

Misconception 1: change causes groups to go off track

The first misconception is that change programmes cause an organization to falter and send it off track. In fact, those in *Off Track* will typically blame the change initiative itself for the poor state they're in. In our research, however, we have found that the conditions leading to failure usually existed well before the change initiative was implemented. In other words, **the upheaval of a change initiative doesn't *cause* organizational dysfunction; it merely *exposes* it**.

That certainly was the case for the change initiative at the global company that we discussed at the beginning of this chapter. Duplication of business processes and inefficiencies existed in each business unit before the change programme had come along. One of the most painful points for employees during the reorganization was the lack of clear employment terms and conditions. This was delayed by global negotiations that had commenced long before the reorganization. The hard truth is that, although change might be a convenient scapegoat for groups in *Off Track*, a close examination of our data reveals that most of those groups were already low performers long before the change initiative took place. In fact, we found that only 15 per cent of groups from higher regions move down into *Off Track* and, of those, most come from the *Unsustainable* zone.

For groups in *High Performance* or *On Track*, building strong capabilities *prior* to a change initiative being implemented is one of the best 'insurance policies' to avoid falling into *Off Track*. As those capabilities become strengthened, the organization becomes genuinely more robust in the face of increased change. Once leadership capability has been developed, for example, it is rare for a group to experience a complete failure across all the drivers of performance that will cause it to fall from the highest levels of performance down to *Off Track* in one pass. Instead, there may actually be a 'bump' upwards in performance when the group is under the pressure of difficult change but then rises to the challenge. Unfortunately, many executives strongly believe in the change management metaphor of going through 'the valley of despair'. Based on Elisabeth Kübler-Ross's work on grieving (Kübler-Ross, 1973), **the metaphor contends that change programmes necessarily go through an initial difficult period, as people work through feelings of denial and anger. Our research, however, has found that performance can actually increase throughout an initiative when the right capabilities are in place**.

These findings reinforce the need for leaders to clearly understand the state of their organizations *before* commencing a major change programme.

It is dangerous and risky to find out, just before rolling out an initiative, that the foundation on which the change programme is being built is weak and unstable, and that groups are already effectively mired in the *Off Track* zone. **It is far better to understand, in advance of a change programme being rolled out, that the foundations are shaky and that people's capabilities and strengths need to be developed.**

Misconception 2: too much change, too fast, is bad

The second big misconception is that groups in *Off Track* are unable to deal with a fast pace of change, and that this is why their performance suffers. The conventional thinking is that too much change, too fast, is the major source of problems for organizations simply not able to keep up. Our research, however, paints an entirely different picture. We have found that, in *Off Track*, less change actually occurs and at a slower pace than in other zones and, wherever change is taking place, the deckchairs are being rearranged without a deeper change in the culture. In other words, staffers often have been promised change, but they see just superficial differences that don't get at the more fundamental issues that need to be addressed. The reason for that is simple. Even though a change initiative might initially start off as being ambitious, the lack of emotional agreement to the vision and poor leadership, such that conflicting priorities are not quickly resolved, have resulted in mixed and confused messages filtering through the organization. People don't know where to go or what to do, so the pace slows down, often to a standstill.

In other words, it is a myth that too much change or change happening too fast is bad. Our research clearly shows that organizations with the highest business performance also have the maximum amount of change taking place. **The optimal pace of change, even for groups on the norm, where business performance and benefits realization are at peak levels and negative feelings are at their lowest, is slightly faster than 'okay' – not too fast and not too slow** (see Figure 4.2). The simple fact is that people want to be stretched and challenged – because it is exciting to embrace new possibilities. All too often, though, management underestimates the amount of change that people can comfortably absorb, and misjudges the pace of change that is needed to keep people motivated and engaged.

So the reverse of conventional thinking appears to be true: an increased pace of change does not cause organizations to go *Off Track*. Instead, the culprit is a lack of change – lots of promises but the inability to make change truly happen, to improve poor relationships inside the organization, to remove organizational obstacles, to overhaul inefficient business processes and so on.

FIGURE 4.2   The optimal pace of change

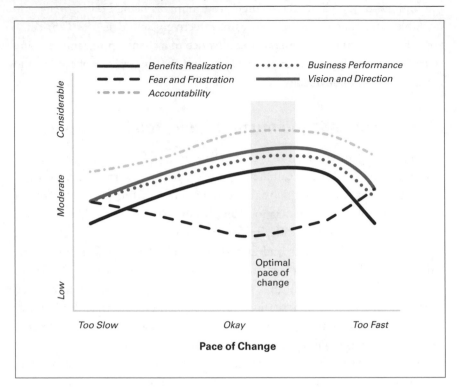

Of course, reorganizations like the one described at the global company cited above are difficult to execute. But we have seen many examples in our database in which organizations have undergone similarly massive initiatives, including major structural changes and downsizings, all while avoiding the *Off Track* zone. What accounts for that difference?

The answer is not surprising. Namely, the fundamental reason that groups end up in *Off Track* in the first place is a failure of leadership. Or, stated in another way, good leadership through all levels in the organization lies at the heart of well-managed change (we discuss this in depth in later chapters). Change simply does not go *Off Track* when people have high trust in good leadership. In all the journeys we have measured, when people lost their trust in leaders the change programme stopped dead in its tracks. The business literature highlights the importance of leadership in organizational change, but our research shows that it is actually *trust* and *confidence* in leaders at all levels and their ability to take quick remedial actions that play the crucial roles, more so than other aspects of leadership, such as the business competence of an individual or the resources that he or she provides.

If leadership – or lack thereof – is the fundamental reason for groups being in *Off Track*, it is also the essential part of the solution for escaping that zone. As we will see, building trust in leadership is one of two main actions that need to be taken for teams to reach regions of higher performance. The other is to lower people's fears and frustrations. Our research clearly shows that the failure to accomplish both of these interrelated actions – and we will see how these play out across the different regions of *Off Track* – will lead to slow or incomplete implementation of change, loss of benefits and even the total failure of the initiative.

Different ways to spiral downward

In the *Off Track* zone, negative feelings tend to run strong, and the temptation is to paint everything with a broad brush. But the truth is that there are a number of varying shades of difficulty and distress, and organizations need to appreciate those differing dynamics in order to intervene in the most effective ways. Just as we saw in Chapter 3 that the different regions of *High Performance* contained different seeds of failure, so do the different regions of *Off Track* contain different seeds of hope and renewal. In addition to the capital city of *Case for Action*, which we describe in the next section, the *Off Track* zone contains four other regions (see Figure 4.1):

- *Downward Spiral:* in this region everything is at its lowest ebb; risks and roadblocks are high; and benefits are non-existent. Relationships with leaders and other group members are fractured, with people feeling completely disconnected from – and angry towards – their organization. Groups are in a no-win situation and the question is, where to start? A lot of listening is needed, first to allow people to release the pressure valve and let off destructive steam, and then to recognize the gravity of the situation they are in. Only then can people begin to consider how they might change.

- *Rocky Ground:* in this region, top management is seen to be driving change, and a programme is in place although the foundations have yet to be built. Some individuals see the benefits resulting from the change, but groups lack the teamwork or trust in managers to make that a reality. People have more faith in top management than in their immediate boss, and they crave clear performance objectives and measurable outcomes.

- *Washed Up*: this region is characterized by sitting, watching and waiting. Think of it as low performance in a deckchair. Groups have all the resources they need, including skills, staffing, systems and processes, but are completely uninvolved and uninformed. Almost no change of any kind is taking place. Unlike other *Off Track* regions, there is little negative feeling, but equally so there is little positive feeling either. People's poor opinions of their local and business unit management are justified by the lack of action seen in this region.

- *Burning Platform*: this region can be seen as a gateway between the *Off Track* and *On Track* zones. In contrast with other *Off Track* regions, people have a high awareness of the need for change and an urgency to get going. Team leadership and accountability are at their highest levels in the *Off Track* zone, but so also are the numbers of people who are thinking of leaving. Groups are making do with few or no resources, although their actions are critically hampered by the lack of business leadership. This region is not frequented often, with just 1 per cent of groups positioned here, and those groups that do find themselves in *Burning Platform* typically move quickly into other higher-performing regions.

Case for Action, a capital city – where the seeds of hope can be found

Having discussed the surrounding regions, we now focus on *Off Track*'s capital city: *Case for Action*, where 6 per cent of groups reside. As with all regions in the zone (Figure 4.1), benefits realization is low and performance is declining. In contrast, as shown in Figure 4.3, the amount of change that occurs in *Case for Action* is higher than for any other *Off Track* region, with particularly high levels of restructuring. In addition, the pace of change tends to be on the 'too fast' side. Everything is seemingly up in the air, and people find it near impossible not to be caught up in the change programme.

On the positive side, people in *Case for Action* are generally aware of the need to change. They receive information from their team leaders, and although trust in team leadership is still low it is one of the best scoring behaviours. People are also open to working with each other, yet unfortunately their efforts are often directed in working together in 'guerilla teams' to oppose the change programme rather than to align with it. Teamwork within individual groups might be present, but the cooperation and collaboration across

FIGURE 4.3 Change map and driver profile for *Case for Action* region

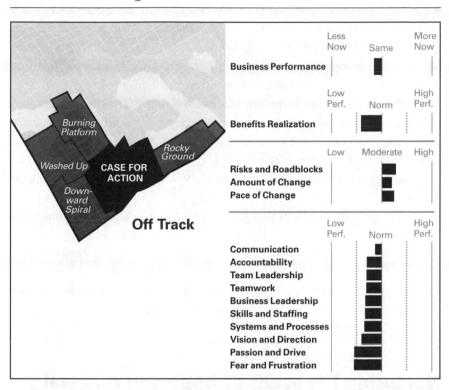

groups and the interaction with management is poor, with an attitude of 'them against us' pervading the workplace.

A major issue in *Case for Action* is the gap between the amount of change taking place and the amount of benefits that people are experiencing, either in the form of improved ways of working or in terms of any growth taking place. Indeed, at this stage any benefits resulting from the change initiative are at their lowest levels. So the proposition to employees is typically a mixed message: continue to endure pain now for the promise of a better future, even though your job might not be guaranteed. Even when downsizing is not involved, many staffers might remain cynical, viewing the focus of the change initiative as taking benefits away from them and delivering them to someone else. Many might feel that change is merely a means to cut costs in the organization. So the question that needs to be answered for employees is this: what's in it for them?

Part of the problem is that, although people have some understanding of the vision and awareness of the need for change, they do not necessarily agree with that vision. Our research shows that, in *Case for Action*, stronger team leadership tends to be associated with lower agreement to the vision – the opposite of what would normally be expected. In other words, team members disagree with the vision and they trust their team leader to fight on their behalf, and that puts the team in conflict with the rest of the organization. Consequently the organization is left without a vehicle for focusing people's energies outwards in a positive direction. Thus the key to unlocking this pattern of poor performance lies in resolving the conflict with team leaders, who must come full circle, moving from opposition to alignment with the vision. Only then can those individuals use their energies in a positive and constructive manner to help lower fear and frustration so that they can assist team members to take ownership of the change initiative and make it their own.

In summary, the upside is that *Case for Action* is where the action takes place in the *Off Track* zone, with numerous opportunities for improvement. The downside, though, is that this is also where the potential for conflict is greatest. Hope is offered, providing a future that is better than the current situation, but a fundamental lack of trust in the business unit leadership and senior corporate execs has done little to erase people's cynicism, with many feeling helpless and undervalued.

Nurturing the seeds of hope and renewal

Once groups are in *Case for Action*, they tend to stay there. In other areas of the change map, 20 to 25 per cent of groups typically stay stuck in the same regions. In *Case for Action*, that figure is 43 per cent, making it the most difficult region to exit. The simple fact is that once groups are locked into a dynamic of poor performance, it is difficult to break that pattern.

Debilitating fear and frustration

Our research clearly shows that the failure to deal adequately with fear and frustration leads to slow or incomplete implementation of change, loss of benefits and even failure. According to our data, benefits realization declines significantly as the levels of fear and frustration increase in the organization (see Figure 4.4). As such, for large change programmes the difference between a team in which no one has feelings of fear, distress and anger versus a team in which most people do have such feelings can translate to millions of pounds in unrealized benefits.

FIGURE 4.4   The effects of fear and frustration

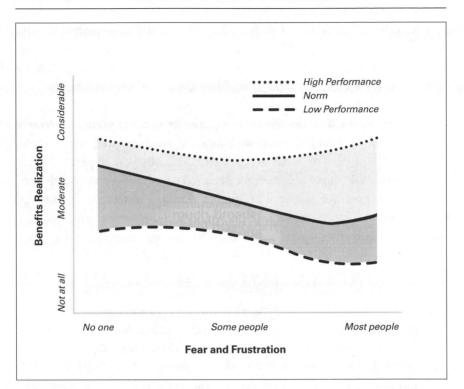

Remember the global company that we discussed at the beginning of this chapter? The company's senior executives developed a detailed strategy to manage various aspects of the change initiative. To better manage its fleet, for example, they took a hard look at truck scheduling and dispatch, and they developed a plan for implementing a new order-fulfilment and tracking system. But those top executives failed to put in place any measures to manage people's fears, not realizing that this single action could have significantly helped the financial bottom line. Instead, they tried to perform tasks over the top of those negative feelings, and they failed.

A deeper look at our research reveals significant differences between how low- and high-performing teams manage fear and frustration. Interestingly, on low-performing teams, a small level of negative feelings can actually be beneficial (see the bottom curve of Figure 4.4), but a 'tipping point' is quickly reached when around one-third of the team starts to experience fear and frustration, with benefits decreasing after that. In other words, although a small level of negative feelings can stimulate a desire to give up the old ways and move forward, too much fear and frustration quickly becomes counterproductive. Recognizing that crucial difference, however, is not always a simple matter.

Consider the example of a company that was implementing a new finance system in Europe. The project team was one month over schedule, costing the firm a considerable amount of money. Moreover, the company had failed to realize the anticipated benefits of the new system and the accountants were unable to sign off on the end-of-year closing because of inaccuracies in the data. In our survey of the project, we found extremely high levels of fear and frustration, but when we presented these results to management, the response was, 'Well, what do you expect? We are restructuring. Of course people don't like it'. Their assumption was that, of course it is normal for people to be anxious during a restructuring – but the level of negative emotions was well beyond that. On further investigation, we found that many staffers feared that the new automated system would replace their jobs, and when we asked the leadership what it had done to manage those fears, the response was, 'We thought it would be better not to tell them; it will distract them from doing their job'. Unfortunately, management had failed to consider that fear and frustration can spread like wildfire. Indeed, staffers had already figured out that they might be losing their jobs, and their fear was pervading everything they did, leading to a substantial decline in performance. As it turns out, the cost of managing fear and frustration would have been a fraction of the cost of the project overrun.

How not to manage fear and frustration

Thus the question becomes, how can groups best manage their levels of fear and frustration? On the surface, the answer for leaders might seem obvious: be clear, logical and factual about the reasons for the change initiative and its implementation. But as we will see, change produces many consequences that are emotional and irrational, and therefore traditional logical approaches can often be woefully inadequate. Specifically, the conventional approach is to communicate, make people accountable, provide the necessary resources and inject passion and drive. But will those actions truly make a difference?

Communicating

In the midst of any change programme, the typical 'go to' strategy is to communicate. That approach seems logical enough: in order to calm and align people with the organization's new direction, tell people what is going on and why it is happening. Thus staffers receive no shortage of e-mails, updates via the company intranet and even a few roadshows featuring top management. **Our data, however, indicates that more communication, especially through formal channels when people are in** *Off Track,* **can often be counterproductive, making people more anxious and even angry.** Interestingly, even in high-performing teams, more communication makes little difference to fear and frustration levels.

The secret of successful communication lies in understanding the primary importance of *how* information is transmitted. That is, the quality of the relationship between the sender and receiver of the communication is the key factor, not the volume of information transmitted. The data shows clearly that strong trusting relationships are the most effective way to transform negative feelings that are blocking a genuine emotional commitment to embrace the vision for change.

Holding people accountable

Another common approach is to concentrate on accountability. Our research shows that this strategy does indeed have more impact than a focus on com-munication, yet its effectiveness is still rather limited until a group's level of performance reaches a higher level. Specifically, for low-performing groups, only an 11 per cent drop in fear and frustration can be achieved by moving from no accountability to very high accountability. For high-performing groups, on the other hand, a larger drop of 25 per cent can be achieved through the same transition. The underlying reason is that people are ready to accept accountability *only* when their emotions have been turned around from negative to positive.

Providing resources

Teams experiencing high fear and frustration will often complain that they cannot meet their objectives because of a lack of resources. But our research paints a somewhat different picture, and it sounds a cautionary note for leaders. **When fear and frustration are high, adding more resources will not solve the problem. In fact, highly negative groups will only waste and squander the precious resources they have. It is only after the level of fear and frustration is lowered through other means that teams can benefit through the addition of resources.**

Injecting passion and drive

Many leaders assume that the injection of positive energy will somehow cancel out any negative emotions. So, when a team's morale is down, an assumption is that managers should organize a social function, plan a fun event off-site and tell employees how valuable they are. Yet although such actions are based on good intentions, they only relieve the symptoms temporarily, leaving the fundamental causes buried deep and undisturbed. Our research shows that, until the root causes of fear and frustration are addressed, symptoms treated in a superficial way will frequently return.

Leaders often assume that fear and frustration are symmetrical to passion and drive – when one is high the other is low. But this is not always the case. Positive feelings cannot simply be poured onto negative ones to make them go away. Although it is true that fear and frustration are strongly linked to passion and drive, the actions required to decrease the former are not the same as those needed to increase the latter. Moreover, it should be noted that negative feelings such as fear and frustration do not have to be eliminated altogether; they need only to be contained to a level at which they do not interfere with people's ability to work productively.

The right way to manage fear and frustration

To understand how best to manage fear and frustration, we can study how successful groups deal with those emotions. For high-performing teams (the top curve of Figure 4.4), benefits initially drop as fear and frustration start to rise, but when a critical mass is reached – around half of the people on the team begin to experience negative feelings – then the will to succeed kicks in and benefits realization is back on the agenda. From that point on, more and more benefits are realized in the face of higher and higher levels of fear and frustration. In other words, high-performing groups rise to the challenge: they are not daunted by facing more difficulties; in fact they thrive on them. As we will see, the skills of the team leader are vital in bringing about this transformation.

The resulting difference between the ways that low- and high-performing groups handle their levels of fear and frustration is startling, accounting for more than a 50 per cent disparity in the amount of benefits they realize. In other words, fear and frustration are huge differentiators, well worth the investment of time and resources to ensure that they are managed properly. The trick is to use negative feelings in a constructive way. That is, leaders should not ignore or attempt to squash negative feelings, because that will simply send those emotions underground. Instead, leaders should find ways to focus that energy and channel it in positive ways, for example, to push through roadblocks and to overcome obstacles.

Leadership – the key for action

In our research, we found that groups that have successfully moved out of *Case for Action* tended to do three important things: 1) be ruthlessly honest about leadership capabilities, 2) creatively manage fear and frustration, and 3) help people to find meaning in change in order to make it their own.

Be ruthlessly honest about leadership capabilities

The first step in helping groups in *Case for Action* is an extensive review of leadership capabilities at all levels. This is the single most-effective intervention for improving performance. Admittedly, the process is difficult to undertake but it offers the greatest potential rewards. Without good leadership, the organization will only continue to stumble.

Consider, for example, the CEO who faced tough choices in the merger of the transport and storage groups of his business after he realized that all those on the leadership team were not up to their jobs. They had come together as a group with executives from both units, but the CEO now recognized that managing people through change was the most critical success factor, requiring role changes to be made. During the next six months, over 50 per cent of the leadership team was replaced, and the result was a dramatic improvement in the progress of the merger, with the business moving up the change map.

Making such difficult decisions is crucial because our research shows that trust in leadership is the key to lowering the levels of fear and frustration and, as we have seen, the failure to deal with such negative emotions can stall, if not completely derail, the implementation of a change initiative. Indeed, we have found that it is simply not possible to lower such negative feelings without first rebuilding leadership trust. Executives and managers should think of trust as the invisible glue that keeps change on track to deliver business outcomes. High levels of trust can enable people to succeed with limited resources, but no amount of resources will make up for a lack of trust.

Our research also shows that each organizational level of leadership is responsible for a piece of the trust 'pie'. Top management holds the emotional commitment to the vision and the keys to staff confidence and optimism. Leaders in middle management, including those at the unit or division level, must manage change effectively and take quick remedial action when things go wrong. Moreover, they must show support, commitment and visible effort in promoting change. Below them, trust in the team leader is the key factor in unlocking the potential of the team members – making them feel recognized, utilizing their talents and enabling everyone to work effectively together to manage change. Most of all, the team leader sets an example through his or her own involvement in the change initiative.

To instill trust, leaders in *Off Track* must have a combination of skills and knowledge that will enable them to sit comfortably in the middle of a difficult situation and to facilitate change, all without becoming overwhelmed themselves. It can be relatively easy for leaders to be effective when things are going well; it is far more difficult when groups are faced with conflict and distress, particularly when the leaders themselves are the focus of negative feelings. This is one of the most difficult challenges of leadership, yet it is exactly what is needed in *Case for Action*.

Although the change literature talks much about the importance of leadership, relatively little has been written on managing the difficult, disturbing and even painful aspects of change initiatives. The assumption is that management's job is to help people get through their negative emotions as quickly as possible. It is almost as if nothing valuable can be learned from travelling down the blind alleys and dead ends that are typical of any major change programme. But the ability to manage a group through the ups and downs of a change journey is of vital importance for any leader, particularly those in the *Off Track* zone. This is where our research with hundreds of thousands of data points provides insight into the effective ways of skilfully managing various setbacks of such journeys, showing how leaders are able to gain the trust of their followers.

To gain a deeper understanding of the human dynamics at play when dealing with difficult situations, it is helpful to seek lessons learned from other fields. In psychology, researchers have found that people can endure much suffering if they can still find meaning in it. This meaning can then support and sustain them for the rest of their lives. Similarly, finding meaning in a change programme is the central task in *Case for Action*, and is vital to sustain the journey when faced with pain and difficulty. In the helping professions, doctors, psychologists, psychiatrists and counsellors are trained to guide people through a range of distressed and difficult states. Valuable insight from these fields can assist change leaders, faced with managing an increased scale, complexity and speed of change. This is one of the most important but the least understood tasks of leadership.

One important lesson is that it is important for leaders to have the capacity to learn from their own life experiences. It is hard to lead others – to empathize and help guide constructive actions – when leaders have little appreciation of what is really going on with their people. For instance, good leaders know that, when fear and frustration are high, employees' energies and imaginations become locked up, and their worldview shrinks. As their anxiety rises, people begin to view the actions of others as more malevolent and threatening to their interests, and they will find comfort in joining with co-workers of a similar worldview. This is the genesis of 'them versus us'.

Of course, change by definition creates uncertainty, and this is where good leaders are essential in establishing strong relationships that can confine the uncertainty, making it manageable and creating an environment in which people can openly discuss and work through their fears and other negative, corrosive emotions. As anxiety levels decline, good leaders are able to tap into people's out-of-the-box thinking to find creative solutions to seemingly intractable problems. Just as high-performing teams contain the seeds of potential failure, low-performance ones contain all the seeds of improvement *if* leaders know where to look. **Good leaders understand that negative feelings are not the enemies of change to be conquered or overcome. Instead, such emotions must be painstakingly worked through to eventually enable progress to proceed.**

Unfortunately, many leaders are not well-equipped to calmly and confidently manage change in adverse conditions. When talking about the change map, we often say that leaders cannot lead from below; they must be higher up on the map in order to bring others along on the journey. When a leader is deficient in that respect, one option is to retain an external coach to help that individual. Obviously, this takes time and effort, but it can be a much less expensive solution than having the change programme continue to founder. In other cases, replacing a leader might be the most effective intervention to bring about change. Specifically, if a leader lacks the necessary capabilities and has little desire to develop them, the toxic conditions he or she creates will squash any chance of the change programme succeeding. Such conditions require decisive actions, including redeployment, organizational restructuring, disciplinary actions and perhaps outright dismissal. In certain cases, recruiting new leaders is the best option.

Creatively manage fear and frustration

When people see change as an attack on their current way of doing things, their natural reaction is to become angry. Moreover, if they believe that the changes imposed by an initiative are unrealistic, that the effects will be harmful and that they lack any viable alternatives, they will feel cornered, heightening their fears and increasing their anger. That anger and frustration can easily boil over when, to exacerbate matters, people are confronted with various obstacles, especially seemingly illogical ones, that impede the ways in which they need to work. A very small percentage of groups fall backwards into *Downward Spiral* as a result of team leaders being unable to master these difficulties.

When an international food distributor was implementing a change programme, senior managers took the time to travel to rural locations and informally address each team, some of which had newly appointed team leaders. The managers explained what they had done and why – and it made a difference. Team leaders had previously struggled to defuse negative feelings in their teams; and senior management's willingness to openly discuss difficult issues helped convince even sceptical team leaders that opposition to change was no longer in anyone's interest. Things were not perfect, but fear and frustration levels had been lowered sufficiently to talk logically about what needed to be done to get everyone back on track.

Savvy leaders view employee anger as a sign of people wanting to improve. Fear and distress will typically cause people to turn inwards; anger is energy turned outwards. Team leaders should begin channelling the strong feelings raised by anger into work that would benefit from the pent-up energy. To do that, though, they must remove any roadblocks that have been adding to people's frustrations. Skilful leaders help their teams to see clearly what the obstacles to their goals are, and then they act as a resource to overcome those impediments.

According to Michelangelo, sculpturing was simple. When looking at a slab of marble, the artist only needs to see the sculpture that already exists within and then chip away everything else. Similarly, leaders working in difficult situations need to 'see the vision within' and chip away, removing the obstacles that are preventing people from completing those tasks that are necessary for the change programme to move forward. In our experience, people generally want to move to a better situation but they are often impeded by various roadblocks. As such, leaders need to adopt Michelangelo's attitude, because it is much easier to remove the barriers that are causing mistrust than it is to try to create a layer of trust on top of underlying cynicism. Trust emerges when the right conditions are in place; it cannot be forced or made to happen.

In summary, **frustration can become the force that drives change, providing the fuel that people can use to push through various roadblocks**. To enable that to happen, though, team leaders must work closely with the business unit leadership and corporate executives to eliminate or at least minimize the obstacles that are in the way of teams moving forward.

Help people to find meaning in change

Fear is a natural emotion of those who undergo change. People are generally afraid of the unknown, and change is typically an unknown quantity. The first step in managing fear is to clarify what people are fearful of, because the things they envision may not always reflect reality. Often, the default mode is to view the changes solely as threats to a group's or individual's needs and goals, and that perspective is typically reinforced when people are relying on rumours for information.

In such situations, direct actions by corporate executives can help to outline the bigger picture – to instill vision and to increase passion and drive. But it is the business and team leaders who first need to work to lower fear and frustration. Business unit leaders can play an important role in the design of policies and procedures to remove obstacles, but the ones who can have the greatest impact in reducing fear and frustration are the team leaders. Our data shows that the combination of strong team leadership and increased passion and drive can lower the level of fear and frustration by more than one-third. Comparatively speaking, that is three times more effective than a focus on communication and nearly twice as effective as increasing people's accountability. Fortunately, for groups in *Case for Action*, the levels of trust in team leadership are generally strong, and organizations would do well to leverage that strength.

Consider the approach taken by the new chief designer of a formerly prestigious automotive and aircraft design firm that had since lost its lustre. The company had strayed too far away from its trendsetting origins, leading to disillusionment among key people, including many former design 'stars'. The new design chief's strategy was to recapture hearts and minds, with a big emphasis on 'hearts'. He listened and listened and listened, taking some of the criticism himself until enough of the frustration was spent, and then he asked what it would take to win back the firm's former design brilliance. Suggestions covered everything from individual design and product ideas to the overall vision, direction and marketing thrust for the company.

The turnaround was both rapid and dramatic. The designers, challenged to make their own ideas real, got right behind the new direction. Yet the total amount of communication had hardly changed. What made the difference was the give-and-take nature of communication and its relevance to everyone's perceived future, which was born of trust in the new chief designer. For his part, the new chief was seen as team-orientated, always accessible and supportive of obtaining resources whenever a good case was made for them.

One reason for the new design chief's effectiveness was that he encouraged people's natural tendency towards teamwork, collaboratively tapping into and better utilizing everyone's skills and expertise. If a team leader is successful at that, then people will begin to take greater ownership of the initiative and, as they begin to feel they have more control over their environment, their fears will begin to dissipate. This process is particularly important when the change initiative requires that people develop new skills, which can be a fearful prospect for many people. Here, the team leader needs to emphasize the value of work that employees have done in the past and then provide the clearest pathway possible for them to acquire the experience and skills that will enable them to be successful in the future.

In certain ways, fear and vision are flip sides of the same coin. As team leaders work to lower fear and frustration, they must also begin to explore what the organization's vision is offering. Specifically, what kinds of advantages and benefits will the change bring to people? In short, leaders need to help people to use their imagination in a positive, constructive manner, and they should leverage their strong relationships to help people to replace the old (fear and frustration) with the new (vision and direction).

The key here is to gain people's emotional commitment to the vision. Simply restating the vision repeatedly, as many management teams do with roadshows and senior executive presentations, will have little impact on building alignment across the organization. In fact, roadshows can easily be counterproductive, generating even more cynicism. Our research has repeatedly shown that what drives benefits realization is not *understanding* of the vision but *agreement* to it because, when people agree with and then attach to the new vision, that means they will necessarily be letting go of the past. Yet many leaders misinterpret understanding of the vision for agreement, leading them to move on prematurely. Faced with distress and an environment of fear and frustration, they try to eliminate confusion too quickly, denying people the opportunity to internalize the change. The result is that staffers end up with an intellectual understanding but not the deep emotional commitment that is necessary to make change happen.

Indeed, well-managed 'confusion' involves a synthesis of the old and the new, eventually leading to empowerment. The transition is one of the most critical phases in change implementation. When it is managed well, people internalize the change, find meaning in it and make it their own. Seen in a positive light, controlled confusion is simply 'work in progress'. Unfortunately, many leaders panic when their groups are engulfed with confusion, quickly becoming reactive and dogmatic. They might impose short-term solutions that actually make matters worse. They could, for example, launch multiple change initiatives to get things done more quickly, but then they don't resolve conflicting priorities, leading to inevitable overruns on schedule and budget. Instead, team leaders need to work with each person, one-on-one, to allay his or her fears and frustrations by communicating the benefits of the change in multiple ways. That said, it should be noted that some people might decide to leave after they gain a better understanding of what is involved with the change programme. The truth is that the initiative may not be for everyone, and people will make choices to stay or to leave based on a number of factors, including their future roles and the people they will be working with.

We have seen evidence that movement out of 'darkness' and into 'light' can be difficult for many people. A study in the United States found a spike in suicide rates during spring and not in the depths of winter, as previously thought (Kposowa and D'Auria, 2010). Apparently, for some people the 'light' of longer days can be more distressing than the 'dark'. Sociologists have attributed the increase to the higher density of human interaction that takes place as people come out of their winter social hibernation. Similar to this phenomenon, though clearly not nearly as extreme, 6 per cent of groups shift from *Case for Action* to *Rocky Ground*, and moving upward is not always as desirable as one might think. Sitting in the midst of difficulties, like hibernating in the 'darkness' of winter, can become a way of life, and for some this is more comforting because it is at least familiar.

Common pathways exiting *Case for Action*

The approach described in the previous section holds the key to unlocking the repetitive, victim-type cycles in which groups in *Case for Action* tend to become mired. As noted previously, 43 per cent of groups remain in *Case for Action* indefinitely. But where do groups go when they succeed in moving out of *Case for Action*? Figure 4.5 shows the most common pathways. We discuss each of those pathways in more depth below, highlighting some case examples. (Note: the examples in this section represent a composite of organizations from our research with similar experiences of change.)

Path 1: moving to Cruising

Although only 1 per cent of groups have made the jump all the way from *Case for Action* in the *Off Track* zone to *Cruising* in the *High Performance* zone, we believe this incredible feat is worth noting. For example, at a regional

FIGURE 4.5   Common pathways exiting *Case for Action*

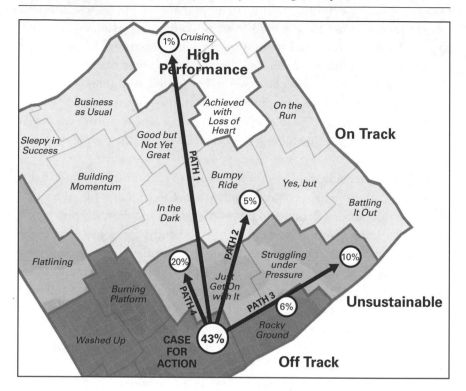

branch of a worldwide producer of building materials, a proven manager was brought in to run a struggling facility. Disruptive employees sensed that they could also be replaced, and a core of still-engaged staff became extremely focused to follow through on their commitment to results. New recruits acted like the 'dedicated few', and production quality and quantity became constant and reliable. A new team leader took the reins and became the driving force behind this change.

Path 2: *moving to* Bumpy Ride

On this path 5 per cent of groups move to *Bumpy Ride*. Here, a vision-led strategy delivers a significant uplift in performance and benefits. For example, when a new CEO took charge at an established national building society, he immediately visited every branch in the country. He observed, and spoke to the organization's key people, constantly asking: 'How do we make this place better?' People connected with his vision and used their energy to make change happen, with few additional resources. While fear and frustration levels were still somewhat high, teams' emotional agreement to the change helped them to persevere in the face of difficulties. To make an even higher move up the map, this group still needed to address resources and structural issues.

Path 3: *moving to* Struggling under Pressure *and* Rocky Ground

A typical strategy is for groups in *Case for Action* to throw resources at the problem. This creates a short-term boost, significantly increasing passion and drive, lowering fear and frustration and delivering improvements in business effectiveness. However, as a government department found out when they restructured their change plans but did not invest in their people, increases in team leadership, business leadership, and vision and direction were not sufficient to move groups higher up the change map, as we will see in Chapter 6. Six per cent of groups take this path and land in *Rocky Ground*, and another 10 per cent wind up in *Struggling under Pressure*, including the reorganization initiative discussed in this chapter.

Path 4: *moving to* Just Get On with It

At the international food distributor discussed earlier in this chapter, when senior managers took the time and effort to meet informally and talk with team leaders openly about negative feelings their teams subsequently moved to *Just Get On with It*, one of the 20 per cent of groups that follow this path. They had made a start and built an alliance to move forward. A significant increase in team leadership enabled fear and frustration to drop, delivering improved customer service levels. Team leaders set achievable targets to focus on improving accountability, teamwork, and passion and drive. However, the big-ticket items such as business leadership, and vision and direction, were 'too difficult' for this stage of the journey and were to be addressed at a later stage.

Tackling deeper-seated issues

Although each of the above common pathways might be effective in attaining short-term boosts in performance, they avoid tackling deeper-seated issues. They do not, for instance, focus on deficiencies with respect to business leadership, accountability, and vision and direction. But, as we shall see in the next chapter, those larger issues eventually do need to be addressed in order to attain additional performance improvements and to move to higher positions on the change map.

SUMMARY FOR CHAPTER 4: KEY INSIGHTS

- In change programmes that go seriously *Off Track* – 10 per cent of our database – benefits are not delivered, performance declines and all change drivers are well below the norm.

- The upheaval of a change programme does not *cause* an organization to go off track; change merely *exposes* the underlying dysfunctions in the organization. The conditions leading to failure existed well before the change came along.

- 'Joke' is the most commonly used word to describe what is happening when a change programme is in *Off Track*.

- Change programmes do not go off track because people are unable to deal with too much change too fast; in most cases too little change is happening.

- The optimal pace of change, where business performance and benefits realization are at peak levels and negative feelings are at their lowest, is slightly faster than 'okay' – not too fast and not too slow.

- The performance of change programmes does not need to go through a dip and then bounce back. When the right capabilities are in place, the best change programmes continuously increase performance across all stages of change.

- When people lose their trust in leaders, change programmes stop dead in their tracks. Change simply does not go off track when people have high trust in leadership. Building trust in leadership and lowering people's fears is the best way forward.

- Forty-three per cent of groups do not make it out of *Case for Action*, as they are unable to manage the debilitating levels of fear and frustration and lack of trust, making it the most difficult region to leave. The cost can translate to millions of pounds in unrealized benefits.

- More communication, especially through formal channels when people are in *Off Track*, can often be counterproductive, making staffers more anxious and even angry. People are ready to accept accountability, to listen to communication about the vision and appeals to reason, only when their emotions have been turned around from negative to positive.

- In *Case for Action*, business unit leaders engage team leaders so that they embrace the vision for change instead of fighting it. Only then can team leaders help their teams to lower their fear and frustration levels and use their energies positively.

- Strong team leadership and increased passion and drive can lower the level of fear and frustration by more than one-third. That is three times more effective than a focus on communication and nearly twice as effective as increasing people's accountability.

- Seen in a positive light, well-managed confusion is simply 'work in progress', where people internalize the change – synthesizing the old and the new to make it their own – eventually leading to empowerment.

Unsustainable
When change is
at the crossroads

05

> *I have noticed that even people who claim everything is predestined, and that we can do nothing to change it, look before they cross the road.* STEPHEN HAWKING

A major utility company was facing a host of challenges: significant changes in the regulatory environment, disaggregation, privatization and corporatization. In addition, the utility had to deal with supply-and-demand issues, competitive pressures, uncertainty over carbon pricing and the rise of the renewable energy market. To tackle some of those challenges, the company undertook a major change initiative to introduce newer systems with smart meters, a reconfiguration of its business processes and a restructuring of its operations. The goals were cost savings, greater efficiency and a lift in the market perception.

On the surface, the change programme was proceeding as planned, with respectable results on various business metrics, including costs, efficiency and customer service. Below the surface, though, trouble was brewing. Unbeknown to the senior executives, the company was suffering a pronounced drop in teamwork, team leadership, communication, accountability and passion, among other key drivers. Before the initiative, the utility's business performance had been solid but not spectacular, and management had hoped to improve on that. But things did not turn out as planned. In essence, the utility, which had been in the *On Track* zone and was hoping to move up the change map, actually fell into *Unsustainable*.

This utility company is among the 16 per cent of groups in our database that have fallen from *On Track* to *Unsustainable*. There are 10 per cent of groups that have fallen further, from *High Performance* to *Unsustainable*. Such drops in performance can happen for many reasons. For example, they could be due to a change in personnel. Key employees may have left, and management might not have realized the importance of those individuals until after their departures. Other workers who have been under considerable stress might quietly give up and simply go through the motions of their jobs. The introduction of new technologies may find some groups coping with the changes but not really using the systems to their full potential. The hard truth is that as change is being implemented it catches people off-guard. The danger of this is that, over time, an organization can lose its essential capabilities for change but not notice any deficiencies until its business performance has eventually plunged.

Unsustainable insights

The *Unsustainable* zone forms the crossover point where groups teeter on the edge between improving and getting worse but have not yet headed in either direction. We have talked about the extremes of change: the very best performance (Chapter 3), where vision and passion are high, enabling groups to achieve their business objectives; and the very worst performance (Chapter 4), where fear and frustration and a lack of trust in leaders make it difficult to achieve targets. In this chapter, we focus on the *Unsustainable* zone, which is located on the change map just above *Off Track*. One out of four groups in our database find themselves in *Unsustainable*, and 41 per cent of those get stuck there. For those unfortunate groups, the change initiative has stalled and business performance has levelled off. In analysing our data for the *Unsustainable* zone, we uncovered two key insights. The first has to do with business metrics, and the second concerns managerial focus.

Insight 1: business metrics can be extremely misleading

When implementing a change initiative, many organizations focus on traditional business metrics such as operating costs and revenue per employee. Of course, those measures are important but they are essentially *lag* indicators, in that they can only provide information about the current outcomes of past actions. Instead, when organizations implement change initiatives, they need *lead* indicators that will warn them of future problems.

At the utility company cited above, executives were caught off-guard when their change initiative stumbled. After we told them that our research had indicated underlying issues that would prevent them from reaching higher performance, their response was, 'But we have been profitable! We thought staff would welcome the new technologies that would make their life easier'. Beyond the issue of profitability, though, our data showed that customer service, business effectiveness and benefits had dropped by around 8 to 10 per cent; risks had slightly increased; and the amount and pace of change had decreased. Still, senior leaders were not overly concerned because their business metrics had showed similar trends. But only with a close examination of the change drivers, which their business metrics did not show, was the full extent of their problem revealed. Business leadership and vision had dropped by around 30 per cent and, even more telling, was this: teamwork, team leadership, communication, accountability, and passion and drive had plummeted by 40 to 50 per cent. Change had gone off track without them realizing; had these metrics – all lead indicators – been available to the senior leaders earlier on, they surely would have noticed the warning signs long before the initiative had stalled.

Insight 2: the past is not a prologue to the future

Some organizations, such as the above utility company, gradually slide down the change map into *Unsustainable*. The problem is typically that leaders have taken their eyes off the ball and are then surprised when all aspects of their group's performance have collapsed. Other groups take an entirely different path to *Unsustainable*, coming up from the bottom of the change map. For these groups, senior executives have built momentum for change, but now they need to shift to a completely new gear to push through to higher performance. In other words, what has worked before cannot be repeated again and again.

In Chapter 4, we saw how groups and organizations move up from *Off Track* using two main strategies. Some groups throw resources at the problem, creating a short-term boost by increasing passion and drive, lowering fear and frustration, and delivering improvements in business effectiveness. Other groups focus on small wins and set achievable targets to increase accountability, passion and drive, and teamwork, along with improved customer service levels for the organization. Both strategies represent steps in the right direction, creating a visible change with performance picking up, particularly with respect to business effectiveness and customer service levels. And both approaches lead to *Unsustainable*, with momentum towards

On Track. In making that transition from *Off Track* to *Unsustainable*, groups experience a huge increase in confidence and optimism that the change programme will lead to future improvements; performance of the business increases by an average of 40 per cent and benefits realization goes up by an average of 27 per cent.

But the reason why these groups are in *Unsustainable* and not in the greener pastures of *On Track* is because their leaders have made a classic mistake. To get out of difficult times, they focused only on short-term fixes, such as reducing headcount to improve profitability, but have failed to build sufficient driver strength to make those improvements sustainable over the long term. In *Unsustainable*, all drivers are still well below the norm. The hope that things will get better exists, but the organization lacks the necessary capabilities to realize it. Unfortunately, senior executives often mistakenly believe that devoting resources to strengthen their teams through training or management development is a luxury that they cannot afford. 'We will invest in people when we get profitable', is the typical response.

Yet it is exactly those types of investments that will enable organizations to make the leap from *Unsustainable* to a zone of higher performance. Remember that business metrics such as profitability, operating costs and key performance indicators (KPIs) are lag indicators. In contrast, the lead indicators are drivers such as business leadership, vision, passion and drive, and lower levels of fear. Unless organizations make the investments to improve those drivers, they will not achieve the desired performance improvements and business benefits, including increased profitability. In other words, **delaying investments in people until certain business metrics have improved is exactly the opposite of what organizations should be doing, akin to putting the proverbial cart before the horse**.

When change is unsustainable

By our definition, 'unsustainable' refers to performance that is improving or at around the same levels, while driver capability is below the norm. The promise of change is there, but it is not yet sustainable. As such, the change agenda begins to stall. The driver profile of the *Unsustainable* zone shows that the best drivers are fear and frustration and both types of resources: systems and processes, and skills and staffing (see Figure 5.1). But even these drivers sit just below the norm. The worst drivers are team leadership, teamwork and communication, which are all close to the levels exhibited by low-performing organizations. In general, vision and direction, and business

FIGURE 5.1   Change map and driver profile for the *Unsustainable* zone

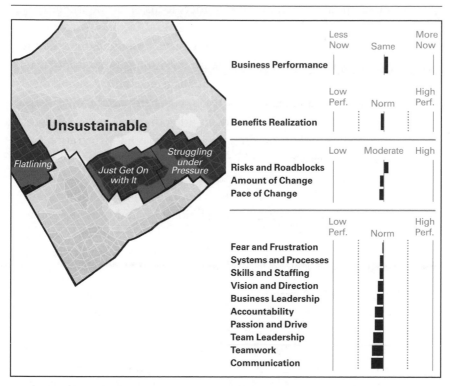

leadership, are at higher levels than team leadership and teamwork, but even they are still well below the norm. Also, risks and roadblocks remain substantial, even as the amount and pace of change have increased slightly.

In *Unsustainable,* the pressure on team leaders is considerable. In the best-case scenarios, senior management supports team leaders, enabling them to develop their capabilities and build strong teams. Without this support, team leaders become the 'meat in the sandwich', stuck between senior executives trying to make change happen and a negative, hostile team that is being dragged kicking and screaming into a change programme they neither want nor like. Such no-win situations can easily lead to team leaders failing, despite their best efforts.

The common theme for all regions in *Unsustainable* is that corporate and business unit leaders have turned a blind eye to building capabilities in critical areas. Within the zone there are three distinct regions, each with its unique characteristics:

- **Just Get On with It.** This region is one of two capital cities of *Unsustainable* and is occupied by 9 per cent of groups in our database. In *Just Get On with It*, leaders focus on accountability, teamwork, and skills and staffing in order to drive performance improvements. These drivers are at high levels. But when it comes to change, people neither like it nor want it. Vision is not a priority, and employees would rather that senior management stop pushing the change initiative and leave them alone. For their part, team leaders stay focused on the tasks at hand, ignoring the need for building positive feeling and for tackling the level of fear and frustration. Tensions exist between the old and new, but teams do not spend time discussing people's emotions or their work relationships, and an atmosphere of blame pervades the work environment. Rather than paying attention to building team relationships and fostering passion and drive – both critical to moving out of *Just Get On with It* – team leaders focus on tasks and they push hard on accountability in order to get that work done.

- **Struggling under Pressure.** This region is the second capital city of *Unsustainable* and is occupied by 11 per cent of groups in our database. In *Struggling under Pressure*, change is project driven, relying on the classic formula of systems, training and vision to drive improvement. This situation is basically the opposite of *Just Get On with It*. The group has the resources required, but they need to build strong teams and address issues with accountability. Otherwise, people will continue to lack the discipline and structure to make change happen. As with other *Unsustainable* regions, the overall driver strength is low. Because change is project driven in *Struggling under Pressure*, organizations rely on strong business and team leadership rather than on the teams themselves to provide the necessary 'horsepower' to implement change. But, as noted earlier, that approach neglects the need to build team capabilities, which becomes the change programme's Achilles heel. Specifically, leaders in this region become distracted by larger, 'big picture' issues and they fail to actively engage with people to gain commitment and buy-in, the key ingredients needed to make change happen. As such, the team leaders in *Struggling under Pressure* often find themselves becoming 'the meat in the sandwich' that was described earlier.

- **Flatlining.** The third region in *Unsustainable* is *Flatlining*, where 5 per cent of groups in our database reside. It is the region where people can see that change is happening. They even understand the vision for change, but they believe that the change does not really concern them. In *Flatlining*, risks and roadblocks are moderate, yet little change is taking place. Teamwork is at rock bottom, while accountability, passion and drive are also low. Because people believe that the change initiative does not concern them, there is little fear and frustration, and no one seems worried that the level of skills and staffing is low. When a group is locked in such lethargy, team leadership is the key to imparting a sense of urgency to move groups to improved performance.

In this chapter, we focus on the first capital city of the *Unsustainable* zone – *Just Get On with It* – and we describe how organizations can build stronger team relationships and foster passion and drive in order to move higher on the change map. In Chapter 6 we concentrate on the other capital city – *Struggling under Pressure* – and we discuss how team leaders need to get out from being caught in the middle, between the expectations of top management and the pressures from their teams. In both chapters, we explain why the two capital cities of *Unsustainable* have become such well-travelled destinations, because leaders and teams frequently try to repeat old solutions in the context of new situations.

Just Get On with It

The name of the capital city says it all: *Just Get On with It*. People's central concern is their work, and they just want to get on with their jobs. They want to do the things they do best and put everything else, including change, onto the back burner. Accountability and teamwork are the standout drivers in this region, with levels above the norm (see Figure 5.2). Team leadership and passion come next, just below the norm. In contrast, the remaining drivers drop further, with vision and direction, fear and frustration, and business leadership at levels indicative of low performance. On the surface, the dynamics of this capital city of *Unsustainable* look very similar to *Case for Action*, albeit in a less extreme fashion, but there are important differences.

Teams gravitate towards – and even leaders drift into – *Just Get On with It* because they just want to focus on their jobs. They know their roles, and they are happy to have targets and be held accountable for those outcomes. As such, team leaders focus on practical, concrete tasks. When problems

FIGURE 5.2   Change map and driver profile of *Just Get On with It* region

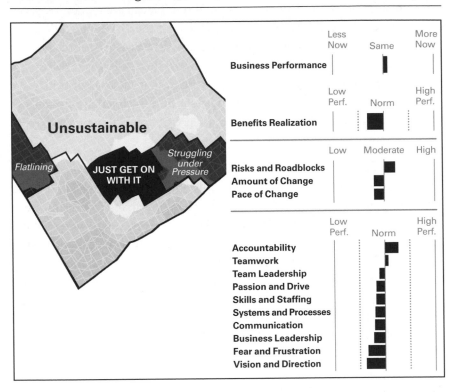

arise, the leaders typically respond with, 'I told you what to do, so what's the problem?' Emotions are not on the table for discussion. Nor do abstract or intellectual debates get high priority. People take pride in their work and are passionate about delivering good customer service. Although resources are below the norm, the level is adequate for people to make do with what they have in order to complete their work.

Similar to *Case for Action*, trust in team leadership is one of the biggest strengths, with people believing that their bosses will fight for them. On the other hand, a mentality of 'us versus them' is also pervasive, with groups forming factions that are closed to outsiders. Not surprisingly, many unionized work groups are prominent in the *Just Get On with It* region, and staff relationships with all higher levels of management are generally poor.

Although there is some agreement to the vision, it is tentative and fragile. In general, people have some awareness of the need for change, but the risks and roadblocks are too high for them to overcome and, even though everyone might be passionate about his or her work, the passion for change is close to zero. Another obstacle is that communication is poor, with rumours a primary source of information. This makes it difficult for groups to embrace the organization's vision and direction. From the written comments in our data, we found that many employees might want to leave but are sometimes discouraged by the ways in which their termination packages are structured. Clearly leaders in this region feel the underlying negativity and try to keep everything under control, but they tend to manage costs better than they do people. Consequently they have trouble sustaining loyalty, given that they have not been taking care of the intrinsic needs of their employees.

The major areas of concern are the predominance of fear and frustration, and low levels of vision and business leadership. Because of these deficiencies, teams find it impossible to look at the bigger picture when change comes along. But the key difference from *Case for Action* is that people in *Just Get On with It* take great pride in their work. The problem, though, is that many are fearful that the change initiative will eventually lead to their losing their jobs. As one staffer remarked, 'The goal from management is that we work harder so that we can achieve savings so that the people who worked hard can be retrenched and replaced with contractors or sold off. It's a lose–lose situation'.

The key to unlocking the dynamics of change in *Just Get On with It* is to leverage the strengths of this capital city – people take pride in their jobs and they want to work, but first they need to know what the change means for them. Vision and direction only attain traction when they become translated into concrete tangible tasks; otherwise, they will remain just 'pie in the sky' – abstract concepts, never realized. Also, people need to know that their jobs are secure. Whether any fear of job loss is real or imagined, it should not be ignored. At a time when creativity is most needed in order to find new and innovative solutions, people's energies should not be tied up in thinking about job security. Unfortunately, low trust in business and corporate leadership does not make matters any easier, especially when team leaders find it difficult to talk about emotional issues.

In *Case for Action*, groups need to establish bonds of trust that will then help reduce fear and frustration, thereby unlocking people's talents and creativity. **In *Just Get On with It*, groups need to replace fear and frustration with passion and drive, which will then provide the energy required to make the push into the *On Track* zone.** How, though, can organizations unlock everyone's passion and drive when employees are afraid of losing their jobs? The case study in the next section provides some answers.

The right way to rightsize

A large financial services company was caught in a business downturn, leaving its dedicated CEO in a tough position. Having spent years building up the business, he was now forced to make painful decisions about which staff would stay and which would go – decisions that were keeping him awake at night. Whether he thought of it as 'downsizing', 'rightsizing', 'retrenchment' or simply 'having to let people go', taking apart the business he had strived to build over the years was one of the toughest jobs that he had ever had to undertake.

In such conditions, when an organization is under pressure to reduce costs quickly, corporate procedures typically take over. A list is drawn up and managers just want to get through the process, so they announce the redundancies and people are shown the door. Throughout such downsizings, executives might try to shield themselves and their colleagues from the emotional fallout as much as possible, but the restructuring takes a toll on the organization as a whole. All this raises a crucial question: is there a right way to rightsize?

In our research, we found that there is indeed a way to downsize that leaves organizations stronger instead of weaker, and in better shape to improve performance. Consider the following tale of two companies. When we tracked the large financial services firm just mentioned, we found that it had started in *On Track*, dropped into *Unsustainable*, but then bounced back. The comparison company, which was not in the same industry but had been dealt the same mandatory requirement to downsize by 10–15 per cent, started in *Unsustainable* and then slid down into different regions of *Off Track* (see Figure 5.3).

As the graphs in Figure 5.3 show, in well-managed workforce reduction, while customer service, cost management and effectiveness may initially drop, they quickly rebound as the organization comes out of the change. In the comparison company's workforce reduction, only cost management improves in the longer term, and levels of customer service and effectiveness fail to bounce back as the organization comes out of the restructure.

The two organizations shown in Figure 5.3 differed in a number of ways, including industry, corporate culture and work environment, but both had started with very similar levels of accountability and resources, including skills and staffing, and systems and processes. As we studied these two organizations in greater depth, we found that a key difference was that the financial services firm had started with a much clearer vision, stronger

FIGURE 5.3   Successful versus unsuccessful downsizing

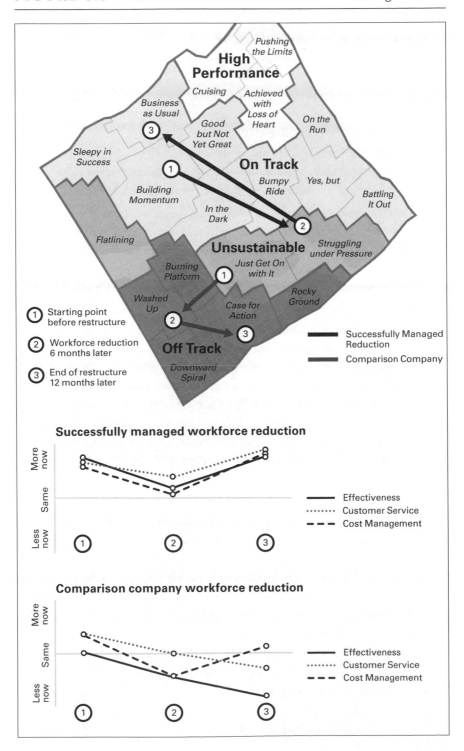

teamwork and better leadership. Moreover, the financial services firm had taken the following actions, whereas the comparison company had not:

- **Keeping change short and decisive**: in a well-managed workforce reduction, change is decisive. Leaders take the necessary action and then work quickly to stabilize the organization and refocus people's efforts in a positive direction. Everyone knows what they are doing and why. It is not just a matter of *what* is done but, more importantly, *how* it is done. In contrast, long, painful, drawn-out downsizings only tend to shake the organization apart, with the impact of decision-making in the early phases continuing to reverberate in the business long after people have left.

- **Quickly removing obstacles**: at the financial services firm, top management worked quickly to remove obstacles so that everyone could move forward after the downsizing. In the comparison company, the risks and roadblocks continuously increased as management failed to resolve conflicting priorities. As a result, the downsizing spiralled out of control.

- **Opening communications in difficult times**: it is important to note that, during a workforce reduction, a gap typically opens between the employees who lose their jobs and those who don't. Frequently, the two groups stop talking to each other, because they are uncomfortable or embarrassed. As such, maintaining open and honest dialogue throughout all levels becomes critical to ensuring a positive outcome. At the financial services firm, executives began holding weekly lunchtime sessions called 'Let's Talk', which were open to the entire organization. No matter what difficult questions came their way, leaders answered them as best as they could.

- **Adjusting the vision as the initiative proceeds**: at the financial services firm, vision suffered an initial hit when staff reductions were announced, but the CEO reframed the vision to include the new reality they faced, keeping everyone connected with the bigger picture even when times were tough. At the comparison company, the level of vision started from a low base and never recovered. Consequently, people lacked the proper context to make sense of the change programme, as management made no attempts to redefine a new future. Consequently, the initiative simply dropped off the agenda.

- **Constantly renewing trust**: not surprisingly, trust in leadership took a hit at both companies when the change initiative was announced. At the financial services firm, though, leaders worked hard to stay engaged with the process and trust bounced back just six months after the staff reduction. At the comparison company, leadership trust levels rapidly declined throughout the restructuring, sending harmful ripples of negativity throughout the entire organization. Building trust is all about being up close and personal, even though talking about emotions can be a messy, difficult process. Employees need to feel included and valued by being listened to and having their concerns acted upon. If instead they are ignored, they are likely to become more negative, disengaged and increasingly likely to be a destructive influence on the organization.

- **Leaving the organization in good shape:** the focus of a downsizing is often on the people who leave, with managers failing to invest the necessary time and resources on the employees who remain. That can be a big mistake. Once a downsizing is announced, employees become suspicious and fearful. Everyone is likely to think, 'If it could happen to others, then it could happen to me'. And even when people understand the reasons for a downsizing, those who remain often resent having to do more with less. Thus, managing the fears and other negative emotions of the people who stay is vital, and doing so often requires leaders to think creatively. We have found that investing in training and building capability reaps rewards over the long term, and the costs involved are significantly less than the savings gained by the staff reduction. At the financial services firm, passion and drive, and accountability, increased by 15–20 per cent from the beginning of the change programme to its end. Teams are the engine for getting things done, and part of that organization's success was due to the ways in which it was able to nurture the teams of employees who had remained in their jobs. In contrast, at the comparison company, accountability, teamwork, and passion and drive were the drivers that took the biggest hits from the start to the finish of the initiative, suffering declines of 40–50 per cent.

Saying 'goodbye' and 'hello'

We can see from the downsizing of the financial services firm cited above that remaining true to the core values of an organization and the personal values of a leader actually matters. Employees may not like what is happening with a change initiative. After all, they or their colleagues may be losing their jobs. However, people can retain respect for a company and even talk positively of its values afterwards *if* the change initiative is managed well. Also, strong interpersonal bonds can develop when people go through difficult times together. They share the challenges, working hard to achieve positive outcomes despite the trying circumstances, and that common experience can build a foundation of enduring, positive values in an organization.

It is important to note that difficult circumstances often cause people to reflect on the things they truly value. By definition, change initiatives challenge the way that things are done. The changes can affect not only work processes and work designs but also people's roles and the individuals they will be working with. This can then have an impact on a person's self-identity and motivation. Past research has shown that finding meaning in the work itself is the number one thing that motivates employees, and the people they work with is number two, with extrinsic motivators such as pay and other rewards having lower importance (Deci, 1975; Pink, 2009; Richmond and Schepman, 2005). It is no wonder, then, why change programmes often evoke such strong emotional reactions. To manage them, leaders must first appreciate that change initiatives challenge, if not altogether break, the existing psychological contract between employees and the organization they work for.

For many groups in *Just Get On with It*, people will stubbornly negotiate over the smallest details as they attempt to ensure that nothing of the old is lost during their move to the new. Small changes to work practices will trigger emotional responses that might, on the surface, appear to be well out of proportion to the actual actions. During a reorganization at one global company, managers were surprised to learn that their seeking a less costly form of end-of-year celebration was perceived by staffers as a direct attack on everything they had worked for. As one employee stated, 'I feel the decision to remove the formal end-of-year Christmas function to be a show of total disrespect to the employees and their partners'. Or, as another employee succinctly put it, 'Destroying the Christmas morale of the staff by offering a very small one-hour BBQ to all the staff for a year's hard work is such a slap in the face!'

Indeed, the way that people work often becomes wired almost unconsciously to their core values, and they might not even be aware of those values until change disrupts them. The loss that someone feels can take many forms. It can be the loss of a sense of security, of being in control, or of being confident about the future. Losing skills and competence can also have a huge impact on a person's self-esteem. Organizations reward people for being right and for being capable, and it is embarrassing for someone to be ignorant or to lack the necessary know-how. Moreover, the transferring of employees to different business units can alter their roles, status and sense of belonging. Their authority could also become diminished or even encroached upon by others.

Not surprisingly, when people are fearful about the future they tend to seek refuge in the past. They could become nostalgic and meet in small groups to reminisce, advocating for a return to the old ways of doing things. They might believe that they can embrace the new while fervently holding on to the old, creating an impossible challenge for leaders, or they might want a guarantee that everything will be alright before they allow themselves to move on. The danger is that team members could unite against a leader who is not sympathetic to their central values. Moreover, if management expresses frustration with those who cling to the past, the response could be indignation and accusations of betrayal. All this, obviously, could lead to a work environment that is far from productive. As one employee in *Just Get On with It* put it, 'This company used to have a real family feel about it. Now all [that people] can talk about is how soon they can retire and get out of here'.

In such situations it is easy to see how passion and drive can become locked up. Although it is healthy for people to acknowledge their feelings of loss and frustration, doing so in *Just Get On with It* is often viewed as a sign of weakness or lack of competence. But **if managers want to unlock the passion and drive needed to support and sustain workforce change, they must first recognize the different forms of loss involved and make plans for people to adequately say goodbye to the past**. To succeed in that, people must acknowledge the way that things were done in the past, identify the central values involved, make decisions about which of those values to keep and which to discard, and begin to find new ways of expressing the important values in the work they do. Part of that process involves encouraging individuals to tell stories and creating adequate rituals for them to say farewell to the past, because change means saying both 'goodbye' and 'hello'.

Unlocking the passion for change

Having recognized the importance of values and emotions, leaders can get on with the challenge of mobilizing passion and drive. From our data, we found that the only way for groups in *Just Get On with It* to eventually reach high performance is to increase their passion and drive, and in doing so they can deliver a 40 per cent increase in benefits. More passion and drive also leads to increased collaboration and improved performance. When teams let go of the old and are open to the new, silos between business units begin to break down, and people's energies can be applied to solving business problems instead of protecting self-interests.

The level of passion and drive is a measure of how much the change programme has captured people's hearts, as well as their minds. When passion is high, people feel good, excited and creative. When they have a high level of drive, they report feeling determined, decisive, proud and even humorous. In other words, passion and drive are the foundation for positive emotional energy in the workplace.

Passion is a set of feelings characterized by being encouraged or 'pulled' by some external force to perform certain actions, and these feelings produce a positive effect on others. Drive is related more to using one's own willpower to make things happen, and the person experiencing it is 'pushed' to do certain things. When faced with change, people's drive begins to become engaged when they start to take an interest in the objectives to be achieved and when they begin to take personal responsibility not only for those objectives but also for any unstated or implied goals that contribute to the effectiveness of the change.

The alignment between feelings of passion and drive is a good indicator of performance. **In high-performance groups, the scores for passion and drive are closely entwined, remaining at high levels across all stages. In low-performance groups, a gap opens up, especially in the latter stages of change, with drive being significantly higher than passion.** In such situations, willpower and determination can override a sense of dwindling excitement, and people's overall mindset might best be characterized by, 'I don't feel like doing this, but I will make myself do it'.

It is commonly thought that passion and drive emerge only towards the end stages of change, as has been previously proposed by other change models. Based on the work of psychiatrist Elisabeth Kübler-Ross (Kübler-Ross, 1973), some of those models contend that people must initially endure a 'valley of despair'. We found, however, that the level of passion and drive tends to remain quite consistent across the stages of change. For low-performance groups, the level of passion and drive starts and tends to stay low, and for high-performance groups it starts and tends to stay high. This is across all stages of a change programme, which emphasizes the importance of starting an initiative with the highest possible levels.

Cultivating passion and drive

So, the key question is: how can groups attain high levels of passion and drive? Unfortunately, many common approaches have limited effectiveness.

Passion and drive cannot be instilled or cultivated simply by preaching to the troops. Nor does more communication help very much. In fact, an increased level of communication has virtually no effect on low-performance teams; its impact seems to be significant only when the level of passion and drive is already high, indicating that people need to be open to communication before it can have an effect. Another motivational approach is to organize a barbecue, drinks, or some other type of social get-together to give people a 'feel good' experience. Although such efforts are well-meaning, they will work only if people are receptive and not still deeply buried in fear and frustration. Moreover, the effectiveness will be limited unless the fundamental causes of low passion and drive have already been addressed.

To develop lasting passion and drive, leaders must expend considerable effort to get people involved in making change happen. Initially, passion and drive can be built by helping everyone to find ways to look forward to the change. People's minds need to be opened to the positive aspects of an initiative, or at least they need to learn how to make the most of a bad lot. A passion for change can be developed through opportunities to become involved in the change, perhaps starting with low-risk projects. Eventually, people can then be coaxed through to the point at which their involvement starts to lead to positive feelings about the change, and about their contributions to it.

Although both business unit and team leaders play an important role in lowering fear and frustration, our research shows that it is the team leaders who are almost exclusively able to mobilize passion and drive. Strong team leadership can transform low levels of passion and drive into highly positive emotional energy, especially in terms of fostering strong levels of teamwork. To support and sustain that momentum, business unit leaders can then help by providing resources, including systems, processes, skills and staffing. Once people become convinced that the attempts to reduce fear and frustration are genuine and sustained, they become open to the logic and practical implications of the future vision and direction. Business unit leaders can also help by gaining people's commitment to the organization's vision and direction. Team leaders may have little direct effect on vision and direction but, through the mobilization of passion and drive, they can generate the energy that fuels vision and direction.

The major interventions that can help to increase passion and drive across the change map include recognizing and rewarding good performance, paying attention to each employee's unique talents, and utilizing every person's strengths to further the cause of the change programme. In *Just Get On with It*, those actions are important but they are just part of the solution. In addition, team leaders must be sensitive to gaining the confidence of their teams as well as the confidence of senior management, which might be desperate for results. So the job of team leaders is twofold. On the one hand, they must be able to conduct the sensitive one-on-ones with team members to calm their fears and frustrations, unlock their passion and drive, and engage their skills and knowledge in the cause of the change initiative. But equally, they must build bridges to senior management, negotiate for resources, and enrol the assistance of top executives to demonstrate that the change is real and authentic, and that it is fully supported by the organization.

Leading by example

When it comes to making change happen through a shift in core values, we have found that some of the most powerful examples occur when leaders themselves change. As a CEO of a resources company once said, 'I personally recognized that, despite my best intentions, the way that I behaved in the pursuit of business success was often creating stress in the workplace, rather than building trust and empowerment. Something had to change! Or perhaps I should say someone had to change! And to my greatest surprise, I understood that the person who needed to change first (and probably most) was me!' For leaders like this CEO, feelings they once ignored can eventually become their greatest asset.

Another example that shows the importance of leaders being open to learning comes from a major IT project at a bank. When we surveyed those involved with the project, we found that the level of skills and staffing was particularly low. We relayed this information to the senior executives and their response was, 'Well, we can't do anything about that because the CIO has announced a hiring freeze while he considers outsourcing'. In other words, the message being sent was, 'We haven't decided yet whether you're going to lose your job or not, but meanwhile please get on with your work'. Not exactly motivating.

Although staffers at that bank might have viewed management as malevolent, what we have more typically seen is that senior leaders just don't think through the impact of their actions. They are too focused on the competition; they look at the numbers; and they develop a proposal that gets signed off by the board. Then they proceed full-steam ahead without really considering the numerous implications of their actions.

There is a fundamental principle in managing people through change: you cannot give what you don't have. **If leaders are down at the bottom of the change map, struggling to manage themselves, they cannot truly lead others further up the map.** More specifically, when leaders themselves are in *Just Get On with It* and are ignoring the emotional impact of a change programme, they will have the same limitations as their staff, rendering them incapable of helping others to move out of this region.

That, however, does not mean that leaders have to remain stuck. When we provided the staff feedback to the bank CIO in our above example, he realized the depth of resentment that he had created, and he changed the ways in which he engaged with staffers by, for example, more actively soliciting their input. Sometimes it takes a jolt of honest feedback to spur people into action. It is like being asleep and then starting to wake up. If you were having a pleasant dream, then you want to return to sleeping. But if you were having a nightmare, then you want to regain enough consciousness to shake it off, because the last thing you want is for the nightmare to continue.

Common pathways exiting *Just Get On with It*

Our data indicates that 9 per cent of all groups reside in *Just Get On with It* and 24 per cent of them get stuck there, unable to adequately address issues of vision and direction, fear and frustration, and business leadership. Let's take a closer look at some of the major pathways leading out of *Just Get On with It* (Figure 5.4). We discuss each of those pathways below, highlighting some case examples in more depth. (Note: the examples in this section represent a composite of organizations from our research with similar experiences of change.)

Path 1: moving to Cruising *and* In the Dark

Only 2 per cent of groups travel straight up the change map all the way to *Cruising*. Performance and all drivers increase along this pathway, with improvements in business and team leadership delivering dramatic increases in benefits. Employee passion and drive rises as the amount and pace of change increase.

Another 7 per cent of groups travel on this path but instead end up in *In the Dark*. Propelled by passion and drive from highly motivated individuals,

FIGURE 5.4   Common pathways exiting *Just Get On with It*

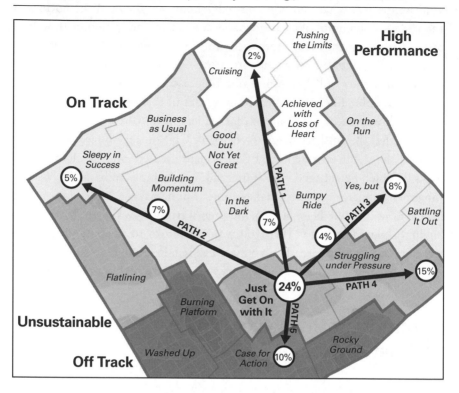

these groups experienced increased skills and staffing and manager communication. At a software company, one group had monthly meetings with their managers. Though the group did not enhance its understanding of the vision or increase trust in business leadership, the meetings enabled the group to negotiate for more resources 'to do their own thing', moving them up the change map.

Path 2: moving to Building Momentum *and* Sleepy in Success

On this path 5 per cent of groups move left to *Sleepy in Success* and another 7 per cent make it to *Building Momentum*. Following the path to *Building Momentum* at an engineering company, some team members joined a consultative committee – an unexpected exercise in participative decision-making. Consequently, people had a much better sense of the vision and direction of the company, and trust in corporate and business leadership increased. Also, the group obtained more resources and boosted passion and drive.

Performance and benefits both improved. In other cases, where employee involvement is lower, groups end up in *Sleepy in Success* – and even though more change is actually taking place, team leadership is lacking, and accountability and teamwork decline.

Path 3: *moving to* Yes, but *and* Bumpy Ride

On this path 4 per cent of groups move to *Bumpy Ride* and another 8 per cent to *Yes, but*. An example of the latter was a large civil engineering project that was running well behind schedule. A well-respected engineer who had risen through the ranks replaced the project head. People wanted to get involved with this new leader to make change happen and so the amount of change rose, as they saw the benefits of a new way of working. Pace of change also increased and, as the project moved back on schedule, people's confidence in the change programme surged. The project leader's efforts in building a better understanding and agreement to the vision had meant more awareness of the need for change. Passion and drive increased as people felt recognized for their efforts, and negative emotions dropped. There were still issues, however, regarding a lack of necessary resources, team leadership quality and accountability problems.

Path 4: *moving to* Struggling under Pressure

On this path 15 per cent of groups move to *Struggling under Pressure*. For example, at a department store chain, executives had implemented a change initiative that targeted growth and new ways of working. Accordingly, trust in business and corporate leadership increased; vision and direction rose; and benefits increased. Confidence in the change jumped dramatically. But the movement was sideways because little change occurred in day-to-day business performance. Part of the problem was that, instead of hiring new staff to meet the change needs, contractors were being retained on an entirely different basis than veteran, loyal staff. Team leadership was at the core of this problem. Eventually, all aspects of accountability dropped as contracted staff kept growing while employees saw no recognition of their loyalty and sacrifice; and people increasingly thought of leaving.

Path 5: *moving to* Case for Action

On this path 10 per cent of groups drop to *Case for Action*. Consider a construction company caught in economic free fall. It wasn't just the impact of a recession; the signs were already there, especially for teams led by a 'toxic' site manager. Under drastic downsizing, everything worsened. All drivers declined, as people could not resolve conflicts. Fear and frustration rose, and more people considered leaving. Effectively, the group had imploded under pressure, and performance and benefits declined. Replacing the toxic leader could have united team members to implement the change, but unfortunately, this didn't happen.

The importance of emotions

This chapter focused on *Just Get On with It*, one of the two capital cities of the *Unsustainable* zone. In Chapter 6 we describe the characteristics, dynamics and challenges of *Struggling under Pressure*, the other capital city. As we will see, although both capital cities are in *Unsustainable*, they each require a different overall approach and a unique set of specific interventions for groups to move up into regions of higher performance.

SUMMARY FOR CHAPTER 5: KEY INSIGHTS

- One out of four change programmes finds itself in a situation where change is *Unsustainable* – where business performance has levelled off through lack of change capability; 41 per cent of groups stay stranded, never making it past this point, neither getting better nor worse.

- Organizations lose essential capabilities long before they show up in plunging business performance. Business metrics such as operating costs and budget are essentially *lag* indicators, reflecting the outcomes of past actions.

- When organizations invest in building people's capabilities, they gain much-needed *lead* indicators that warn them well in advance of future problems.

- It is tempting for leaders to push harder to ensure they meet business targets as performance levels off, but this only produces short-term gains. The secret to achieving much greater levels of performance lies in building people's multiple capabilities to manage change continuously.

- Senior management risks losing good team leaders, who fail despite their best efforts, when it turns a blind eye to building team leaders' capabilities to manage emotions.

- What leaders have done in the past is not the prologue to future success. 'Change or die' does not motivate in *Unsustainable*, as it did in *Off Track*. This approach needs to be replaced by more attractive alternatives and a genuine sense of excitement.

- Leaders who help their teams to say goodbye to the past (overcoming fear and frustration) before saying hello to the future (engaging passion and drive) unlock the energy needed to push towards *High Performance*.

- In high-performing groups, passion and drive are closely entwined, remaining at high levels across all stages. In low-performing groups, a gap opens up, and people feel much more determined than they do excited.

- 'You can't give what you don't have' is a fundamental principle in managing people through change. Leaders who struggle to manage themselves struggle to lead others towards high performance.

- Downsizing can be painful for those who stay as well as those who leave the organization, but trust can be retained by keeping change short and decisive, by quickly removing obstacles, by opening up communication, by adjusting the vision as the initiative proceeds, by constantly renewing the meaning of core values and by investing in those who stay.

- Everyone watches what leaders do. Some of the most powerful changes occur when leaders openly and honestly recognize that they themselves need to change.

Struggling under Pressure
When teams falter

06

> I've always hated the danger part of climbing, and it's great to come down again because it's safe... But there is something about building up a comradeship – that I still believe is the greatest of all feats – and sharing in the dangers with your company of peers. It's the intense effort, the giving of everything you've got. SIR EDMUND HILLARY

At the executive level, the reorganization at the bank seemed to be progressing smoothly one year into the initiative. Benefits were being realized, and various business metrics such as cost management were experiencing significant improvements. But at the staff level, the picture was not so rosy. Many employees who had already been working full-time schedules were struggling with an additional 20 per cent more work, and teamwork and accountability were sorely lacking. As a result, staffers had become disenchanted with the change initiative. 'To be brutally honest', noted one employee, 'the amount of organizational and procedural change has been staggering and unwelcome. This, coupled with an exceedingly large work programme, is past the point of burning out our most committed people'.

To be sure, the bank's change programme was ambitious. Executives wanted to adopt new technologies to improve time to market, exploit growth opportunities, increase efficiency and improve employee engagement.

Accordingly, a new operating model was implemented across the IT functions of the bank. Other goals were to decrease supplier costs and improve the return from strategic partners. Throughout the initiative, roles and responsibilities were redefined for a staff of 1,300.

As it turned out, hierarchical levels throughout the organization had become seriously misaligned in their actions and expectations. Executives of the bank were in *High Performance*; managers were in *On Track*; and team leaders and employees were lower on the change map, immersed in the *Struggling under Pressure* region (see Figure 6.1). In analysing our database, we found that 11 per cent of groups and organizations reside in *Struggling under Pressure*. There, people have resources but lack the discipline needed to utilize them to their best advantage. Team leaders, especially, struggle under pressure as they try to juggle the demands from senior executives to deliver results while managing the role confusion in their teams. They are caught in the middle and desperately seek to improve the accountability and teamwork of their staffers.

FIGURE 6.1   The locations of different groups in a change programme

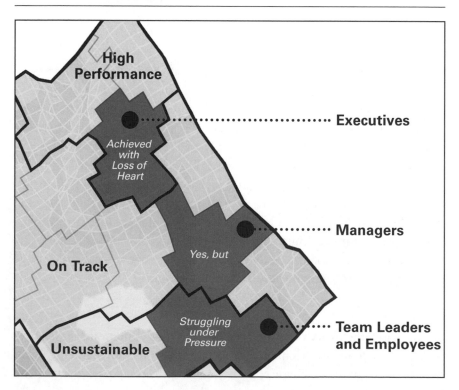

Struggling under Pressure is one of two capital cities in the *Unsustainable* zone – the crossroads for groups between improving or getting worse. In Chapter 5, we described the characteristics of *Unsustainable*, and we also focused on *Just Get On with It*, the zone's other capital city. In that region, we saw how organizations needed to build stronger team relationships and foster passion and drive in order to move higher on the change map. In this chapter, we focus on the characteristics, dynamics and challenges of *Struggling under Pressure*.

Struggling under Pressure insights

The bank cited above was eventually able to move up the change map from *Struggling under Pressure*, saving over US$30 million in technology spending across the three-year transformation. Many groups, however, are not that fortunate. According to our database, 26 per cent remain stuck in *Struggling under Pressure*. As we shall see, the challenges in this region can be daunting, particularly when people lack the discipline, structure and drive to make change happen. From our research, we have found that the key to unlocking the dynamics of *Struggling under Pressure* is to gain alignment among stakeholders on what the issues are and what actions need to be taken to help team leaders effectively to lead their teams. This is because senior executives and business unit leaders can only do so much to improve the functioning of teams at the lower levels of the organization. Specifically, in analysing our data, we uncovered two key insights about teams that can greatly aid those who find themselves in *Struggling under Pressure*: 1) good teamwork is driven by high levels of accountability, and passion and drive; 2) accountability must be driven primarily by team leaders.

Insight 1: good teamwork is driven by high levels of accountability, and passion and drive

Teamwork is not a 'fluffy' or 'fuzzy' concept of people getting along and having a good time doing their jobs. Instead it is a highly disciplined use of energy aimed at achieving clear organizational targets. Moreover, strong team leadership is vital to good teamwork. A crucial key in *Struggling under Pressure* is that team leaders must instill accountability, and passion and drive, in their team members.

Insight 2: accountability must be driven primarily by team leaders

Although alignment among leaders at all levels is needed to ensure high levels of accountability throughout an organization, accountability must be driven primarily by team leaders. Many organizations make the mistake of trying to drive accountability at the executive or business unit level, but that can often be counterproductive, leading to increased resentment among staffers. That said, team leaders cannot drive accountability in their teams without clear direction, guidelines and support from the leaders above them. The expression that 'you can't give what you don't have' sums up this situation. As we shall see in the bank example, when the attention of senior executives is directed elsewhere, this creates an almost impossible task for team leaders and they suffer as a result. Taking steps to ensure alignment in the early stages of change – rather than finding out in the middle of an initiative that there is a problem – is one of the best investments that management can make.

As mentioned earlier, much of the focus in *Struggling under Pressure* is on team leaders because they are the individuals who are best positioned to help groups to move to regions of higher performance. As we shall see, though, team leaders are typically under intense pressures from above, with senior management often impatient for results, and this makes it difficult for them to manage their teams in the most effective ways.

The characteristics and dynamics of *Struggling under Pressure*

In *Struggling under Pressure*, groups improve all aspects of business performance, including cost, customer service and effectiveness. People take pride in their work; they want to do a good job; and they try to remain loyal to their customers in the face of the changes taking place. Benefits are being realized, although nothing like the full potential that was outlined in the business case. The reason for the difference is because people's roles have been restructured and reorganized, but a new way of working has yet to emerge.

That certainly was the case at the bank we discussed at the beginning of this chapter. An IT manager in that change initiative likened the situation to 'a game of constant musical chairs as vacancies open and get filled'. Or, as one team leader noted, 'Even though numerous additional resources have been added, skills and knowledge are watered down now that expertise is sprinkled across multiple areas. I am unable to see how this new model can possibly be cheaper given all the additional layers'.

The big issues in *Struggling under Pressure* are teamwork, accountability and the communication necessary to build both (see Figure 6.2). The level of fear and frustration is also an area of concern, and it is important to note that all these drivers are the primary responsibility of team leaders. On the positive side, resources are available; business performance hasn't suffered; and the benefits of change are still being realized. Although risks do exist in the face of the amount of change taking place, they are only at a moderate level. The level of business leadership is only a little higher than that for team leadership, which is below the norm, and this poses a potential challenge. Managers in *Yes, but* and executives in *Achieved with Loss of Heart* struggle to manage their own issues. In *Struggling under Pressure* they are effective in providing resources and taking quick remedial actions on broader organizational issues, but in doing this they can lose sight of the need to support their team leaders.

FIGURE 6.2 Change map and driver profile for *Struggling under Pressure* region

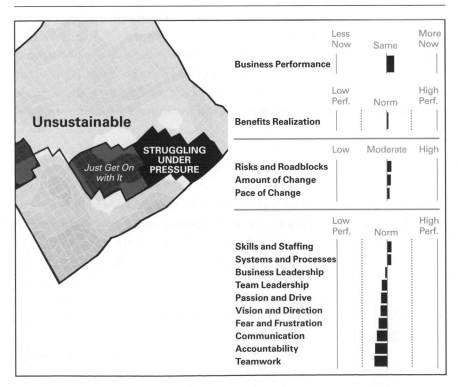

In *Struggling under Pressure* people talk a lot about their frustrations, pressures and stresses, and they frequently complain about the hours they are working and the lack of recognition and rewards. Expectations are on everyone's mind, and the words 'motivation', 'delivering' and 'performance' appear frequently in comments from those in this region. There is a sense of immediacy regarding the present, with little focus on the future and very minimal reference to the past.

A huge problem for groups in this region is that nearly everything around role clarity and objectives seems to have been neglected. People often find themselves in new teams and are not sure of who's who and how to get things done. Unfortunately, involvement in planning and implementing change is low, and managers don't provide important information about what is needed by whom and when. It is a confusing place to be because people cannot connect with the 'big picture', and they don't have a clue about what change means for them and their teams.

Team leaders under pressure

In some cases, for team leaders new to their role and often promoted because of their technical expertise, their lack of managerial skills and experience can make it difficult to get things done. As a result, trust in the team leader is much lower than trust in upper management. Not surprisingly, teamwork suffers, leaving people feeling impatient, distressed, stubborn and afraid. Positive feelings dry up, with passion and drive at low levels. Most of all, people lack an awareness of the need for change, as team leaders struggle to get staffers involved in making the initiative happen. Regular information updates from management do not seem to occur and individuals operate as best as they can, but in a vacuum. Yet, in spite of these difficulties, people in *Struggling under Pressure* are not thinking of leaving. Instead, they want to stay with the organization and make the change initiative work.

A huge issue is that **team leaders are caught in a double bind. From the top down, they face unrelenting management expectations to deliver results. From the bottom up, they must deal with a lack of accountability and teamwork.** Unless team leaders delegate tasks, build accountability and invest time to strengthen their teams, they cannot reduce the load they carry. Yet doing all that takes considerable time – time that team leaders don't believe they have. It is no wonder, then, why so many of them become burned out in the process.

Clarifying roles and responsibilities, and improving teamwork, are the keys to reaching a region of higher performance, and team leaders are the

linchpins for accomplishing that. To understand the crucial importance of accountability, teamwork and team leadership, let's consider the extreme example of mountain climbing, in which decisions often have life-or-death consequences.

Lessons from Mount Everest

Climbing Mount Everest is among the most demanding of human endeavours. Mountain climbing is a journey that is inherently fraught with danger, as travellers can unexpectedly encounter numerous events that cannot be predicted in advance, including quick changes in the weather conditions, avalanches, injuries to team members and other accidents. What makes the difference between surviving such expeditions and perishing on the mountain? Sir Edmund Hillary, who was the first to climb Everest, stressed the importance of 'building up a comradeship' and the significance of 'sharing in the dangers with your company of peers' (McFadden, 2008). In other words, teamwork in mountaineering has both a human, affiliative effect as well as a more utilitarian purpose: it is simply more efficient and effective to work as a unified team.

Hillary and Tenzing Norgay, his sherpa, may have been the first to reach the top of Mount Everest, but their success was the result of a much larger, well-organized expedition. Base camps and supply chains were set up at strategic points across the mountain. Colleagues and expert guides provided support at each stage. Planning and coordination behind the scenes involved many teams, managing resources across many countries. Early on in the expedition planning, Hillary gained confidence that the leaders of those teams knew exactly what they were doing, and he was impressed with John Hunt, who headed the overall expedition. According to Hillary, '[Hunt] brought a series of detailed plans which I reluctantly had to admit seemed to hit the nail on the head every time... it was quite obvious that the organization was going ahead at great speed and that our equipment was to be the best that could be achieved' (Hillary, 1955: 118). In organizational terms, Hillary saw that the different levels of individuals involved in the climb were aligned from the earliest stages.

Contrast that historic effort with another expedition – the ill-fated Everest climb led by Rob Hall in the spring of 1996. That expedition, recounted in the best-selling book *Into Thin Air* (1997) by Jon Krakauer, ultimately resulted in the death of 12 people. Krakauer, a member of that team, said he lost confidence in the expedition early on when he observed the following misalignment between the leadership and team members:

> I soon learned that on Everest not even the rope – the quintessential climber's accoutrement – was to be utilized in the time-honoured manner. Ordinarily, one climber is tied to one or two partners with a 150-foot length of rope, making each person directly responsible for the life of the others; roping up in this fashion is a serious and very intimate act. In the Icefall, though, expediency dictated that each of us climb independently, without being physically connected to one another in any way. (Krakauer, 1997)

To be sure, organizational change initiatives do not typically have the same life-or-death consequences, but the process is nevertheless inherently difficult and demanding. In the bank example cited above, the signs and signals of misalignments were visible in the very early stages of change, but management failed to see them until much later. Consequently, people found themselves in the midst of change having to sort things out on top of confusion and resentment. In any change initiative, priorities can rapidly switch, and crises can come from many directions. In such situations, clear roles mean faster response times. Precise, shared objectives mean that everyone is heading in the same direction and, if something goes wrong, people will know what needs to be done without having to refer to a higher authority. Teamwork means that problems are tackled collectively, rather than alone.

Unfortunately, teamwork and accountability are easily eroded in the context of poorly planned change programmes, and the problem is exacerbated when different managerial layers have widely varying perceptions of what is actually happening. In mountain climbing and organizational change, however, teams can ill afford to have their members working independently with little accountability to one another.

Organizational disconnects

As mentioned earlier, different groups involved in a change programme – for example, executives, senior managers, team leaders and team members – can have varying perceptions of how the initiative is progressing. For that bank discussed earlier, we tracked the company's change programme across three years at five different points in time. Using that data, we could position the different groups of participants on the change map in order to understand how each group reacted and responded to change. By the second cycle, staff teams had moved across from *Just Get On with It* to *Struggling under Pressure* to join the team leaders who were already there; managers were in

Yes, but and remained there; and executives had moved upward from *Yes, but* to *Achieved with Loss of Heart*.

By analysing details of the disconnects between those groups, we could better understand how such misalignments ultimately led to increasing pressures on the bank's team leaders. As it turned out, staff teams, managers and executives all saw business performance as improving, with executives having an especially rosy view, perceiving very high levels of improvement in cost management, effectiveness and customer service levels. For benefits realization, though, the disconnects were more pronounced. Managers, and especially executives, saw considerable benefits being delivered, above the norm and close to the levels of high performance. In contrast, staff teams viewed the benefits realization as much lower, sitting around the norm. In terms of the amount and pace of change, executives saw a considerable amount of change taking place at a pace that was too fast. At lower levels at the bank, managers and staff teams viewed the restructuring as the main changes taking place but without any accompanying growth or new ways of working and, for them, the pace was fine. Also, managers saw more risks and roadblocks than did those at other levels.

Many executives would look at these results and say, 'Well, what do you expect? The programme is on time and on budget, so what's the problem?' But exactly whose view holds the most weight when it comes to successfully managing change? Executives' perceptions were around 6 per cent of the data we collected; managers were about 29 per cent; and staff teams were around 65 per cent. If we believed only executives and managers, then no actions would be necessary. That, however, was clearly not the case.

A case example showing disconnects

The different driver profiles for the bank reveal details of how the separate groups had very different views of the change initiative (see Figure 6.3). First, if we look at resource levels, even though groups were positioned in different parts of the change map, everyone except the team leaders agreed that resource levels were around the norm. But there were important differences. For teams, the best-scoring drivers were skills and staffing, and systems and processes. For executives and managers, these were the worst-scoring drivers. When managers perceive that staffing levels are just below the norm, the logical solution is to hire more people. But what use will that be for teams that say they already have sufficient staff and instead really need help with accountability and teamwork? In such cases, additional staff might only confuse the situation. Furthermore, team leaders specifically said that they

FIGURE 6.3   Driver profiles of different groups in a change programme

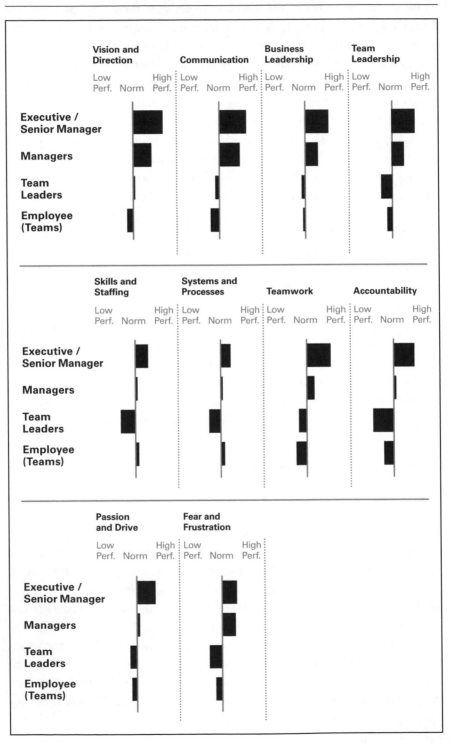

lacked skills and knowledge, so there was a disconnect between what people in their team said they had and what was needed by the team leaders.

If we look across vision and direction, and communication, we see that these drivers were high for managers and executives at the bank but lower for team leaders and teams. As such, managers who had information and who understood the vision were on a collision course with team leaders who didn't fully know where the initiative was headed. As one employee at the bank complained, 'People are hearing about the changes but I'm not sure how much is truly being absorbed because it's coming at us too fast. Since the overall plan has never been communicated, we learn about other activities requiring our time when an invite lands in our inbox'. On the plus side, though, people were not relying on the rumour mill for whatever information they did obtain.

When managers have a high level of information they can easily sit down with team leaders to share it with them. But as can be seen in Figure 6.3, this did not happen at the bank. What managers there didn't realize was that, by not closing that information gap, they were sending the following message to team leaders: figure it out on your own. Given those circumstances, it is no wonder that the bank's team leaders struggled.

This pattern of disconnects between organizational levels is typically repeated across other drivers for groups in *Struggling under Pressure*. Accountability, and high fear and frustration, are much bigger issues for team leaders than for anyone else, and they are typically alone in their concerns. **To move into the *On Track* zone, groups need an increase of at least 40 per cent in accountability and teamwork as well as in passion and drive**. It is important to note that these drivers are already high at the executive level, yet organizations fail to capitalize on these strengths to help team leaders build their and their staff's competencies and capabilities.

Gaining alignment and fixing disconnects

Taking a systemic view – understanding how all of the parts interact to jointly determine outcomes – is vital to managing risk in change programmes. Some disconnects are easy to fix and require little effort and cost. Communication, for example, might not require much beyond certain individuals sitting down and talking. Other disconnects require an investment of time or resources. Accountability and teamwork, for instance, require a considerable commitment of time and effort from team leaders. Furthermore, whenever organizations need to rebuild trust that has been broken, they must ensure that leaders have the necessary experience and skills. As mentioned earlier, groups in *Struggling under Pressure* require substantial increases in both accountability and teamwork in order to move into the *On Track* zone. Let's now take a closer look at what the research tells us about how organizations can accomplish that.

How to increase accountability

Many organizations view accountability merely as an exercise in which managers just have to set goals and objectives. If only things were that simple. In our research, **we have found that high levels of accountability are driven through strong relationships among the team members, including the team leader**. In fact, targets mean very little without open communication and the trusting relationships needed to achieve them. Targets might define the goals but team members need one another to get the job done, and communication is not so much a driver of accountability as it is a mechanism to confirm what has been agreed upon between team leaders and their teams. Once accountability has been established, providing resources – systems and processes, and skills and staffing – helps to support and sustain the momentum. Even when the systems and processes have inadequacies, people will find creative ways around those shortcomings *if* they are supported by their team and team leader. It should be noted that vision and direction, and passion and drive, play almost no direct role in increasing accountability.

Accountability is a measure of whether team members do their jobs and take responsibility for their own objectives and outcomes. Improved accountability requires an increase in all of the dimensions we measure:

- How clear are your roles and responsibilities within your team?
- To what extent does your team have clear performance objectives and measurable outcomes?
- How much are people on your team held accountable for achieving their objectives?

Increases in accountability cannot occur without getting people involved in understanding their roles in making change happen. First, leaders need to spell out for each team member, one-on-one, what is expected of his or her role in terms of responsibilities, duties and boundaries with other roles. An important part of this conversation is a discussion of how the changes will be affecting that person's role as well as their impact on customers' expectations. Involving team members in this way is crucial to work through the implications of the objectives and outcomes set for them.

FIGURE 6.4   Accountability compared to benefits realization and fear and frustration

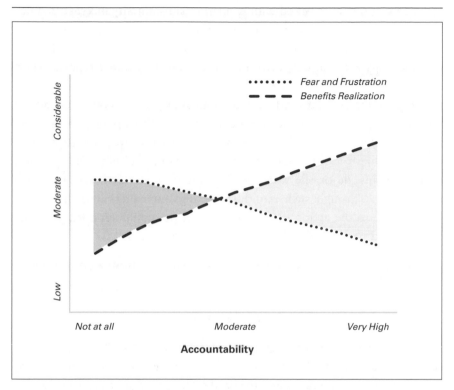

When people embrace responsibility for what happens in their workplace, the gains are considerable for the team, as well as for the organization. Specifically, **stronger accountability helps deliver benefits – a 41 per cent improvement from the norm** (see Figure 6.4). It can also help lower the level of fear and frustration, which is typically an issue in *Struggling under Pressure*, by as much as 25 per cent from the norm.

It is also important to note that for high-performing teams – that is, for those in *Cruising* or higher regions – increasing accountability is what takes benefits from mid to very high levels. On the other hand, **for low-performing teams increased accountability only improves benefits realization up to a certain point, and then the effect flattens out**.

Accountability makes a huge difference in terms of how people react to a set of outcomes. Do they respond fatalistically or helplessly, or do they act decisively to try and influence those outcomes? Do they often say 'It's not my job' and 'What do I care?', or do they ask 'What can I do?' and 'How can I help?' People making the decision to act on something that might seem to be out of their control will often lead to a vastly different outcome than the alternative of abject inaction.

One executive we worked with wanted to substantially increase people's accountability while a change programme was taking place at his organization. So he insisted that all of his team leaders and managers have face-to-face meetings every month with their direct and non-direct reports. These sessions would have a very specific structure. The first step was to review the previous month – what worked and what didn't. The second step was to set business priorities for the coming month. The third part, and the most interesting step, was to ask people to come up with three different action plans to achieve the business targets. If a person couldn't think of three different plans, he or she was told to come back the next day with that information. Through such monthly meetings, managers and their staffs would agree to the action plans that both parties could support, and both business and personal development needs were discussed to reach the best outcomes. Thanks to these meetings, accountability in that group increased considerably.

An investment of time and energy

So why is it so difficult for groups in *Struggling under Pressure* to build strong accountability? Team leaders are faced with many pressures, pulling them in different directions, and the hard truth is that increasing the level of accountability – and teamwork, as we will see in the next section – requires a considerable investment of time and energy. Because both quantities are typically in short supply, team leaders end up rarely talking to their teams. Indeed, our research shows that the level of face-to-face and written communications is one of the lowest scoring behaviours in *Struggling under Pressure*. But leaders cannot take for granted their communication with their teams; they have to somehow make the time for real conversations about what is actually occurring in the workplace.

When a team's accountability is low, a big temptation is for business unit leaders to jump in and try to fix the problem. This intervention might seem logical in that business leaders would be well positioned to help teams connect their objectives to the larger organizational vision and direction. Our research, however, shows that business leadership can often play a contentious role in its effects on accountability. For most regions, business leadership has no effect on accountability; in other regions, including *Struggling under Pressure*, it has a negative effect, reflecting a 'them versus us' perspective between teams and upper management. In such cases, business leaders who get directly involved can strike a discordant note, undermining the authority and credibility of team leaders and breaking the pact between them and their teams.

Ideally, business leaders and team leaders work collaboratively to implement the change programme. The former helps the latter by assisting them to define team accountabilities, by supporting their actions through good policies and procedures, and by providing important resources. It cannot be stressed enough that **having the right team leaders is the most significant single intervention for improving staff accountability in *Struggling under Pressure*.** The selection and recruitment of people with the necessary skills for those roles is the obvious first step but, when that is not possible, organizations should consider coaching for those individuals. Moreover, putting in place a professional development system can help ensure that employees have the required skills and experience before they are tapped to lead a team.

How to build strong teams

Everyone has heard stories of how a collection of individuals can coalesce into a tightly knit group bent on a common purpose. Movies have been made and stories told about how a motley collection of personalities can sometimes meld into a synergistic and focused team of people who, under seemingly impossible conditions, undergo personal transformations and bond together to accomplish remarkable feats. But is this how it really happens? We investigated the teamwork of thousands of groups by asking two interrelated questions:

- Within your team, how involved are you in planning and implementing changes?
- How would you rate the level of teamwork in your team?

The results show that the foundation of teamwork consists of two building blocks: 1) accountability, and 2) passion and drive. Interestingly, communication and business leadership have little effect on developing teamwork. But that is not to say that communication is unimportant. As we have mentioned, communication is the vehicle to get things done. It plays a role in shaping and confirming accountabilities and linking objectives and outcomes to the unified organizational vision and direction.

Team leaders play a critical role in bringing together those two important but seemingly opposite attributes: accountability, and passion and drive. Bringing discipline, focus and structure together with the pure energy of excitement and drive can be like trying to tame a wild horse, and getting the balance right is tricky. Too much accountability with little energy can easily lead to lacklustre performance. On the other hand, abundant energy with no structure can quickly result in chaos. To avoid that, teams need a focus on an end goal for their actions. This is where vision and direction can play an important role by creating a target that stretches the team beyond achieving their day-to-day objectives.

Many leaders have a natural bias either towards managing tasks or managing people. At a senior level, those orientated towards tasks believe that change issues can be resolved by structural interventions, technical solutions, new processes, or a combination of those. In contrast, those orientated towards people will focus first on the culture. The belief is that, 'If we get people fired up, then we'll find a way through'. **When implementing change initiatives, the best leaders are those who have a natural balance between managing both tasks and people.**

When teams work well, high-performance leaders don't wait to be told what to do; instead they continuously seek information to share with their teams and actively shape their future. Often, teamwork is enhanced under the pressure of a challenge – overly aggressive deadlines, stretch goals or people's lack of experience in performing the tasks that need to be done. Sometimes, a group has no precedents for what it has to do and yet, despite all the odds, it perseveres and achieves success through good, solid teamwork.

But what about those cases in which teamwork is sorely lacking? Following a pattern similar to that for accountability, **business unit leaders can best help their team leaders build teamwork by providing support and, in some cases, resources, all while avoiding the temptation to interfere.** If, for example, a business leader is a trusted and competent coach, he or she can work with team leaders to build their skills. Also, when teams get to the point at which they start to look beyond their own boundaries, business leadership can play a major role in facilitating cooperation and synergy across and between teams. The problem, though, is when the relationship between business leaders and team leaders breaks down. In such dysfunctional cases, the danger is that well-respected team leaders can unite their teams against both the business leadership and the organization itself, bringing change to a standstill.

Difficulties with teamwork

Because fear and frustration run high in *Struggling under Pressure*, any attempts to mobilize teamwork on top of those negative feelings can quickly turn into sessions of blaming and complaining. That is, unless the level of fear and frustration is lowered first, people will have difficulty hearing messages in a logical and rational way. The situation becomes all the more tricky during a restructuring in which new members must be absorbed into a team. But when the team can make those individuals feel accepted, they could bring new perspectives to old problems.

Good team leaders help their teams to discuss openly their objections and criticisms so that those issues can be worked through and resolved whenever possible. Unfortunately, many team leaders are themselves struggling under the pressure of a heavy workload, making it difficult for them to facilitate team-building. They simply may not have the capacity to engage the team in constructive discussions, and they may even succumb to the pressure and join in the complaining themselves.

It is important to recognize that even the most levelheaded of individuals can lose their ability to think clearly under relentless pressure. In Chapter 3, we saw from the America's Cup example that, even under the intense pressure to win, Captain John Bertrand encouraged his team members simply to do what they had been trained to do, nothing more. Accountability and teamwork bring the discipline required to repeat patterns that have been learned and built up across long periods of time. But even the clearest thinking can evaporate under stressful conditions, and this needs to be factored into leadership plans. In the America's Cup story, Bertrand knew that his crew might lose their judgement under pressure, so he built crosschecks into the system of teamwork. For instance, each crew member was trained to watch others of their team and shout out key words to bring them back on track whenever they saw people losing their focus.

When a group is failing, the kneejerk reaction is to replace its leader. 'Heads must roll' is the mantra that captures that sentiment. But such situations are typically far more complex than that. The data emerging from thousands of change journeys shows us that teamwork is not just a result of team leadership but the product of many factors, only some of which are under the control of the team leader. Thus, when a good leader buckles under pressure, management needs to take a hard look at what is going on in the wider change programme, or even across the organization as a whole. It is always dangerous for senior executives to be out of touch with the reality of what is happening on the ground. Rather than immediately blaming a team leader, they need to each ask themselves the following question: what role did I play in that team leader's failure, either by my actions or inactions?

Sometimes, team leaders lack the credibility or competence to manage their teams. They might, for example, be incapable of dispelling fear and frustration, or lack the skills to have the difficult discussions needed to build accountability. In such situations, upper management needs to become more proactive. Recognizing the competence of team leaders, and adjusting their change strategy accordingly before people crack under pressure, is one of the most critical tasks for business unit leaders in this region, and is well worth the investment of time and effort. Should the current team leader be impervious to coaching and counselling, the business leader must find someone who isn't. **All of the evidence from our research shows that putting the right team leader in the right role can rapidly accelerate teams out of** *Struggling under Pressure*.

The importance of good governance

Organizational culture and good governance set the conditions that enable people to operate at their best. Without them, even strong individuals and teams can fail. One of the problems with the fateful Everest expedition led by Rob Hall was that he was essentially wearing two hats. As the team leader, he was continually trying to decide what was best for his team in a particular situation at a given time. But as a business leader, he was also trying to assess what was best for the company running a commercial expedition with the responsibility of taking people up Everest. Such lack of role clarity, which is typical of many change initiatives, can easily confuse decision-making.

Moreover, when organizations change, people often abandon established practices and procedures, exposing vulnerabilities in the organization that may not have been visible before. People often claim that 'the change caused us to fail', but our experience is that the 'cracks' already existed before the change came along. In the bank example cited earlier in this chapter, for instance, all the signs of misalignment were visible in the first cycle results; they had just never been put under pressure. Part of that pressure can come from new team members who do not think and act the same as others who have been there for a while. New blood can be a great source of inspiration, but it can also be the single biggest cause of frustration. Also, discipline and deep knowledge can easily be lost.

Looking at the broader question of organization governance, we find it useful to refer back to the differences in the perceptions of staff teams, managers and executives at the bank cited above. Each of those groups had its own legitimate point of view, but the problem was that, if the staff perceptions were not addressed and the senior executive position held sway, the change initiative would have veered badly off track. The data shows that confidence in executive leadership is boosted by four factors: the staff's agreement with the vision proposed by senior executives; their willingness to take quick remedial action when systems and processes fail; the overall perception of how well they are managing the change process; and whether or not the benefits of change are being realized. As such, senior executives must take into account the perceptions and opinions of their constituencies, or else they are failing to meet their own responsibilities and are modelling poor accountability to the workforce.

Unfortunately, team leaders can easily forget the importance of teamwork and accountability while managing large projects, yet their own accountability for the success of those efforts is constantly on display to all stakeholders. We cannot stress enough that teamwork along with team leadership are core capabilities of any high-performing organization, regardless of the changes that are taking place. Our research shows that change initiatives that start with strong teamwork do better, and those that commence with low teamwork do worse. Both teamwork and accountability are not significantly affected by change, and **teamwork makes little difference to benefits realization but it can have a huge impact on everything else when it is neglected.**

Common pathways exiting *Struggling under Pressure*

Struggling under Pressure is the most common destination on the change map. Our data indicates that 11 per cent of groups reside in this region, with 26 per cent of them getting stuck there, unable to adequately address issues with team leadership, teamwork and accountability. Let's take a closer look at some of the major pathways leading out of *Struggling under Pressure* (Figure 6.5). We discuss each of those pathways below, highlighting some case examples in more depth. (Note: the examples in this section represent a composite of organizations from our research with similar experiences of change.)

FIGURE 6.5   Common pathways exiting *Struggling under Pressure*

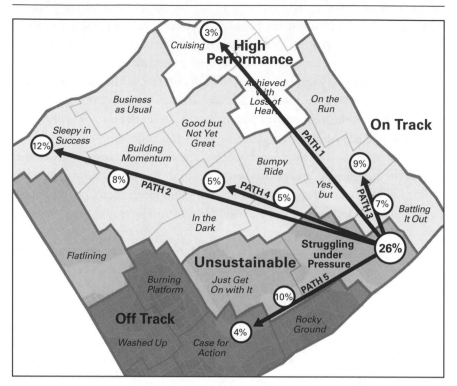

Path 1: moving to Cruising

Only 3 per cent of groups in *Struggling under Pressure* make the transition to *Cruising*. They do so by tackling the difficult issues of teamwork, accountability, and team and business leadership, which all increase significantly. As a result, vision becomes clearer, and fear and frustration decreases dramatically.

Path 2: moving to Building Momentum *and* Sleepy in Success

On this path, 8 per cent of groups end up in *Building Momentum* and another 12 per cent move further left to *Sleepy in Success*. As an example of the latter, at a public service organization, leaders focused on the broader vision and communication around the change initiative. Negative feelings dropped considerably, even though the amount of change through restructuring and growth continued to increase. In essence, people gained a wider perspective on the changes taking place and more comfort in them. However, little else changed in the drivers, and deep-seated issues of team leadership capability were not addressed. Because of the failure to address accountability and teamwork issues, the move into *On Track* was deceptive, as groups continued to function as they had before but in a less pressured environment, becoming *Sleepy in Success*.

Path 3: moving to Yes, but and Battling It Out

On this path, 9 per cent of groups move to *Yes, but* and 7 per cent to *Battling It Out*. Consider a biotech firm with two divisions initially in *Struggling under Pressure*. Each division took a different path. In the first division, teams had resolved issues around teamwork and accountability, and understood the vision and direction to move forward. All drivers improved significantly except for systems and processes, and skills and staffing. However, it was these issues with resources, along with numerous risks and roadblocks, which ground the change to a halt, landing this division in *Yes, but*.

The second division was on the same trajectory out of *Struggling under Pressure*, with all drivers improving significantly. In this case, though, working in the division had become exciting and frightening at the same time, like a war zone. Results were being delivered but at a cost. Action had become everything, as leaders lost their strategic perspective in the midst of day-to-day tactical urgencies. Moreover, the level of fear and frustration increased, and the division found itself in *Battling It Out*.

Path 4: moving to In the Dark and Bumpy Ride

On this path, 5 per cent move to *Bumpy Ride* and another 5 per cent to *In the Dark*. As an example of the latter, at a mining company's laboratory with more than 40 chemists and chemical engineers, a team leader worked with all his section leaders and conducted one-on-ones with his key staff, simply listening as they expressed their concerns about a change initiative. As a result, teamwork, accountability, passion and drive, and fear and frustration all improved significantly. But the team leader was not clear on the vision and his boss wasn't supporting him. Consequently, people lost trust in the organizational leaders and the change stalled. In such situations, further movement requires greater acceptance and clarity of the vision and direction.

Path 5: moving to Just Get On with It *and* Case for Action

On this path, 10 per cent end up in *Just Get On with It* and 4 per cent fall to *Case for Action*. A retailer's warehouse provides an example of both. The front office at the warehouse had succeeded in lifting accountability and teamwork but, because of a rush of orders before Christmas, change had moved off the agenda. Vision and direction, and the reputation of the warehouse manager, who was always out on the road, declined. Resources became scarce, and this put pressure on the office teams. Under these conditions they found it difficult to cope, and landed in *Just Get On with It*. Meanwhile, in the warehouse itself, a lack of resources and the apparent absence of concern from the warehouse manager plunged people even deeper into despair to *Case for Action*.

Towards the *On Track* zone

In this chapter and Chapter 5 we described the two capital cities of *Unsustainable*, where groups find themselves at a crossroad between improving and getting worse. In that zone, the promise of change is there, but it is not yet sustainable as people struggle with low levels of team leadership, teamwork and communication. Even so, many groups are eventually able to improve their performance and climb up the change map to the *On Track* zone. In the following Chapters 7 through 11, we describe the different regions of that zone, including its five capital cities. As we shall see, groups in those regions experience improved performance with driver strengths above the norm. For them, though, performance may be acceptable but still far short of great, requiring a concerted effort and the right strategy to make that final push to *High Performance*.

> ### SUMMARY FOR CHAPTER 6: KEY INSIGHTS
>
> - Team leaders – caught between the unrelenting expectations from the top down to deliver results and the bottom up to communicate and build accountability and strong teamwork in their teams – quickly get burnt out unless they get help to build their management capabilities.

- When team leaders feel unsupported by top management and business leadership, the danger is that well-respected team leaders can unite their teams against the organization, bringing change to a standstill.

- Change causes 'cracks in the system' to become obvious that may not have been visible before. When good team leaders fail under pressure, problems in the organizational culture and poor governance are where the real problems lie.

- Disconnects in communication show up long before trust breaks down. Taking steps to ensure alignment among leaders in the early stages of change – fixing small problems before they become big ones – is one of the best investments that management can make.

- To move up from *Struggling under Pressure*, groups need an increase of at least 40 per cent in accountability and teamwork, as well as in passion and drive. Team leaders are the key for accomplishing that.

- High levels of accountability are driven through strong relationships, teamwork and team leadership. Resources are also needed to support and sustain accountability as it develops.

- Having the right team leaders in the right roles – those who naturally balance managing both tasks and people – is the most significant intervention to build accountability.

- Increased accountability helps high-performing teams to deliver greater benefits and make the push into *High Performance*, but in low-performing teams any benefits gained quickly flatten off.

- Teamwork is driven by strong discipline (accountability) fused together with positive energy (passion and drive). Team leaders play a critical role in bringing together these seemingly opposite attributes. Even the most level-headed individuals can lose their ability to think clearly under relentless pressure. Accountability and teamwork bring the discipline required to repeat positive patterns that have been learned and built up across long periods of time during periods of high pressure.

07

On Track
Win the war for resources and move out of the middle ground

> *Take care of physical health and stay where there are plenty of resources. When there is no sickness in the army, it is said to be invincible.* SUN TZU

Many leaders who have moved their groups into *On Track* have reason to celebrate, while others have cause for concern. It all depends on whether their group has risen from a lower region of performance or fallen from a higher location.

Consider the following example:

A division head in a large utility had moved her group out from *Just Get On with It* to *Yes, but*. Realizing that the shared services organization had been set up in record time and that leadership had not paid sufficient attention to what was happening with employees – their feelings and how they were working together as teams – she sat down with her managers to clearly rearticulate the vision: what they were doing and why. Then she worked to gain people's emotional commitment in order to connect the head and the heart of the organization. It was a difficult process, rebuilding core values across

▶

the organization, but her efforts eventually paid off. People genuinely felt they could let go of the old and move to a better future. They felt more positive, and old patterns of criticizing and blaming dropped away.

In contrast, the leader of a new sales organization was unpleasantly surprised to learn that his area sales teams had dropped from *Cruising* to *Yes, but*. Caught off-guard when business conditions changed, he realized that he had neglected to build management capability in his managers while he was busy trying to hit record sales targets. His regular communication sessions to staff had dropped off the agenda, and he had not delivered on his promise to implement a new performance management system. Although he still had the confidence of his managers and staff, he was now faced with the challenge of building capability under much tougher market conditions.

In both cases, leaders found their organizations in the *On Track* zone, located right in the middle of the change map. This is where the majority of groups spend most of their time. Our database indicates that 55 per cent of all groups reside in *On Track*, compared with 25 per cent in *Unsustainable*, 10 per cent in *High Performance* and 10 per cent in *Off Track*. *On Track* is the largest area on the change map, consisting of various regions where groups reside in the middle ground – not yet at *High Performance*, but well away from *Off Track*. This is a world where things are mostly okay and where everything appears to be variations on 'normal' – the change initiative seems to be progressing as planned, and everything is going well but not exceptionally well. In the face of change, business performance is generally improving, as indicated by dimensions vital to company performance, including cost management, customer service and effectiveness. Indeed, performance is mostly good, sometimes very good, and on a few occasions getting close to great.

On Track insights

In *On Track*, all drivers are above the norm (see Figure 7.1). The level of fear and frustration is low, close to high-performance levels, as people are not under threat as they were in the lower regions of the change map. Moreover, team leadership, teamwork, accountability, and passion and drive are all strong. That's why we consider the *On Track* zone to be the powerhouse of

FIGURE 7.1   Change map and driver profile for *On Track* zone

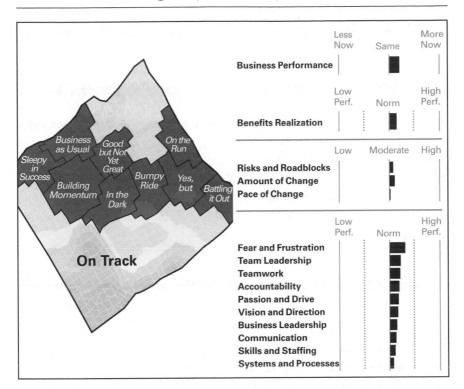

change – where most groups are and where most change takes place. Among the lowest-performing drivers are systems and processes, skills and staffing, and communication. Business leadership follows close behind and, as we will see in this chapter, the responsibility to move from *On Track* into *High Performance* lies primarily with the business unit leaders winning the war for resources, with crucial support from team leaders and senior executives.

Our database shows an optimistic, not pessimistic, view of how change is progressing in *On Track*. People see that benefits are being realized; they have capability above the norm; and the factors that typically cause employees to leave are generally low. Evidently, most organizations in our database in this zone, most of the time, do alright at change. This makes some intuitive sense; otherwise, organizations would generally not be moving forward and there would be little evolution of any kind taking place.

When we examined the movement of groups in *On Track*, we found that only 12 per cent of them make it up to *High Performance* while 19 per cent drop down to either *Unsustainable* or *Off Track*. The remaining 69 per cent do not leave the zone; they simply shuffle around reactively in regular patterns within *On Track*. It is almost impossible for an organization to sit still. The days when organizations had the time and luxury to 'unfreeze' and 'refreeze' before dealing with the next change programme are clearly over; most of the movements inside *On Track* are variations on being around the norm. It should be noted, however, that remaining within the *On Track* zone can be a perfectly acceptable strategy. For many organizations, making the jump to *High Performance* may not be in line with their business aspirations. After all, not everyone needs to be an Olympic athlete or Nobel laureate. But for those groups that do see the need to move higher on the change map as part of an aggressive business strategy, their journey can be made considerably less difficult if they first understand two key insights about the *On Track* zone, the first having to do with motivation and the second relating to resources.

Insight 1: to reach high performance, business leaders must motivate using excitement rather than fear

Our research indicates that leaders must take on different roles as groups move up or down the change map. In Chapter 4 we saw how business leaders need to build strong relationships with team leaders in *Off Track*, and in Chapter 5 we discussed how they need to provide support for team leaders to build their management capabilities in *Unsustainable*. When it comes to the *On Track* zone, business leadership must take a far more visible and active role.

In *On Track*, people work hard to do their jobs, but they need help to lift their sights beyond the day-to-day 'operational grind' to imagine a bigger and better future. **Mobilizing the passion and drive in teams can be an important source of positive energy but, in order to tap into it, the business leadership needs to ensure that people are appropriately resourced and connected into the 'big picture' – that is, the vision for change. A huge challenge for business leaders in *On Track* is that they need to shift gears and motivate people using excitement rather than fear.** Many struggle to do this. Some leaders are skilful at business turnarounds, putting the hard facts and figures on the table while outlining the dire consequences: 'If we don't cut costs, we will perish'. But they flounder when disaster is averted and people revert to a normal day-to-day existence where there is less difficulty and pressure. When 'cut costs or else...' no longer motivates staff, business leadership must instill a vision that inspires people.

The old expression 'can't see the forest for the trees' sums up the challenge of moving from *On Track* to *High Performance*. People often get so caught up in small details that they lose sight of larger issues. But true leaders are able to help others to see the bigger picture by capturing their imagination so that they don't let the future slip by.

Insight 2: people often underestimate the importance of resources

When asked why change programmes fail, people often cite bad communication, lack of vision, poor leadership, management resistance and so on. Inadequate resourcing is almost never included on the list, yet our research indicates that **the lack of resources and the failure to reprioritize around the limited resources people have at their disposal are among the critical issues for groups in *On Track*.**

By 'resources' we mean two things specifically: systems and processes, and skills and staffing. The level of systems and processes is a measure of whether team members have the means to do their work and achieve their objectives. One part of this is having effective processes and procedures in place with respect to human resources, decision-making, reporting lines and so on. The other component is systems, including equipment, information technology (IT) and knowledge-management tools. Skills and staffing are a measure of whether teams have the necessary skills and the right people in the right roles. That is, do teams have sufficient staff with the skills, talent, ability, knowledge and, perhaps most importantly, capacity to learn those things required to carry out their roles effectively?

When we conducted our research, the results provided feedback to leaders at all levels about the user experience – the usability and reliability of systems and processes. We also obtained valuable data describing the intangible but absolutely vital areas of skills and staffing. This information was then benchmarked along with other drivers to show the level of resourcing needed to attain high performance. The results were unequivocal: in order to make the jump from *On Track* to *High Performance*, groups need a significant increase in resources with respect to both systems and processes, and skills and staffing. **In most organizations, people fight to get resources and it is the job of business leaders to help their teams win that war – to either obtain additional resources or to reprioritize work efforts so that staffers can creatively make the best use of the limited resources they have in order to achieve their objectives.**

Five core dynamics and five capital cities

On Track is the zone where performance is improving. At the lower boundary of the zone, near *Unsustainable*, the driver strength is near the norm as compared with the rest of our database. At the upper edges, bordering on *High Performance*, the driver strength moves to its highest levels, along with increased benefits realization and much-improved business performance. In total, the *On Track* zone contains nine distinct regions, reflecting different common patterns of being just okay, good and close to great. Similar to life in the developed world, for the most part we all tend to live around the norm. Mostly we are fine; we all do some things well; we strive for greatness; and each of us has areas where development is needed. Some groups, for example, have good team leaders but are not well-resourced. Others have business leaders who are committed to the vision but fail to get people involved in making change happen. The regions are named in order to reflect these patterns. *In the Dark*, for example, highlights that all drivers are in good shape, except that people don't understand or agree with the vision and direction.

Of the nine regions in the *On Track* zone, five are capital cities: *Yes, but*; *In the Dark*; *Sleepy in Success*; *Building Momentum*; and *On the Run*. Looking at the dynamics of these cities as well as their adjacent regions, we find that there are five main challenges for successfully moving to the *High Performance* zone – as shown in Figure 7.2. There is no such thing as 'one size fits all' when it comes to getting out of *On Track*, and organizations can unintentionally go around in circles when they fail to recognize that different strategies are needed:

Challenge 1: sitting on the sidelines while change goes by. In the regions of *Sleepy in Success* and *Business as Usual*, 14 per cent of groups in our database face the challenge that people sit on the sidelines while change happens around them. Complacency is the biggest risk when things are going well. Groups understand the bigger picture but lack the discipline, teamwork and accountability to make change happen.

Challenge 2: no leadership, no change. In *Building Momentum*, 11 per cent of groups in our database face the challenge that change is simply not possible without strong business and team leadership. Groups face a crisis of confidence and cannot go much further without leaders who have what it takes to get there.

Challenge 3: no vision, no progress. In the regions of *In the Dark* and *Good but Not Yet Great*, 8 per cent of groups in our database face the challenge that their teams are doing great; emotional energy is

FIGURE 7.2   Major dynamics to address in the *On Track* zone

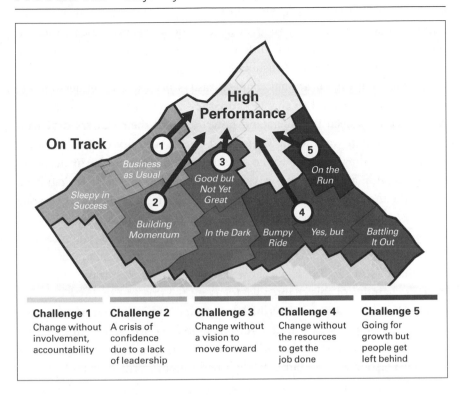

Challenge 1	Challenge 2	Challenge 3	Challenge 4	Challenge 5
Change without involvement, accountability	A crisis of confidence due to a lack of leadership	Change without a vision to move forward	Change without the resources to get the job done	Going for growth but people get left behind

high; but they have gone as far as they can go without business leaders telling them exactly where they are going and why.

Challenge 4: resources are limited. In the regions of *Battling It Out*, *Bumpy Ride* and *Yes, but*, 18 per cent of groups in our database face the challenge that people want to change; they see the vision; leadership is strong; but teams lack the resources needed to drive change. In addition, fear and frustration complicate things and people have to fight for what they want. They encounter risks and roadblocks that are too high to overcome.

Challenge 5: going for growth. In *On the Run*, 4 per cent of groups in our database face the challenge of rapid growth. In the rush to grow the business, the leadership forgets to communicate and leaves people behind because they lack accountability and adequate resources.

Although we live in a digital age, the dynamics that our research has revealed show that the secrets for moving out of *On Track* are archetypal and have actually been known for centuries. This is well illustrated in the case of Miyamoto Musashi, an expert Japanese swordsman and rōnin of the 1600s. To rise above others, Musashi relied on his teacher's words for his mantra: 'Whether people were great or not, there was not much variety in their inner life experience. Any difference lay merely in how they dealt with common human weakness' (Yoshikawa, 1981).

In managing organizational change, leaders need a deep understanding of how people respond to change, how they grow and how they develop. Moreover, they need to understand how they and their staffers deal with 'common human weakness'. When faced with a scarcity of resources, for example, will they succumb to the urge to give up? Or will they instead rise to the occasion and figure out ways to overcome that obstacle? Recognizing vulnerabilities and weaknesses as a source of strength is the key. Everyone has these and the strongest person doesn't hide them nor pretend they are not there. Moreover, they don't sit passively by either – they take personal responsibility and systematically build capability, step by step. Across the next chapters in *On Track*, we show how successful organizations do this. In the remainder of this chapter, we focus on the first of *On Track*'s capital cities – *Yes, but* – and we describe how groups and organizations can best unlock the resources they need. (Note: The box feature later in this chapter '*Bumpy Ride* and *Battling It Out*' describes two other *On Track* regions that also have resource issues but with slightly different characteristics.)

Yes, but: change without the necessary resources

After making changes to safety management practices, senior leaders at a government organization were alarmed by the high number of occupational safety incidents there. In addition to the human cost, the financial burden of such workplace incidents was significant. The leaders realized that, before doing anything else, they needed to uncover the systemic and behavioural causes of the accidents. What they needed was data in order to put the facts on the table.

When we checked the status of the programme across the staff of more than 15,000 people, we found that the majority of divisions were in *Yes, but*. With both staff and leadership teams in that capital city, it quickly became clear that the number of safety incidents was not an anomaly but part of a larger pattern, revealing why the organization as a whole struggled to implement any type of change. The main culprit: a lack of resources – systems and processes, and skills and staffing. Typical of groups in *Yes, but*, the dynamics of the organization could best be described as, '*Yes*, we understand and agree to the vision; we are passionate; and we want to move forward. *But* we don't have the resources needed to achieve our objectives'.

In the *Yes, but* region, where 10 per cent of groups reside, people see that benefits will be delivered and they feel involved in making change happen. As such, change takes place in an environment in which business performance improves, and people do take seriously the need to deliver on expectations. Yet, although change takes place, it is a restructuring rather than growth or a new way of working, and the benefits have yet to be fully realized. Moreover, the pace of change is typically around 'okay', which is below the optimal pace for many staffers.

One of the greatest strengths in *Yes, but* is that communication flows smoothly. Team leadership and business leadership are also strong drivers. In addition, people generally feel valued, rewarded and recognized. Staffers openly discuss issues and can mobilize the support and commitment needed from their managers. If things start to go wrong, it is a 'can do' culture; people can count on quick remedial action. Consequently, few think of leaving the organization. In short, people have a 'nose to the grindstone' attitude and will keep trying to make a change initiative work.

That said, teams do not feel confident that they can achieve what is being asked of them. This is because of a lack of training, skills and knowledge; poor processes; inadequate systems; and the wrong people in the wrong roles (see Figure 7.3). As such, passion and drive, and accountability, also suffer. In addition, higher-than-normal risks and roadblocks make it difficult to get things done.

The bottom line is that, even though the vision is sold, its reality has not yet come to fruition. **The 'pull' to move forward and realize the vision is resisted by the 'fight' to get the resources required, with the resulting tension impairing team performance.** Everyone feels the stress, with unrelenting expectations to keep within budgets and meet targets on the one side, and an ongoing lack of resources that demotivates them on the other. To make matters worse, people struggle against bureaucracy in order to get things done; silo mentalities are a challenge; and leaders have difficulty resolving conflicting priorities across the organization. Not surprisingly, common words that occur in comments about this region include 'clarity', 'administrative', 'targets', 'operational', 'efficient' and 'fail'. In the battle for scarce resources, constantly bumping into the 'but' has left people asking themselves, 'why bother?'

FIGURE 7.3   Change map and driver profile for *Yes, but* region

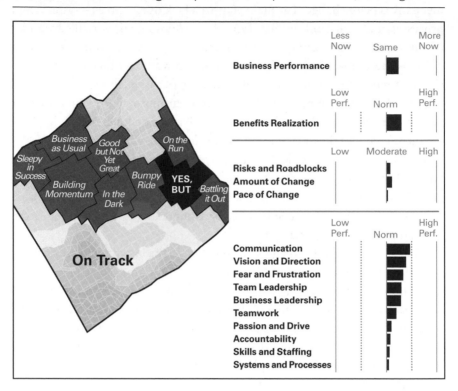

Returning to the above-cited government organization that made changes to safety management practices, we found that employees there had clearly embraced the bigger picture. They understood and agreed that the changes would deliver benefits, including fewer injuries, a reduced number of incidents, improved risk management and better hazard identification. That was the 'yes'. The 'but', though, came from cumbersome organizational processes needed to get things done. As one employee noted, 'The largest issue... is the increasing amount of time that is required to be devoted to administrative paperwork. Many of the new procedures seem to be there purely to cover someone's backside rather than improving our skill or preparedness'.

On the surface, this might seem like a simple matter of making changes to the processes. But, looking deeper, we found systemic issues that were ingrained in the organization's culture. In the government organization, a 'can do' attitude had traditionally enabled managers to get recognized and promoted. The mentality was basically this: fix the problem; don't complain; just get things done. What was not fully appreciated at the time was that the new safety management practices were countercultural. With an already high workload stretching work–life balance to the limits, managers now had to file a three- or four-page assessment every time an individual saw a potential hazard. Because of this clash between the new practices and the organization's culture, people viewed the safety procedures as obstacles – not enablers – to success, and they resisted the adoption of the practices even though they basically thought that they were good ideas in concept.

The example of the government organization provides an important lesson about organizational change, particularly with respect to the *Yes, but* region. In many cases, whatever appears to be the main problem is not the fundamental issue that needs to be addressed. The new procedures at the government organization might have seemed like the problem, and managers put the blame there for not successfully implementing the change, but it was the culture clash that was the underlying issue. In essence, the change initiative was never set up to succeed in the first place.

Three keys to better resource management

In our research, we have observed many groups and organizations in *Yes, but* undergo struggle after receiving feedback that additional resources are needed. We have often met with executive teams saying, 'You have done a great job of selling the vision; you have strong leaders; and your people are engaged. But your change programme is under-resourced', only to find little receptivity to that message. One CEO, for example, responded by saying, 'Good... I don't want my staff to think that they can get any more resources'. Another CEO, after being warned that leaders were thinking of quitting, said, 'Let them leave, we need [fewer] people in senior roles'. They dismiss the feedback on resources, automatically thinking that they have to spend more money on systems or hire more people. What they don't realize is that the creative management of limited resources is the critical issue that re-quires their attention.

Of course, it is not easy for groups to move from *Yes, but* to a higher region. In fact, only 17 per cent make it up to *Cruising, Achieved with Loss of Heart* or *On the Run*. Leaders who have made the transition recognized that they needed to more skilfully manage the distribution of resources they had. Specifically, they took a hard look at resource management at all levels, from operational to strategic. In general, the strategic issues were the most difficult to resolve, coming up against big questions of culture, conflicting priorities and the difficulty of creatively using what is almost always a limited amount of resources. A closer look at each of these in turn reveals key lessons and actions needed.

Moving from operational to strategic thinking

During the global financial crisis triggered in 2007, in the battle for scarce resources many organizations focused on operational efficiency, excelling at practical, task-orientated activities. The goal was to improve quality while eliminating waste and reducing costs. In such environments, change programmes were often implemented on top of lean organizational cultures, resulting in groups finding themselves in the *Yes, but* region.

Although cost-cutting may be good for the bottom line, **a culture that prizes efficiency above all else can become the biggest impediment to successful change**. Unfortunately, what is considered to be wasteful often includes the very things that change programmes require – time for people to talk, efforts to build trust, a plan to lower fear and frustration, and so on. For staff on the receiving end of change, this can mean that little or no time is allowed to actually manage the change. The result is that people who are already stretched to the limits are then expected to implement an initiative in their 'spare time' without added resources – even though change, by its very nature, involves new unknowns and often unpredictable setbacks that can run counter to organizational efficiency. This can then become a nightmare for even skilled managers, leaving the initiative doomed from the start.

In the fight for resources – successful change versus lean efficiency – change almost always loses. Williamson Murray, the noted US historian researching how change takes place in defence organizations, writes, 'the rhythms and culture of most bureaucracies are antithetical to successful adaptation... They are more about efficiency than effectiveness' (Murray, 2011). The dilemma is that adaptation, flexibility and responsiveness are needed to win a war but a culture of efficiency and effectiveness is everything in peacetime. Leaders become 'prisoners of pre-war assumptions and perceptions', making disastrous decisions during war. Rather than exercise 'their minds and mental agility' they pay with a loss of life on the battlefield. The same issue plays out in most organizations today when agility is one of the most prized organizational assets, yet a culture of efficiency prevails. While the symptoms of this conflict play out on the 'front line' with customers and staff, the responsibility for resolving conflicting priorities between 'change and lean' lies clearly with senior executives.

Indeed, one of the biggest risks to successful change in *Yes, but* is when leaders cannot think beyond their lean and highly operational mindsets. But, as one CEO of a global corporation stated, 'Any idiot can reduce costs. You just say "No!"' The CEO went on to say that the real challenge for leaders is to manage costs without impeding business growth. Saying 'yes' and exploring what that might mean is the way forward, yet we see that innovation and the willingness to challenge conventional ways of doing things are low when a group or organization is stuck in *Yes, but*. **In fact, we frequently see senior leadership teams positioned in the same location in *Yes, but* as their 'troops', indicating that they are locked into the same short-term, day-to-day operational mindset.** In such situations, more gifted leaders are able to get themselves out of the 'trenches' and up the change map to think more strategically and less operationally. As we have noted in earlier chapters, it is impossible to lead from behind, and only through strategic thinking can executives begin to overcome resource limitations.

Resolving conflicting priorities

In *Yes, but*, conflicting priorities and the presence of a silo mentality can become major bottlenecks. As such, high-level leadership is needed to ensure the smooth allocation and flow of resources. The problem, though, is that leaders are both slow to take action, and to know where it will be most effective. Often, they are forced to make assumptions about where resources should be allocated without really understanding the critical issues. Working on systems and processes, and skills and staffing, might sound simple and straightforward – just provide them or fix them, and everything will be fine. Our research, however, shows that the solution is far more complex than that. It is not just about getting more resources but about how they get managed, as well as the other factors that need to be taken into consideration to bring about lasting change.

When it comes to systems and processes, leaders need to pay close attention to those resources as any period of change evolves, because what worked in the past can easily fail in the future. Even if an organization's heart is in the right place and it cares deeply about its employees, those good intentions can come to naught if the systems and processes are not able to place people in positions where they will do the most good under the change programme.

In our research, we have found that the strongest driver of systems and processes, by a wide margin, is skills and staffing. What this means is that organizations need to match 'people' with 'things' because it is employees who will use those systems and follow those processes. People's emotions, reactions and responses play an important role in their acceptance of and ability to utilize those systems and processes to achieve business and change objectives. Business leadership is the second driver, because its primary role is to perform the matching between 'people' and 'things'. This occurs at the business unit level, not at the team level, as the business leadership helps define employee roles and their responsibilities, puts all the people-related systems in place and ensures that no human resources are wasted.

If skills and staffing is the strongest driver of systems and processes, what in turn is the strongest driver of skills and staffing? The answer, not surprisingly, is systems and processes. This again highlights the importance of matching people with things. Accountability and business leadership have a much smaller impact on skills and staffing, although local goals and objectives, the outcomes of clearly defined roles, and the products of accountability can have a significant impact.

An important thing to note here is that in terms of both drivers – systems and processes, and skills and staffing – the common focal point is business leadership. It is business leadership that bears the responsibility for ensuring the provision of resources to teams. Business leaders look upward to those who prioritize and allocate resources, and they look downward to those whose accountability depends on proper functioning resources. The role of business leadership is vital in linking and connecting people, their relationships and their outputs, from the beginning of work at the team level to the final destination towards delivering performance and realizing business benefits.

Sometimes resources cannot be provided during change because, for example, systems are being rebuilt or new staff are being hired. In such cases, business leaders must manage people's perceptions and ensure that workloads are appropriately rethought or reprioritized. Their failure to do this will have damaging repercussions for those reporting to them. Team leaders without adequate resources are set up to fail, and this is one of the fastest ways to burn out good managers.

Looking at how this important dynamic plays out in *Yes, but*, we see that although trust in business leaders is high, as those individuals provide moral support and commitment for the change those same leaders nonetheless fail to provide the material resources needed by teams to achieve their objectives. In other words, business leadership 'talks the talk' but doesn't 'walk the walk'. The problem is that when business leaders are under pressure to deliver results on time and on budget, they can easily forget the importance of their connecting-and-linking role across and between groups for which they are responsible. That role, however, is of crucial importance.

Using resources creatively

Looking at the use of resources at a team level, we recognize that it is not always possible for individual team members to influence factors such as the amount of change taking place, the level of resources and the training they receive. But, given the right information, they can rethink and reprioritize activities, and work more creatively within their constraints. Indeed, **our research shows how some groups achieve extraordinary results with very limited resources, while others achieve very little, even when they are well-resourced.**

In Figure 7.4, we see that, on average, benefits realization doubles as teams obtain the resources they need to achieve their objectives. For low-performing groups, though, increased resource levels create an initial boost but then quickly plateaus. The lesson is clear: throwing more resources at the problem when groups are in low performance is a wasted investment. As we have seen in previous chapters, when groups are in *Off Track* and

FIGURE 7.4   Skills and staffing compared to benefits realization

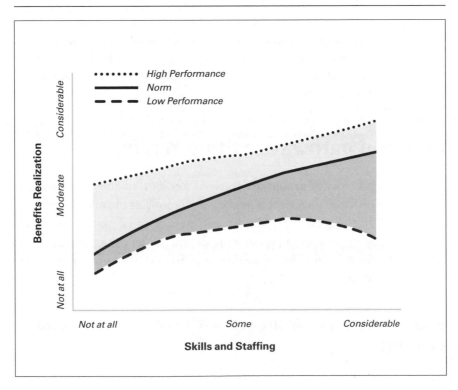

Unsustainable, other interventions such as lowering fear and frustration, and developing increased trust in leadership, have a much greater impact.

For high-performing groups, greater business benefits are realized continually through increased resource levels. Interestingly, though, such groups rely much less on resources for their success. Figure 7.4 shows that, even with very few resources, they achieve a very similar level of benefits to what groups on the norm achieve with very high levels of resources. That result is supported by many examples not only from business but also from other areas, including the military battlefield, where the ways in which people creatively deal with resource constraints can literally have life-or-death consequences.

In the Second World War, during the North Africa campaign, the 28th Maori Battalion captured and held the Tebaga Gap in southern Tunisia against fierce mortar bombardments from the crack Panzer-Grenadier Regiment led by Field Marshal Rommel. The story of that battle amply illustrates how people can overcome even severe resource limitations:

> When Ngarimu (the leader) was running low on ammunition and grenades, his men used stones. At night the Germans would mistake the stones for grenades and scatter... This annoyed the heck out of the Germans. Not knowing whether the stones were real or not. Then having to get up and start all over again. The Maoris would just grin and mix it up a bit, chuck a real grenade... The Maoris were feared because of their fierce fighting spirit... Field Marshal Rommel, the Desert Fox, was reputed to have said, 'Give me a division of Maori and I will conquer the world'. (Reedy, 2012)

Common pathways exiting *Yes, but*

Twenty-five per cent of groups get stuck in *Yes, but*, unable to adequately deal with resource challenges. Let's take a closer look at the major pathways exiting *Yes, but* (Figure 7.5). We discuss each of those pathways below, highlighting some case examples in more depth. (Note: the examples in this section represent a composite of organizations from our research with similar experiences of change.)

Path 1: moving to Achieved with Loss of Heart and Cruising

From *Yes, but*, 5 per cent of groups make it to *Achieved with Loss of Heart* and 6 per cent of groups make it to *Cruising*. One example is a retail chain's

FIGURE 7.5   Common pathways exiting *Yes, but*

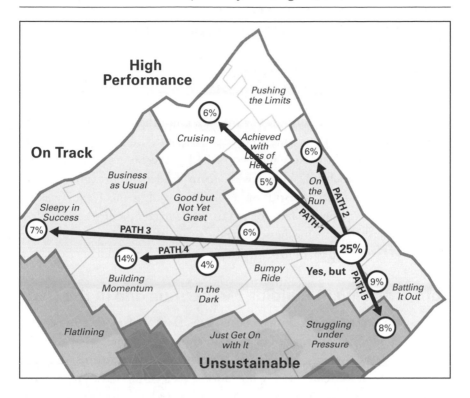

Southeast Asian branches, which underwent a massive refurbishment across all stores. At the 'go-live' stage, managers were stretched to the limit, overseeing change and running business as usual. The breakthrough came when the change programme manager suggested that the best managers lead the 'showpiece' stores, irrespective of where those individuals were located. That change led to impressive results. After a short interval, business performance began to rise. In addition, increases in business leadership, and vision and direction, lifted people's sights to higher goals, as the pace of change increased to optimal levels, landing them in *Cruising*.

Path 2: moving to On the Run

Six per cent of groups move to *On the Run*. For example, when an airline hired a new chief operating officer (COO), she provided a boost of energy, energizing her business leadership and even teams on the ground, as she spent time with air crews and maintenance teams. The amount and pace of change increased. Vision and direction, passion and drive and team leadership significantly increased, as did accountability and teamwork. However, due to the urgency of the mission, there was still a need to keep people together in the confusion of the coming changes.

Path 3: moving to Sleepy in Success and Bumpy Ride

On this path, 6 per cent of groups travel to *Bumpy Ride* and another 7 per cent to *Sleepy in Success*. For the latter, in other parts of the airline cited above, particularly among administrative staff, the amount of restructuring and growth increased, but people had yet to be engaged. Manager communication declined, along with team leadership, teamwork and accountability. Fear and frustration levels improved as insolvency was no longer a threat. Yet, people felt isolated from the bigger picture and had lost confidence and trust in business leaders, causing them to retreat from the change, and increasingly think of leaving.

Path 4: moving to Building Momentum and In the Dark

On this path, 4 per cent of groups move to *In the Dark*, and another 14 per cent head to *Building Momentum*. For the latter, consider a major bank implementing new IT systems. Its infrastructure overhaul was so massive that leaders partly neglected everyday operations. As a result, trust in team and business leadership both dropped. The bank's leaders had forgotten that keeping alignment with their direct reports was important, even in the midst of turmoil, and focus on the change was lost, with decreases in the amount and pace of change. Executives immediately put more people on the change, but because they were focused on daily operations, they did not engage those people properly in the change. In effect, more resources simply meant more confused people who started to think about leaving.

Path 5: moving to Struggling under Pressure and Battling It Out

On this path, 9 per cent of groups migrate to *Battling It Out*, and another 8 per cent move downward to *Struggling under Pressure*. An example of the latter happened on a major IT implementation at a government organization. Business leaders were buried in minutiae of the IT implementation and conflicts with suppliers and subcontractors, leaving teams to work things out on their own. Resources were not so much the issue as the inability to make effective use of them. Everyone seemed to have lost sight of the big picture. Communication dropped dramatically, along with the understanding of the vision and direction. As a result, fear and frustration increased, followed by a collapse in teamwork, team leadership and accountability. Not surprisingly, performance and benefits declined and the amount of change decreased as hard-earned gains in new ways of working evaporated.

Beyond resource limitations

In this chapter, we focused on the first of *On Track*'s capital cities – *Yes, but* – and we described how groups can overcome issues with resources that are indicative of that region. In Chapters 8 through 11, we focus on the four other capital cities of *On Track*: *In the Dark*, *Building Momentum*, *Sleepy in Success* and *On the Run*. There, resources are not the primary problem, yet each of those cities (and their surrounding regions) face other challenges that can be equally daunting, if not more so. As we have learned in this chapter, making the jump to the *High Performance* zone is no simple matter, requiring organizations first to identify the fundamental issues and then apply the right interventions at the right time.

Bumpy Ride and *Battling It Out*

The capital city *Yes, but* has two surrounding regions – *Bumpy Ride* and *Battling It Out* – that share many of the same characteristics and dynamics. But in these two regions, fear and frustration complicate things, making it more difficult to resolve issues with resources.

Bumpy Ride

In *Bumpy Ride*, people are highly involved in planning and implementing change, but the going is tough because a tremendous amount of change is happening at a very fast pace. Nevertheless, business performance improves, while teamwork is good, along with communication and accountability. People can see the vision and want change, but high fear and frustration cloud the picture. Moreover, teams lack the systems and processes, and skills and staffing, to make change happen. As such, benefits are not being realized and people perceive the change as being poorly managed. Not surprisingly, business leadership scores are low in this region and the speed of remedial action is viewed as too slow. Although team members feel the urgency for change and are actively involved, poorly managed change has thwarted their efforts. Positive feelings easily turn to cynicism and anger, and the number of people who are thinking of leaving is high.

Despite these problems, people cope as best they can with a curious mix of pride and creativity. Many groups develop coping strategies such as the use of 'black humour'. With rumours running high, though, there is also a tendency to act first and ask questions later, without taking the time to really see if action was needed in the first place.

Over 30 per cent of groups remain in *Bumpy Ride*, making it one of the most difficult regions to leave. Doing so requires support from senior management to overcome the risks and roadblocks. Top executives need to get people to agree to the vision, not just understand it. Moreover, dealing with conflict has to occur in a positive way, along with removing roadblocks to get people's energies flowing in the right direction.

Battling It Out

Groups in *Battling It Out* achieve close to *High Performance* levels of business performance and benefits realization, but they do so under very high amounts of fear and frustration. To complicate matters, risks and roadblocks get in the way and, with so much change occurring, initiatives and programmes can easily spin out of control.

Although there is a high level of buy-in to the vision for the future, this region is unusual in having both high levels of excitement and high levels of fear. In this respect it is somewhat similar to *Yes, but*, with all the characteristics of a 'war zone'. In *Battling It Out*, people constantly refer to 'them' and 'us', and conflicts easily develop as teams see the achievement of their objectives as being under constant threat. But the fear spurs them on to overcome obstacles. In all other regions on the change map, high passion and drive combined with low levels of fear and frustration help to drive better business performance. In *Battling It Out*, high passion and drive together with high levels of fear and frustration drive up business performance. That said, achieving results in such an environment of high turbulence comes at a cost, with conflicts sometimes leading to an environment of blaming and even sabotage.

In *Battling It Out*, leaders become very operationally focused, often getting involved personally in resolving day-to-day conflicts. But leaders also need to get out of the trenches. The best equipped leaders are able to show tactical flexibility while at the same time conducting longer-term planning to 'win' the war. Furthermore, they need to maintain the morale of their troops.

In short, the adverse environment of *Battling It Out* requires leaders with an intense operational focus along with good strategic capabilities.

Continually overcoming the challenges of *Battling It Out* can be very difficult over extended periods of time. That is why 24 per cent of groups tend to remain in the region. Groups that do move out typically do so by giving up the fight – the negative impact on everyone and their colleagues becomes too high, or they run out of resources. Either way, leaders need to take a strategic view of the battle in order to best direct their troops.

SUMMARY FOR CHAPTER 7: KEY INSIGHTS

- Fifty-five per cent of groups reside in the *On Track* zone, where everything appears to be variations of 'normal' and the change initiative seems to be progressing as planned. Indeed, performance is mostly good, sometimes very good, and in some instances getting close to great.

- The *On Track* zone contains five core dynamics within it, including issues related to resources, complacency, leadership capabilities, vision and rapid growth.

- While improvements in team leadership are needed to move up into *On Track*, business leadership must take a far more visible and active role to move from *On Track* into *High Performance*. Mobilizing passion and drive, clarifying the vision for change and ensuring that people are appropriately resourced are the keys.

- Some groups achieve extraordinary results with very limited resources, creatively making the best use of those they have in order to achieve their objectives, while others achieve very little, even when they are well-resourced. For low-performing groups, throwing more resources at the problem is a wasted investment.

- Managers are often set up to fail in change, without adequate resources. While the symptoms of a lack of resources play out on the front lines between staff and customers, the responsibility lies with top management to resolve the deeper questions of organizational culture and conflicting priorities.

▶

- Creatively using limited resources is the biggest challenge in *Yes, but*, as innovation is often systematically discarded from an organization's culture.

- When people say they do not have enough resources, it is not just about getting more resources. People's emotions, reactions and responses play an important role in creatively using what is almost always the limited amount of resources they have.

- People often cite bad communication, lack of vision, poor leadership and management resistance as the reasons why change programmes fail. Inadequate resourcing and the failure to reprioritize around the limited resources available are almost never included on the list. Yet our research shows that these are the most critical but least discussed reasons why change fails to deliver benefits.

- For a culture that prizes efficiency above all else, this can become the biggest impediment to successful change. Unfortunately, what is considered to be wasteful often includes the very things that change programmes require – for example, time for people to talk, efforts to build trust and a plan to lower levels of fear and frustration.

In the Dark
Mobilize around the vision

08

> " *It was a routine job. The fishing net was ready and now they would just have to pull the herrings up. Suddenly the fishing net was pulled away. It must have been 100 tons of fish – 300,000 herrings. 'Think about 300,000 propellers that take off', says Geir Nikolaisen, who owned the boat. 'I don't know what happened but I think herrings suddenly noticed a killer whale nearby. Then they got scared and swam away.' Three-hundred thousand fish pulled in the same direction and sank M/S Steinsholm – the 70-ton boat foundered and the masthead light hit the water. She disappeared into the waves. 'The last thing we saw was the lights', says Nikolaisen.* JOACHIM KERPNER, AFTONBLADET*

Many people might consider innovation to be an uncomfortable directive for public service organizations. For the research group at one particular government agency included in our data, though, innovation was what their employees did best. They were scientists and innovation was integral to the way that they approached business. Despite working against the backdrop of the global financial crisis triggered in 2007, and while facing staff and funding cuts, the research group had achieved impressive results. The productivity of staff, for example, had surged 28 per cent across a three-year period, as considerable attention was paid to building the right internal environment to support science and innovation.

In bureaucracies that emphasize planning and control, and where decision-making is dominated by larger political 'realities', new ideas and creativity can have difficulty flourishing and taking hold. Novel ways of working, such as flatter structures and self-directed work teams, offer considerable promise in overcoming these obstacles. Moreover, the management team at the government agency had the insight to recognize that innovative organizations are driven by great visions, and the ability to attract superb people who are motivated to innovate through collaboration. Midway through its change programme, though, the promise of a new way of working had hit a major roadblock, and people at the research group found themselves stuck in *In the Dark*.

Part of the problem was that strong teams had been mobilized at the government agency with each focused on its own scientific interests, and people's loyalties were to their work and colleagues, not to the research group itself. Convincing such independent individuals to become part of a divisional team committed to a larger, collective vision was not easy. In such situations, the expression 'herding cats' can be a painfully accurate description. Our feedback to the CEO was blunt: 'You have gone as far as you can go towards high performance without uniting everyone around a clear vision and gaining their emotional commitment.'

In the Dark insights

In Chapter 7, we described the *On Track* zone, where groups are positioned in the middle ground of the change map, and we discussed *Yes, but*, one of that zone's capital cities. In this chapter, we focus on another capital city of the *On Track* zone: *In the Dark*. Here, groups have been doing well but have run into problems in uniting everyone around a common vision, and now need help from business leadership to get people's buy-in and commitment for the next phase of the change journey. *In the Dark*, and the nearby region *Good but Not Yet Great* (see Figure 8.1), are noted for groups with strong levels of team leadership, accountability, teamwork and emotional energy, but business leadership has failed to provide the 'big picture' vision that is necessary to move the organization into the *High Performance* zone.

According to our research, only 8 per cent of groups are in either *In the Dark* or *Good but Not Yet Great*. Our analysis of those two regions of the change map led us to two key insights, the first having to do with organizational vision and the second relating to employee commitment.

FIGURE 8.1   Regions in *On Track* where the key issue is vision and direction

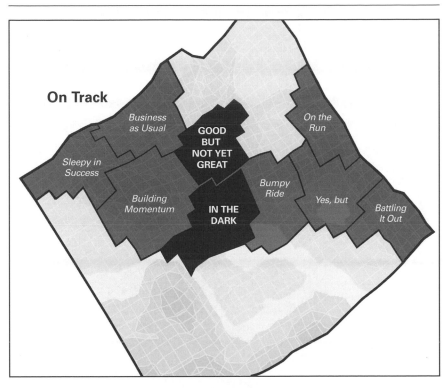

Insight 1: groups can get a long way without a vision – then they really need it

As we discussed in Chapter 2, the level of vision and direction is a measure of whether people embrace the bigger picture of what the change programme is trying to achieve. It is not just about intellectual understanding but also about a heartfelt agreement with the overall direction. Are people inspired by the vision and direction? Will they work hard towards achieving those goals? Of course, a lot depends on how much staff members trust and believe in the executive leadership. We discuss this topic later in this chapter and describe it in more depth in Chapter 10.

In the Dark lies roughly midway between the *Off Track* and *High Performance* zones, and it is in this capital city that the level of vision and direction is lowest. If we look at a three-dimensional change map with the vertical axis representing vision and direction (Figure 8.2), we see a deep

FIGURE 8.2   Three-dimensional change map for vision and direction

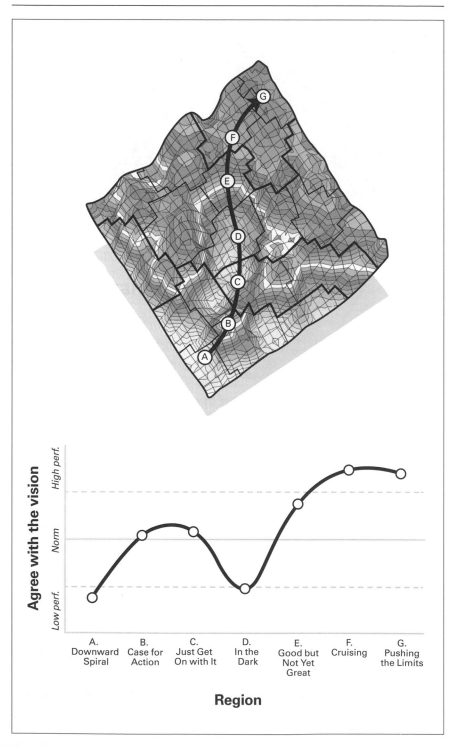

valley through the middle of the map, and that region is *In the Dark*. To reach *High Performance*, there is only one way to go – up – and the climb is neither gentle nor gradual. We see that the topography is clearly non-linear, and taking an organization from *In the Dark* to *High Performance* involves a steep upward trajectory. The good news is that once management tells people where they are going and gets their buy-in, things can change rapidly. In other words, **groups either embrace the vision and direction, or they don't, and if they don't they simply will not make it to the highest regions of the change map**.

If we look at a cross-section drawn through the 3D map going from *Downward Spiral* up to *Pushing the Limits* (see Figure 8.2), we again note that *In the Dark* is the worst region when it comes to vision and direction. Interestingly, the cross-section shows a spike for groups in *Case for Action* but, as we learned in Chapter 4, they are not really in a position to capitalize on that strength.

Another important thing to note from the cross-section is that **organizations can make it halfway up the change map, right into *On Track*, while still having very low levels of vision and direction**. This insight will come as a surprise to many, given the importance that the change management literature tends to emphasize on clarifying and communicating the vision, particularly in the early stages of change. In fact, that task typically occupies a significant part of change activities in most programmes. But the 5 per cent of groups in *In the Dark* and the 3 per cent of groups in *Good but Not Yet Great*, respectively, show that vision and direction are not really necessary to attain satisfactory levels of business performance and benefits realization.

To reach the *High Performance* zone, though, high levels of vision and direction are necessary. That definitely was the issue with the research group at the government agency we described at the start of this chapter. When we informed the CEO of that, he was surprised. 'But we have a vision that was communicated to staff at the beginning of the change', was his response. What the CEO didn't realize, however, was that vision is dynamic and that leaders need to maintain continual dialogue with the staff in order to formulate and reformulate it throughout the change initiative.

Insight 2: in high-performing groups, the 'commitment curve' accelerates change by working in reverse

The second insight is that **the highest-performing groups gain an emotional agreement to the vision *before* understanding comes along**. People emotionally commit to the journey before they fully understand where they are going.

Capturing people's 'hearts and minds' is expressed in that order for a reason: hearts first and minds second. Our analysis confirms that the critical success factor driving much higher levels of benefits is people's emotional agreement to a vision – and not necessarily their understanding of that vision. As we have seen in Chapter 2, the level of vision and direction is the key driver of benefits realization, having nearly four times more importance than any other driver. More specifically, it is the question, 'How much do you agree with the future direction?' that is the main factor. Understanding of the vision hardly plays a role. Unfortunately, many leaders have this backwards. So, when implementing a change programme, they ask, 'Do you understand the vision?' and if the answer is 'yes' then they walk away happy, thinking they have done their job. But what they fail to realize is that understanding of the vision is only the tip of the iceberg. Indeed, appreciating how the patterns of 'understanding' and 'agreement' play out across the stages of change makes a huge difference between ending up in *Off Track* or *High Performance*.

In traditional approaches to change management, leaders rely on the 'commitment curve' to determine change readiness. (Note: there are many variations of the commitment curve. See, for example, Conner, 1993.) The model assumes that people move through the following four stages:

1 They become aware of the need for change.

2 They gain an understanding of the change.

3 They 'buy into' the change.

4 They commit to the change.

But does the commitment curve truly describe how organizations adapt to change?

Based on our research, Figure 8.3 plots four quantities: awareness of the need for change; understanding of the vision; agreement to the vision; and trust in top management. The graph for the low performers shows that awareness is high through all stages of change: first rising, then plateauing and then rising again. Understanding and agreement follow a similar pattern, but drop significantly in the end stages of change. Also, understanding is at a higher level than agreement, particularly in the mid to late stages of change. The level of trust and confidence in top management follows the same pattern as understanding and agreement, but at a much lower level. These three quantities – understanding of the vision, agreement to the vision and trust in top management – end close to or below the level at which they

FIGURE 8.3 Vision and direction for high- and low-performance groups across the stages of change

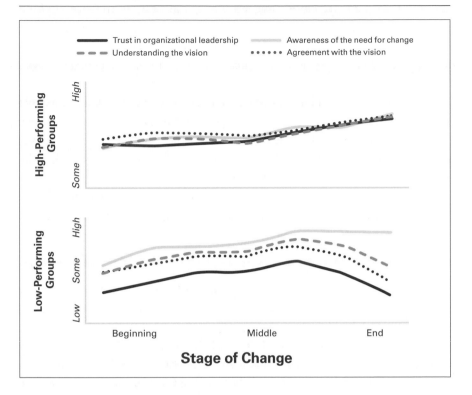

started. Apparently, it is difficult for people to sustain their enthusiasm for a vision or even remember why they started on the journey if business performance – customer service, cost management and effectiveness – is still declining after all their hard work. This behaviour of low performers reflects an approach based on the commitment curve: first leading with raising awareness of the need for change, followed by providing information so that people understand the change, with communication targeted at obtaining buy-in and trying to build commitment. As we can see from the graphs in Figure 8.3, however, the commitment is tentative and not sustainable; it peaks then quickly falls off.

The pattern for high performers is markedly different. First, it is important to note that agreement to the vision is higher than understanding of the vision, particularly in the early stages of change. In essence, an emotional 'yes' is followed by 'please tell us where we are going' as the change initiative progresses. In other words, people do not need to know everything in advance in order to start the journey; instead they can figure certain things out along the way. Second, awareness, understanding and agreement all go hand in hand, and are closely aligned through all stages. Anchored in high levels of trust in top management, they steadily increase across the stages of change, finishing at higher levels towards the end. This reflects how the vision keeps unfolding and new possibilities continue to emerge – even towards the end of the journey.

In Chapter 4, we talked about Michelangelo looking at a block of marble and saying the sculpture already exists – it is the artist's job to set it free. This is the approach that high performers adopt. Given specific market circumstances, the competitive environment and available resources, the vision for the organization to prosper already exists – it is the role of top executives to find that vision and present it in such a way that people can connect emotionally with it. Then people's energy will take over as the vision unfolds in front of them and becomes their own. Top management's role is to continually remove the obstacles to keep that vision alive.

Our research clearly shows that **strong trusting relationships with senior leaders, especially in the early stages of change, are the important ingredient that radically transforms vision from a mere understanding into a deep emotional commitment**. And it pays dividends for the organization: according to our research, **as groups move from a low-performance capital city such as *Case for Action*, to a high-performance capital city like *Cruising*, there is an average rise in trust across the three leadership levels of nearly 50 per cent. This is accompanied by a rise in business performance by about 40 per cent, and in benefits realization of nearly 70 per cent**. That is not to say, however, that blindly following the vision is the answer, and this is where trust and vision are intimately linked. In an open, trusting relationship, decisions and the direction taken can be questioned; critical issues can be discussed; and course corrections can be made if needed. High trust enables fluidity, and this is why it is so important to build, nurture and sustain trust, particularly in times of change.

The two insights set out above can help organizations substantially to improve their levels of business leadership, and vision and direction. Moreover, such knowledge can help leaders to overcome the specific challenges that groups face in *In the Dark*. (Note: for a description of the neighbouring region *Good but Not Yet Great*, see box 'Good but Not Yet Great* – inadequate systems and processes'.)

Good but Not Yet Great – inadequate systems and processes

Groups in *Good but Not Yet Great* face similar issues to those in *In the Dark*. All drivers are well above the norm, but what holds people back is more than just low levels of vision and direction and business leadership. Groups in this region must also contend with insufficient or ineffective systems and processes. Unfortunately, change in this environment is viewed as a distraction. As such, teams are often critical of the company vision and direction, and drivers outside a group's immediate control or experience tend to score significantly lower. It is almost as if teams operate in isolation from the rest of the business. The result is that people's disaffection with an initiative can result in stubbornness or a stoic resignation to the changes and to what is expected of them. To help groups in *Good but Not Yet Great,* senior managers must show that they are there to support and help, take immediate action on problems raised at their level, work with teams on inadequate systems and processes, link the vision and its objectives to team outputs, and communicate such information widely to everyone.

In the Dark – like 'herding cats'

The name '*In the Dark*' accurately summarizes the dynamics for this capital city. Although most aspects of team capability are above the norm, the level of vision and direction is close to that of low-performing groups, and business leadership is also lacking. As a result, the level of passion and drive suffers, hovering around the norm, and there is simply not enough energy to move up into *High Performance*.

As shown in Figure 8.4, *In the Dark* is characterized by groups with low levels of fear and frustration, high skills and staffing, and strong accountability, with people having role clarity and measurable goals. In addition, trust in team leaders is high, and face-to-face communications from managers is good, as people get the information they need to get on with their jobs. The level of teamwork is also high, and the number of people who are thinking of leaving is low.

This strong team capability helps explain the effectiveness of groups carrying out emergency types of work or highly specialized tasks without the need for a longer-term vision or interventions from more senior levels of

FIGURE 8.4   Change map and driver profile for *In the Dark* region

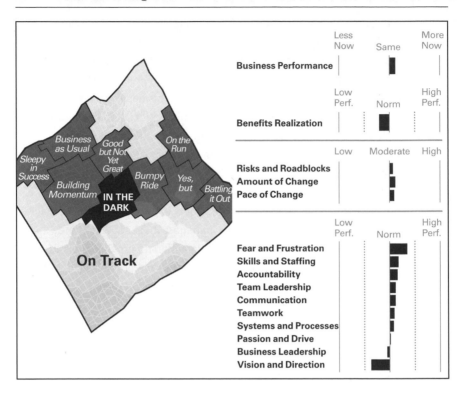

leadership. In fact, we often see highly technical, individualistic people in *In the Dark*: IT specialists, medical staff, business analysts, engineers and computer programmers. They perform well at what they do best. They value safety and routine, and they seem to be content living within their areas of expertise, without really having to deal much with the larger world.

While *In the Dark* groups focus on improving business performance, benefits realization hits its lowest point in the *On Track* zone, being well below the norm. Furthermore, the pace of change may be at optimal levels but restructuring takes place without being accompanied by a new way of working or a feeling of growth in the business. In summary, **In the Dark groups are highly motivated teams that have taken things as far as they can without an understanding of the vision and, more importantly, without the support of their business leaders**.

As we have stated, the phrase commonly used to describe the management situation here is 'herding cats' – the challenge of bringing together individuals to work for a common cause even though they are primarily driven by their own autonomy. When analysing our database, we found that the language used in this region is centred around the present, with less attention on the past or future. People talk about their 'strengths', 'accountability' and 'productivity', all with the underlying message of 'what's in it for me?' As such, the words 'promotion', 'security' and 'contract' occur frequently in people's comments, and a common complaint is the lack of being 'valued'. On the other hand, people highlight the importance of 'community', 'relationships', 'folks', 'shared goals' and communicating more through informal networks than through written communications. Perhaps most importantly, though, change is not on people's agenda and, indeed, the awareness of the need for change is below the norm.

Consequently, visible and well-publicized top-management support is needed in order to make change happen, but trust in business unit leaders tends to be low and people feel that senior management is unsupportive of their goals. The result is that staff are unwilling to exchange the positive feelings in their teams for a less engaging and compelling vision from the organization. Those who are ambitious or want to challenge the status quo may express a desire to leave. A danger here is that, although people in *In the Dark* have few negative feelings, they can easily become critical of top management when it doesn't support their group's activities and needs. Such groups do not make it easy for top management to 'sell' their vision. Often, these senior leaders settle for what they can get from this kind of group, but they may also be frustrated and puzzled by the lack of responsiveness. They might consider replacing certain individuals or they could give up on the group, perhaps even disbanding it.

Moving into the light

To move forward from *In the Dark*, organizations must target two main areas: 1) vision and direction; and 2) business leadership. Groups simply cannot move to higher-performance levels without an increase in these two drivers. Even a small improvement in vision and direction can produce a striking increase in benefits. Figure 8.5 shows how the level of vision and direction has a positive impact on benefits realization regardless of the overall level of a group's performance.

FIGURE 8.5   Vision and direction compared to benefits realization

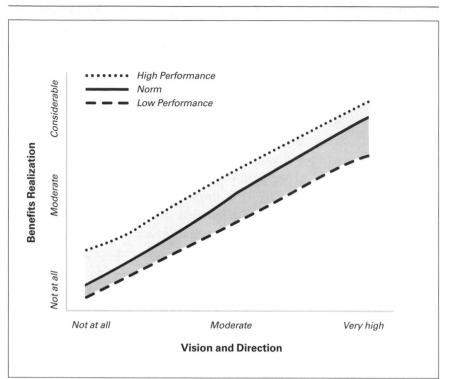

Reasons for low vision and direction

Groups can suffer low vision and direction and a lack of support from business leaders for a number of reasons. In some cases, management has simply forgotten to inform key stakeholders or to involve them in the vision formulation. The language used in global corporations can also be an obstacle. In one company we worked with, we realized that the groups that were positioned in *In the Dark* were the ones that spoke only the local language.

In other situations, executives fail to realize that the vision is alive and continually unfolding. **Outlining the vision once at the beginning of the journey is simply not enough; it is a story that needs to be told and told again at different points along the way.** At one company, it was only at the midpoint of the transformation that we saw staff become receptive to hearing the vision, even though it had been communicated many times before. The leaders recognized that they had previously been communicating too narrowly, saying the same message over and over in the same way.

It is also important to remember that what works in one phase of a change journey might fail in another stage, and that different types of change require different strategies. Vision is an abstraction, and abstract concepts hit home only when the immediate context supports them and people start to internalize what those concepts signify. So, for example, a concept such as 'adapt or die' might be effective in the early stages of a change initiative but then lose its resonance towards the latter stages.

At times we have seen that vision and direction were lacking not because of a failure to communicate but because the vision was never formulated in a meaningful way to begin with. To be effective, the vision for change should present the primary purpose of the business and its longer-term visionary goals, and it should also express the core values to which the organization is committed. The vision needs to inspire people, painting a clear picture of what the organization intends to become and achieve at some point in the future.

Disconnects that ripple though all organizational levels

Unfortunately many leaders who are trying to increase the vision and direction in their organizations mistakenly believe that the process is a simple matter of just explaining the vision and telling people, 'Get on with it!' The assumption is that the vision will magically cascade down through the levels, with everyone understanding and agreeing to it in order to become fully aligned. Looking at our numerous client examples, however, we find that it does not really happen that way.

Figure 8.6 shows data for the research group at the government agency we described at the beginning of this chapter. In the diagram, the disconnect between the executive level and the unit managers who lead the teams below them is starkly highlighted.

At the government agency in question, people on the executive team had a good understanding of and strong agreement with the vision, yet their opinion of how others trusted them was around the norm. A level below that, the unit managers understood the vision but did not agree with it, and trust in the executive team was well below the norm. Still lower in the organization, team leaders and their teams did not understand nor agree with the vision, and they had even less trust in the top executives. This disconnect in alignment was clearly reflected in one team leader's comments: 'Upper senior management doesn't pull together or agree for the overall common good of the organization. They are too insular and concerned for

FIGURE 8.6   Research group results across levels for vision and
direction and communication

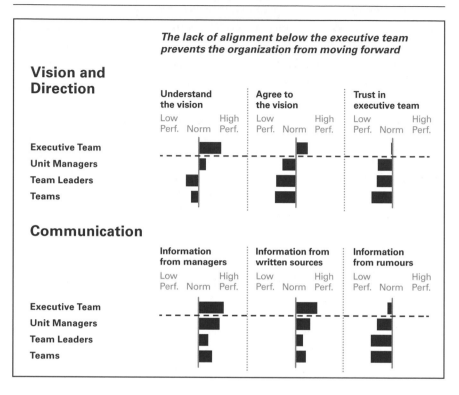

building up and protecting their own domains and departments with their
own political agendas'.

When it comes to vision and direction, an astute question to ask a senior
leader is this: 'How are you going to gain agreement to the vision four levels
below you?' For the government agency in Figure 8.6, results of the organizational disconnects led to a series of intense discussions between the top
executives and their unit managers to redefine and broaden the scope of the
vision. Without any alignment between these two groups, there was no way
that the change programme would reach a higher level of performance and
increased benefits. Indeed, a lack of trust and alignment between leaders will
slow down any change initiative and even bring it to a standstill. In many
cases, this can lead to the burning question, 'Are you on the bus or not?'

It is also important to note that the level of understanding and agreement
was low at the government research group but not because of a lack of
communication. The results in Figure 8.6 clearly show that both written and

face-to-face information was high across all levels. Rumours, however, were also high in the groups below the executive team. Leaders often fail to appreciate that it is not merely a matter of transmitting the message as much as building trust to gain an emotional agreement to the message. More information makes little difference when it comes on top of low trust.

Even given such challenges, our research indicates that these issues are some of the easiest to resolve quickly for groups to leave *In the Dark*. Indeed, only 12 per cent of groups remain there, while 15 per cent make it to *High Performance* and another 45 per cent move to higher areas within *On Track*. To arrive at a higher position on the change map, we have found that organizations must do three fundamental things:

- Get corporate and business unit leaders to take an active role in driving vision and direction.

- Put in place effective communication strategies targeted at gaining an emotional 'yes' to the vision so that the right messages get to the right people at the right time.

- Build strong communities where people feel their best talents can be utilized so that they can 'live the vision'.

Understanding what drives vision and direction

Of the different levels of leadership in a typical organization – corporate (top management), business (unit or division) and team – **we have found that trust in corporate leadership holds the keys to unlocking people's power and potential when they are in *In the Dark*.** People will not embrace the vision and direction without high trust at the most senior levels of the organization. For *In the Dark* groups, trust in corporate leadership is close to low performance, the lowest of all the leadership levels. Consequently, corporate leaders need to tackle this issue as their number one priority as they go about setting the overall vision and direction.

Corporate leaders, however, cannot do this on their own. Corporate leadership might be responsible for setting the overall vision and direction, but it is business leadership that must help transform that into a clear understanding of the big picture and agreement with what it means for the organization. Equally, business leadership provides the glue that binds together teams and work units synergistically, pulling together people's hearts and minds in order to realize the vision and direction. As such, our research has found that **business leadership is by far the most important driver of vision and direction**.

Communication, teamwork, passion and drive, and team leadership also play a role in driving vision and direction, but to a much lesser extent. As we have seen in the research group example, communication is important as the means to deliver a message, but it is not the main driver. Moreover, e-mails and other traditional means of communicating tend to be of limited effectiveness if business leadership is lacking. For lower-performing groups, teamwork helps to build momentum for change, even when the vision seems far away. As groups move up the change map, clearer roles and relationships become a way of life, and are more closely aligned with the vision and direction. Passion and drive tend to work in a similar way, having a stronger role in driving vision under low-performing conditions than they do when groups move into *High Performance*.

Communicating effectively

To be effective, communication needs a central focus and a set of relationships. From our research, we found that team leadership, business leadership, and vision and direction are clear drivers of communication across all levels of performance. Our data is unequivocal: communication cannot flow if the message is blocked by poor relationships. It is important to note that communication is part of a 'package' and not a separate activity that can simply be outsourced to a communications group in the organization. Consequently, its score rises when team leadership and business leadership are strong, and when the vision and direction are able to deliver a powerful message to those undergoing change. Moreover, communication works most effectively when people are hearing a consistent message across different management levels. Unfortunately, such alignment is often not the case for *In the Dark* groups.

Interestingly, our analysis reveals a counterintuitive finding that organizations tend to communicate more when fear and frustration levels are higher. There can be many reasons for this, especially in areas of lower performance: more e-mails are sent out when leaders see people become more fearful; the hardnosed realism of a manager's speech may be followed by more face-to-face discussion; and so on. This increase in communications, however, can easily be counterproductive if leaders do not have a good understanding of which communication modes are most and least effective at any given stage of a change initiative.

Patterns of communication across the stages of change

Figure 8.7 shows how the different forms of communication – face-to-face meetings with managers, written information and rumours – play out across the different stages of change. For groups with performance around the norm, information received from managers increases across the stages of change, peaking between the middle and end stages and then dropping towards the end. Written information follows a similar trend but at a lower level. Meanwhile, information from rumours remains at a constant level, dropping just slightly towards the end stages of change. Our research shows that this is the most common – but not necessarily the most effective – pattern that organizations follow across the stages of change.

In contrast, **high-performing groups start with and maintain very high levels of face-to-face communications with their managers through all stages of change, and those communications are closely supported by**

FIGURE 8.7   Communication patterns of groups across the stages of change

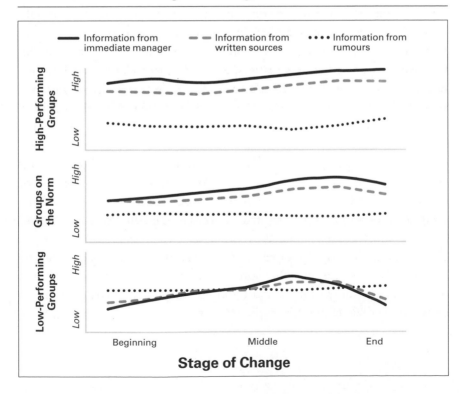

written information. In such groups, leaders actively work to reduce rumours in the early stages of change, and they then maintain a large gap between face-to-face and written communications versus rumours through all stages of change. In other words, high-performing leaders do not wait for information to come from the outside. Instead they continuously seek out information to share with their teams and actively work to confront and discredit inaccurate rumours. High-performing groups want to know what support is being provided to help them sustain their efforts, and they appreciate when leaders look beyond the immediate business horizon to the broader competitive landscape, warning of potential risks and events that may cause them to go off track.

When it comes to communication channels in low-performing groups, rumours are sadly an important source of information across all stages of change. Face-to-face communications from managers and written information both start at low levels in the early stages of change, then they rise as the change programme progresses, peaking in the mid to end stages of the initiative, only to quickly drop off again. They provide too little too late.

A mistake that organizations often make when they see that rumours are running high is to increase their communications. Our research shows that this does not help and can sometimes make the situation worse. Specifically, we have found that a high level of rumours is linked with a large amount of frustration and poor role clarity, not the desire for more information about the vision or other business matters. Improving role clarity and lowering fear and frustration are more effective interventions if an organization is serious about reducing rumours. Another thing to remember is that information coming from rumours is uncontrolled in its quantity, quality and trustworthiness. Further, the feedback mechanism is generally poor, with employees unable to query the source of a rumour and no one held accountable for the veracity of the information. As such, it makes more sense for organizations to take control of that feedback mechanism by supplying accurate information from a trusted source. Here, credibility is paramount, and the most credible source is often a trusted immediate manager. The more that the task of information dissemination is vested in an immediate boss who is highly credible, the more a group will perceive the information to be accurate and pertinent, and the more encouraged people will be to query that individual for any clarifications they need.

Management roadshows

Another communication channel that organizations often use is the management roadshow. In the best-case scenarios, roadshows provide inspiration that makes people optimistic about the future and helps them move forward. In the worst cases, they only serve to cement employee cynicism. For groups in *Off Track*, where building trust is fundamental in gaining commitment to the change, insufficient communication or the wrong kind of communication quickly leads to cynicism and rumours. 'They still didn't answer our real questions', 'They are trying to outmanoeuvre us' and 'They are not telling us the real picture' are the typical kinds of comments we hear. In this zone, talking about *how* the journey will progress is just as important as talking about *where* the organization is going. Unless executives really lay their cards on the table, including uncomfortable truths, and build a new level of empathy between themselves and their audience, our research tells us that simple show-and-tell roadshows don't work when change is *Off Track* or in *Unsustainable*. They really only deliver value when groups are *On Track* or higher up the change map, where there is already an underpinning emotional commitment to change in place.

Building strong communities

The last challenge for *In the Dark* groups is ultimately about building strong communities. Teams located in *In the Dark* are typically close knit, skilled, competent and effective, reporting to a respected and trusted leader. Even if they understand the corporate vision and direction, they will typically resist trading strong team unity in order to be part of the larger organization. To overcome that reluctance, leaders need to create a larger and more engaging community, or 'big team', of the entire business working together in a single direction and towards a common purpose.

With that in mind, one of the key tasks of top management is to shake up the status quo and find new and creative ways to assemble all of the pieces of a larger puzzle. The goal is to break down silos by, for example, having research and development (R&D) connect with the marketing department, or getting the sales force to collaborate with manufacturing. *In the Dark* teams are doing the best they can and they need a tempting incentive to trigger their desire to be part of a bigger effort. That incentive should leverage the key themes of connecting, linking and joining. Instead of individual roles, people become concerned with team roles. Instead of linking individual objectives, they are now linking team objectives, and even unit and divisional objectives.

All this might seem contradictory to the nature of people who are typical of *In the Dark* – highly individual and opportunistic employees, all with their own self-interests. But to recall the epigraph at the beginning of this chapter, a striking event recorded in a Swedish newspaper helps show the power of overcoming this dilemma. A fisherman with 300,000 small herrings in his nets was pulling his catch in when a killer whale passed by. Frightened, the fish all quickly swam in the same direction, which happened to be down and away from the boat, causing the 70-ton, 50-metre vessel to be pulled over onto its side and into the water, sinking it (Kerpner, 2004).

The main lesson from that story is not necessarily that fear is a strong motivator. The larger lesson is that individuals might have little impact working alone, but when aligned their collective power can be enormous. The challenge for *In the Dark* leaders is to harness people's collective effort. Strong communities built around shared values and purposes have the power to create tremendous momentum for change. It is not enough simply to understand the environment; an organization should also try to influence it. Part of the rationale for a change initiative must include why and how people need to modify the operating environment for the organization, and every employee needs to understand the importance of doing so. What threats will likely come from competitors and from impending government decisions? How is the business going to grow and evolve? What new product ideas are in the pipeline? How is everyone going to take advantage of the new processes?

Leaders must encourage and support these larger communities with effective systems and resources; otherwise people's enthusiasm will quickly fizzle out. In the research group example, it was clear that empowering the leaders of project teams also meant providing them with IT systems that supplied the full range of management information. This information included finance and budgeting, management templates for contracts, travel document-ation, strategic planning objectives, client databases and information about team competencies.

Another important mechanism for building a sense of community is for leaders to talk directly to the most important issues, with statements along the lines of, 'This is how we will deal with the lack of resources' and 'These are the steps we are taking to build greater alignment around the vision'. From the very beginning of a change process, people need to be able to read about the initiative from a number of sources, both electronic and paper. E-mail and the company intranet can help explain the initial reasons for the change, how the change is progressing and what success stories are occurring along the way. Blogs, podcasts, company social networking platforms and short videos can also help, especially when the source is a credible one, such as a trusted senior manager or executive. Moreover, the sharing of knowledge, including lessons and best practices that have been learned, further strengthens the sense of community across different groups and individuals. In tribal cultures, storytelling helped ensure that new generations benefited from the wisdom of tribal elders.

Common pathways exiting *In the Dark*

In the Dark is one of the most transient regions on the change map as only 12 per cent of groups get stuck there, unable to adequately address the lack of vision and issues with business leadership. Let's take a closer look at the main pathways leaving *In the Dark* (Figure 8.8). We discuss each of those pathways below, highlighting some case examples in more depth.

FIGURE 8.8   Common pathways exiting *In the Dark*

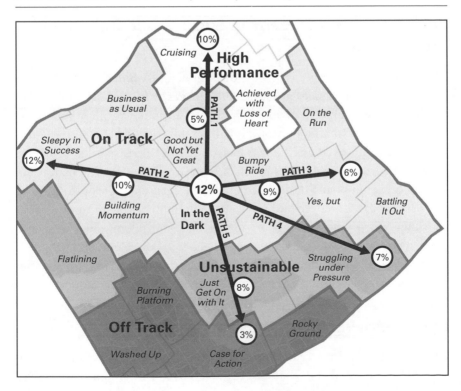

(Note: the examples in this section represent a composite of organizations from our research with similar experiences of change.)

Path 1: moving to Cruising and Good but Not Yet Great

On this path, 5 per cent of groups make the upward move to *Good but Not Yet Great* and another 10 per cent jump from *In the Dark* to *Cruising*. In that move to *High Performance*, a significant rise in business leadership boosts vision and direction, leading to increases in performance and benefits. Such was the case in the industrial division of an international food corporation. Executives travelled extensively to every country site, explaining the vision and direction for the global expansion of the business, and the implications of it. Everyone would be working together, staff and management, to grow the industrial business. This freed up people's emotional energies to focus on the changes ahead. Business leaders communicated effectively and provided support and resources to enable their people. The result was that people actually began to enjoy the challenge of becoming part of a 'big international team'.

Path 2: moving to Sleepy in Success and Building Momentum

This pathway has 10 per cent of groups moving to *Building Momentum* and another 12 per cent of groups landing in *Sleepy in Success*. An example of the latter was an international charity transitioning from a volunteer-dependent group to a more professional organization. There, performance and benefits improved and the amount of change increased due to higher growth. Awareness of the need for change increased, but with so many new staffers being on-boarded, the pace of change eventually dropped but was still reasonable. Moreover, business leadership improved, with those leaders providing more time and support for change, and taking quick remedial steps when action stalled. However, all aspects of teamwork dropped, and team leadership suffered as trusted local leaders were removed from the initiative. Consequently, the charity ended up in *Sleepy in Success*.

Path 3: moving to Yes, but and Bumpy Ride

On this pathway, 6 per cent of groups move to *Yes, but* and another 9 per cent of groups make it to *Bumpy Ride*. Here, the amount of change dramatically increases, and moves at a very fast pace. Take, for example, the staff at a community care centre that had to absorb the patients of two nearby facilities, all with just a minimal increase in resources. Vision and direction rose significantly, and staff went from knowing nothing to knowing perhaps too much. Because staffing levels were too low, trust in team leaders dropped, and passion and drive fell. The net result was that cost management was the only aspect of business performance that improved.

Path 4: *moving to* Struggling under Pressure

Here, 7 per cent of groups travel to *Struggling under Pressure*. This happened to a furniture manufacturer that stumbled when implementing a new corporate strategy. The executive team announced the new vision and direction to employees, which helped to increase trust in top leadership. However, the executive team failed to implement the new direction operationally. People understood 'what' the change was but not the 'how'. Subsequently, accountability, teamwork and communication collapsed. Fear and frustration skyrocketed, as people felt a sense of loss of old routines without clear new ones to replace them. Senior leadership had the best of intentions, but a lack of support for teams resulted in the change initiative going off course.

Path 5: *moving to* Just Get On with It *and* Case for Action

On this path, 8 per cent of groups wind up in *Just Get On with It* and an additional 3 per cent fall further down to *Case for Action*. Here, life in the organization gets much more difficult. All drivers are low and have become worse. More obstacles get in the way of accomplishing work as resources are taken away. Teams are left in a pressure cooker, as the softer aspects that make business work – relationships and emotions – are not valued. In such a demoralizing environment, the number of people who think of leaving increases substantially.

Embracing the big picture

In this chapter, we have seen how a lack of vision and inadequate business leadership can leave groups stuck in *In the Dark*. In this capital city of the *On Track* zone, groups typically have strong levels of team leadership, accountability, teamwork and emotional energy, but business leadership has failed to provide a compelling vision that engages everyone. In essence, teams have been doing well but have gone as far as they can without better business leadership. In Chapter 9, we focus on another capital city of the *On Track* zone: *Sleepy in Success*. There, teams have embraced the bigger picture but struggle with overwhelming complacency and problems with discipline, teamwork and accountability.

SUMMARY FOR CHAPTER 8: KEY INSIGHTS

- Organizations can make it halfway up the change map, right into *On Track*, while still having very low levels of vision and direction. But then they simply will not get any further without gaining people's buy-in.

- Vision and direction is by far the strongest driver of benefits realization, followed by business leadership. An emotional agreement to the vision is what makes the difference, not simply an understanding of it.

- Our research shows that high-performing groups maintain very high levels of face-to-face communication, supported by written information and maintained across all stages of change. For low-performing groups, rumours are a main source of information with generally inadequate face-to-face and written communication.

- Buy-in to vision is not an incremental process but a step jump – people either get it or they don't.

- Building trust pays big dividends for the organization: as groups move from low performance to high performance, there is an average rise in trust across the three leadership levels of nearly 50 per cent. This is accompanied by a rise in business performance by about 40 per cent, and in benefits realization of nearly 70 per cent.

- The 'commitment curve' works in reverse for high-performing groups, capturing people's 'hearts and minds' – in that order. People gain an emotional agreement to the vision before a logical understanding occurs. Low-performing groups follow the commitment curve – awareness, understanding and then buy-in.

- *In the Dark* groups are highly motivated teams that have taken things as far as they can without the support of their top leaders and a clear vision.

- Trust in corporate leadership holds the key to unlocking people's power and potential when they are in *In the Dark*. Unless it is corrected, a disconnect just below top management, where business leaders understand the vision but do not agree, will almost always be fatal to change.

- Rumours are not driven by a lack of communication; rather they are linked with team frustration and poor role clarity.

- Communicating vision is not a one-time activity at the beginning of a change journey. The vision is a living expression of change, and needs to be stated and restated in different ways as change unfolds.

- Good communication in low-trust environments is more a matter of removing the barricades that prevent people from truly receiving the messages, rather than sending the message out.

Sleepy in Success
Get back
in the game

09

> *So many people live within unhappy circumstances and yet will not take the initiative to change their situation because they are conditioned to a life of security, conformity and conservatism, all of which may appear to give one peace of mind, but in reality nothing is more dangerous to the adventurous spirit within a man than a secure future.*
>
> **JON KRAKAUER**

A 'wakeup call' was needed. A large utility company was implementing a new geospatial data conversion system and the project was lagging more than six months behind schedule. Like many IT initiatives, the implementation had promised much but executives had underestimated the myriad challenges with people, organizational culture and data. More than 1,000 staff across the business were using the new system – called the Geographic Information System (GIS) – on a regular basis, and an additional 300 used personal navigation devices with the GIS data loaded. People did not trust the accuracy and reliability of the GIS, and they became frustrated. Moreover, the GIS group itself was struggling with conflicts between contractors and full-time staff, as people lacked the necessary focus to move the initiative forward. In essence, the utility found itself stuck in *Sleepy in Success*.

Sleepy in Success is one of the five capital cities of the *On Track* zone. In Chapter 7, we described how groups in *On Track* are generally in an acceptable middle ground (not great but good), although business leadership and resources might be lacking. **In the *Sleepy in Success* region, groups might understand and agree with the vision and direction of a change programme, but they lack the discipline, teamwork and accountability to implement that initiative effectively.** *Sleepy in Success* is the most common destination on the change map, with 12 per cent of all groups residing there. As the name implies, life is relatively easy there: the levels of risks and fear are low; employees are not worried about their work; and few are thinking of leaving the organization. The challenge, though, is that people are not actively involved in making change happen. It is as if they are on the sidelines waiting for something to happen, when management needs them in the game. Indeed, **complacency – being content with merely acceptable performance and the status quo – is the biggest obstacle, with 26 per cent of groups not making it out of this region the next time around.**

Sleepy in Success insights

To be sure, the GIS implementation at the utility company cited above was hardly a trivial matter. The project involved mapping the location of more than 500,000 poles, about 28,000 substations and kiosks, and more than 46,000 kilometres of underground cables and overhead conductors. Furthermore, the mapping had to be done to an accuracy of less than 1 metre across a geographic landscape with more than 1.6 million customers and a network supply area administered by more than 40 local government authorities.

Yet although the technical challenges were daunting, this was familiar territory to most of the managers and project staff. Many had grown up in the organization and been trained for these roles. The much larger issue, though, was in bringing about change. The initiative required people to do things differently and, in a heavily unionized environment with over half of the workforce having been with the company for more than 20 years, a significant cultural change was needed to transform the staff mindset. To speed up the implementation, the utility brought in a new general manager.

Eventually, over the course of four years, the utility was able to get the project headed back in the right direction. The accuracy and consistency of the data capture improved to almost 100 per cent; the data update time decreased from 180 days to within 5 working days; and annual productivity improvements have averaged 28 per cent, translating into operational savings of over US$15 million across the time frame of the transformation.

Exactly how was the utility company able to accomplish those impressive results? In studying that organization, as well as in our investigation of other *Sleepy in Success* groups, we uncovered two key insights that can greatly help those in that region move to positions higher on the change map, the first having to do with the role played by team leaders and the second in translating 'soft' issues into 'hard' outcomes.

Insight 1: team leaders hold the keys to work groups breaking out of complacency

Our research shows that **team leaders typically act as gatekeepers between their managers and their staff. As such, they hold the keys to unlocking the power to change.** They can either help or hinder change, and management needs to do everything in its power to get the right team leaders in place with the right skills and knowledge. It is one of the wisest investments that an organization can make.

Insight 2: translating 'soft' issues into 'hard' outcomes unlocks the power to change

Management often needs to translate the 'soft' people side of the organization into 'hard' outcomes. At the utility company cited above, many employees were technical people doing technical work, and they took great satisfaction in solving problems. In such an environment, the change map resonated with staff, especially those who were used to dealing with geospatial data. The map enabled people issues that were previously intangible and invisible to be quickly quantified so that they could be more easily discussed and addressed. Furthermore, all teams could compare their position against others and determine where they wanted to be in the next cycle, leading to a competitive dynamic among people.

As the leadership team worked through the technical challenges associated with the GIS implementation, it systematically took decisive actions across all areas of the business. During the business restructuring, some employees were redeployed or dismissed, while others were coached for sub-par performance. More importantly, for the first time, a new strategy was formulated with input from staff across all levels. In addition, the much-needed managerial skills were developed in a new breed of individuals that would take over the business, and the impact was made visible for each team. Thanks to those actions, the progress for the entire group was remarkable, moving up from *Sleepy in Success* all the way into *Cruising*.

Characteristics of *Sleepy in Success*

In *Sleepy in Success*, most things are fine but not great. (Note: for a description of the related region of *Business as Usual*, see box 'Business as Usual'.) For instance, employees care about customer service and want to do a good job, but they might not realize that their work needs to be done better. Moreover, the fundamental problem lies in embracing change. People have no sense of urgency and little awareness of the need for change. In fact, the level of involvement in planning and implementing change is among the lowest scores for any location on the change map. This is odd given that this region has a lot of change occurring, particularly with respect to restructuring and growth. It is as if staff are sitting on the sidelines, hoping that if they wait long enough the change will proceed without their having to get involved and the initiative will simply pass them by.

Business as Usual

As we discussed in Chapter 7, both *Sleepy in Success* and *Business as Usual* contain similar dynamics in that teams are not involved and held accountable for making change happen, but the latter is one step further up towards *High Performance* than the former. In *Business as Usual*, almost every score is high, except change is not on the agenda. Even so, benefits are being delivered and performance is improving.

Groups in *Business as Usual* are well-resourced with strong team and business leadership. Everyone seems happy with the status quo; the level of fear and frustration is very low; but, as in *Sleepy in Success*, people run the risk of sitting on the sidelines of change. Employees do a good job and have settled into roles and relationships that work and deliver results, but people want to keep on doing things the same way that they have done them before. Trust in all levels of leadership is actually very high, with people happy to go along with what management says, and this is reflected by the fact that agreement to the vision is higher than the understanding of it.

The problem in this region is that the focus is on the short term rather than the long term. With things going well and everyone settling into their daily business routines, few are really looking ahead at what needs to change. As such, the level of vision and direction is low; awareness of the need for change is lacking; and people are not really involved in the planning and implementation of change. Top management, for its part, may complain about business units being in silos with a lack of cooperation and synergy between units.

The danger here is that, although organizations may not want to change, in today's world it is impossible not to be affected by market conditions. Organizations either proactively embrace change or they are forced to change because of deterioration in their business performance. This region is unusual in that only 2 per cent of our database lives here and only 10 per cent of those groups remain for a second measurement cycle. It is simply not possible to maintain a state of 'business as usual' for very long, with 30 per cent moving up the change map to *High Performance* while 60 per cent drop into lower regions.

The driver profile in Figure 9.1 shows a very low level of fear and frustration. Also, people have a reasonable understanding of the vision and direction, and business leadership and communication levels are above the norm. Groups in this region receive the necessary support and commitment from business leadership and, when problems arise, quick remedial action is evident. By and large, teams have the systems and processes needed to do their job, along with sufficient skills and staff.

A disconnect, however, is revealed when we take a closer look at the strength of leadership at different levels. Business leadership is much stronger than team leadership, and this is where we find indications of deeper problems, with teams lacking a sense of teamwork and having little accountability. The real shortcoming here is an inability on the part of team leaders to build these capabilities in their teams.

In *Sleepy in Success*, team leaders display little interest in measurable outcomes and in giving people feedback about their performance. In fact, this region has some of the lowest scores for team members feeling rewarded and recognized, and for utilizing their talents. The failure to fully utilize people's talents means that many employees are likely to just sit around and wait for things to happen. The team leader should be an exemplar for making change happen and for mobilizing this untapped potential, but it just does not happen. Problems with accountability go unresolved, as leaders want to keep these issues beneath the radar, and thus gaps in the skill base remain hidden. In addition, the level of written communications is low, as if teams do not want information in writing or they do not see the need for this.

FIGURE 9.1   Change map and driver profile for *Sleepy in Success* region

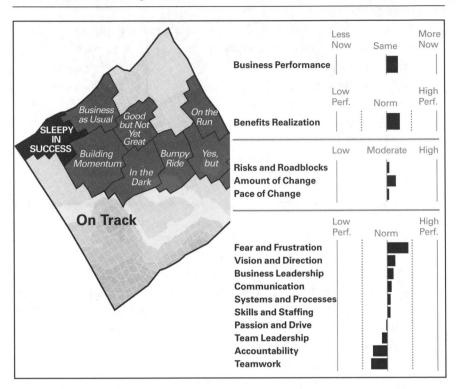

Words that are commonly used in this region are 'connect', 'enjoy', 'helpful' and 'accept', reflecting that teams try to keep the status quo and that team leaders are certainly not pushing their teams to perform beyond expectations. Nor are they trying to address skill gaps or seek out new opportunities critical to moving higher on the change map. 'Desire' is also a frequently used word, in terms of people talking about achieving their personal desires or about something not having the desired effect. It is as if employees feel that they have little power to achieve outcomes, and believe that things are basically out of their control.

In some cases, team leaders try to shield their staff from change, or they may be fearful of the consequences of too much change at once. In other cases, they simply do not have the skills needed to manage change effectively and to build strong accountability and teamwork. Sometimes they might even actively collude to prevent higher management from detecting inadequate performance – their own and that of their teams.

Consequently, outsiders to a team will often find it difficult, if not impossible, to bring about change. In effect, change programmes seem to bounce off the team, and leaders managing large-scale initiatives feel as if they cannot gain any traction and yet they do not quite know why. The business unit leader has perhaps the best chances of bringing about change inside teams under his or her purview, but as we have learned in previous chapters that approach can sometimes backfire.

Getting the right leaders in the right roles working in the right direction

In *Sleepy in Success*, team leaders hold the keys to unlocking the power to change, but a common problem is that they lack the necessary skills and capabilities for that position. Often, they have been promoted into their roles on the basis of their technical expertise or seniority, neither of which is sufficient for helping teams to break out of the status quo or to excel under turbulent change conditions. When we measure team leadership, we ask team members to assess the capabilities of their immediate boss in terms of leading change and performance management. In essence, we are interested in what it is like to be on the receiving end of a leader's leadership. To determine that, we ask team members specific questions along the lines of:

- How would you rate your immediate boss's ability to lead change implementation – building and mobilizing people's commitment?
- How would you rate your immediate boss's performance management – coaching people to develop their potential?
- How confident and trusting are you in your immediate boss's leadership?
- To what degree do you feel your full talents and capabilities are being utilized?
- How recognized and rewarded do you feel for achieving results?

The perceptions of team members are much like 360-degree feedback, and that information enables us to build a clear picture of a team leader's skills and capabilities.

In our discussion of *Struggling under Pressure* in Chapter 6, we highlighted that a team leader does not function in isolation from other levels of management. Our driver analysis clearly shows that team leaders are strongest when they have competent business leaders above them and when they have built strong foundations of accountability and communication in their teams. Managing emotions – nurturing high passion and drive, and lowering fear and frustration – and addressing their root causes are also important, but they are secondary to ensuring high accountability and good communication.

Strong business leadership plays an enormous part in transforming low levels of team leadership eventually into high performance – and the converse is true. It can be tempting for business leaders to blame team leaders for poor performance (or vice versa) without seeing their own role in such failures. Low support from business leadership typically results in team leaders and their teams adopting a siege mentality – us against the rest of the organization.

The most powerful combination for change comes when team and business leaders work together synergistically. A vision and direction backed by those two levels of leadership will be far more credible than that supported by just one level. **Business leadership is responsible for communicating the benefits of the change to the audiences under their control, especially the team leadership, refreshing and reinforcing that message in different ways. For their part, team leaders are responsible for helping to translate what the vision means for their teams and for their team members' roles.**

Managing in 'bear' conditions

In times of difficult change, it makes all the more sense for the business leadership to help team leaders find their way forward. After all, business leaders typically have a better view of the vision and direction, and they may be better placed to see the final product of the change, as well as being better informed about many of its aspects. In steady-state conditions, it might be perfectly acceptable for the business leadership to leave team leaders alone, letting them get on with the tasks at hand. For groups in *Sleepy in Success*, however, the problem is that team leaders have often been left alone for too long. In many cases, team leaders have inherited or have been promoted into comfortable leadership positions and are then left unprepared for change. Like stockbrokers who have only ever experienced a 'bull' market, they are thrown off-balance by 'bear' conditions. **The ultimate test of a team leader's mettle is managing change – leading a team in conditions where the previous way of working no longer exists, where no one is quite certain what the final state should look like, and where great uncertainty exists regarding people's roles.**

Team leadership is also high when accountability and communication are strong. Unfortunately, many team leaders who inherit teams that historically have issues in those areas often see no reason to change and just keep going in that fashion. In some cases, they lack the skills to maintain discipline when the levels of complexity, ambiguity, uncertainty and risk increase. Indeed, team leaders who were perfectly competent when things were simpler and more clear-cut can quickly run into trouble when these confounding factors have to be dealt with confidently and with equanimity. Maintaining an infectious sense of excitement and building levels of passion in their teams are also more challenging under such conditions.

In terms of the communications required, team leaders should focus on building awareness of the need for change and on establishing linkages between people's regular work and the changes taking place. This concerns not only benefits to the organization, but also what the initiative means for the individuals themselves and their teams. **Problems that arise from the change programme also typically bring about new opportunities and possibilities to expand people's horizons and stretch their talents. Without strong team leadership to recognize these opportunities and turn them into reality, they can easily slip by**, leaving teams impoverished as a result. To make a difference in *Sleepy in Success*, change needs to come from within teams and, until that happens, our analysis shows that adding resources, systems and processes, and skills and staffing from the outside will do little to improve team leadership.

The benefits of strong team leadership

Team leadership directly affects benefits realization, particularly for groups that are in *On Track* or *High Performance*. In fact, teams scoring around the norm for team leadership gain most from improvements in that area (Figure 9.2). For low-performing groups, though, increased team leadership capabilities only improve benefits up to a certain point, then the impact flattens off somewhat. It is only through addressing all the elements of the package – accountability, communication and fostering strong positive emotions while combating negative feelings – that team leadership reaches high levels of performance.

Now that we have looked at the main characteristics of *Sleepy in Success*, let's take a closer look at the role of the team leader in dysfunctional teams, the importance of trust in leadership during times of change, and the impact of both performance management, and reward and recognition, in mobilizing people's potential.

FIGURE 9.2   Team leadership compared to benefits realization

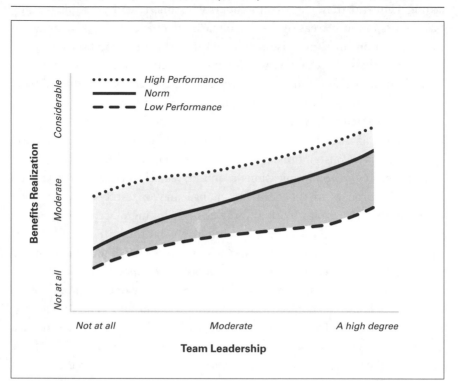

Recruiting the right leaders for difficult situations

The importance of strong team leaders cannot be emphasized enough, and the process starts with effective recruiting, ensuring that the right individuals are selected for those positions. All too often, though, organizations find out only in the middle of a change initiative that they have the wrong team leaders in key roles. As one team member remarked, 'My supervisor is in way over his head: zero people skills and horrible communication skills. His boss is stretched too thin to notice. More attention should be given to selecting supervisor and team leads'.

Training, coaching and even counselling can help build the capabilities that a team leader needs, but there is no point in trying to develop an individual who is not receptive or who is incapable of acquiring the necessary skills. The person may simply not have the natural temperament or innate capacity to perform a certain role. In such situations, the business leader must replace that individual with someone who is right for that position. Our research shows that replacing team leaders in such cases can have a dramatic impact on the performance of teams.

If, however, an organization does not address problems with team leadership, then toxic conditions can quickly develop. When teams suffer a leadership vacuum, for instance, self-entitlement and self-interest will often fill the void. Left unchecked, this can then escalate into destructive actions such as sabotage, which can take many forms. When groups are in *Off Track*, the saboteurs typically seek to deliberately harm the organization. When groups are in *On Track*, the sabotage is often more related to protecting an individual's self-interest. Even when self-interest does not take the form of sabotage, its effects can still greatly hinder a group, especially when the team leader is the guilty party. As one staff member in our study commented, 'My supervisor has a tendency to serve personal ambitions before our team. It seems very clear that there is no care or concern for the individual on the team but rather if we achieve the desired result and make our supervisor look good. It is a discouraging feeling'.

The role of the team leader in managing 'damage'

Across the course of our research, we examined more than 50 different emotional states and discovered that the feeling of being 'bored' was clustered with that of being 'humiliated' and 'guilty'. That result led us to the conclusion that being 'bored' was not the same as the common understanding of being detached or uninterested. In other words, it is not a passive condition in organizations but part of an active state in which very deep emotions are at play. We termed this state 'damage'.

'Damage' is distinguished from other negative, more transitory feelings because of its much more permanent nature. For example, 'fear' or 'anger' levels usually drop quite rapidly when the event causing those emotions changes. In contrast, someone who has been 'humiliated' will still feel 'humiliated' long after being removed from that situation. Indeed, people will often talk about such incidents as if they had happened recently, even though they might have occurred years ago. Deep feelings of damage can have a very disruptive effect, and are often found sitting under the surface in toxic work groups. We have found, for example, that small amounts of damage in an organization are linked to higher occupational health and safety incidents.

Once 'damage' has been done, staffers find it very hard to move forward, as it colours the way they see the world. Providing logical, rational information does little to help them change; in some cases it will only reinforce their underlying cynicism. To mitigate these kinds of negative feelings, a new emotional experience is needed, one in which people feel there is genuine empathy for their situation and which enables them to work through the emotions that have come from what might have been a humiliating incident. The team leader or another trusted person must sit down with staff and talk through their experiences at a deep emotional level. Only then can they begin to recover from the damage they have incurred.

To manage damaged staff, team leaders must have their fingers on the 'pulse' of the team, and they must not be afraid to take strong actions when necessary. The truth is that staffers want to see leaders take action, as evidenced by one team member's comments, 'The new manager noticed lack of discipline and lack of work ethic or morale and advised that this will not be tolerated. I consider that as a positive approach as people within the team often get frustrated that someone is working hard, while others don't and the whole team's work suffers'.

Our data indicates that replacing dysfunctional team members or leaders who are completely out of their depth can reap considerable benefits. At the utility company discussed above, when a key personnel change was made in its GIS team it took months for people to regroup. During that time, the team slid down from *Sleepy in Success* to *Struggling under Pressure* (Figure 9.3) because the team leader lacked the skills to manage this type of situation effectively. That individual was then replaced by a new leader who was promoted from within the team, and she effectively tackled the underlying issues, rebuilding trust through one-on-one and team discussions. Thanks to her efforts, the team was able to move from *Struggling under Pressure* to *Cruising*, a jump that only 3 per cent of groups have managed to accomplish.

The importance of trust in team leadership

In earlier chapters, we highlighted on numerous occasions the importance of trust in leadership as we discussed the other capital cities. In this chapter, we focus on trust in the team leader, and in Chapter 10 we will talk about trust in business unit leaders and the invisible 'trust grid' that needs to be in place between team, business unit and corporate leaders for the organization to stay fit, healthy and highly responsive to change.

FIGURE 9.3   Path of GIS team at a utility company

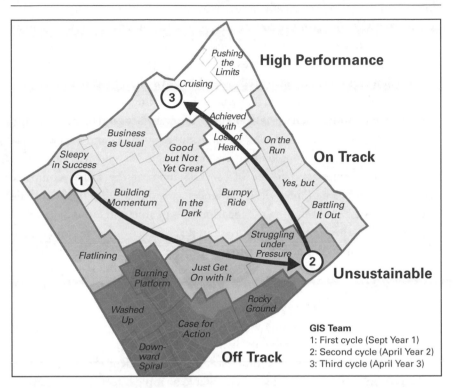

Our research shows that trust and confidence in team leaders are driven by three critical factors. Specifically, trust and confidence are high when team leaders:

- **have strong, well-developed capabilities to lead change (building and mobilizing people's commitment);**

- **regularly conduct performance management sessions (establishing role clarity and coaching people to develop their potential);**

- **communicate face-to-face on a regular basis with their teams.**

To a much lesser degree, other factors that contribute to trust in the team leader are strong teamwork, the staff feeling recognized, people being rewarded for achieving results, the lowering of fear and distress, and the building of passion and drive. Trust in team leaders is also helped when the business unit leaders above them take quick remedial actions to address identified problems, and when they are actively supporting the changes taking place.

When it comes to leading change, it helps if the team leader is not only thinking through the relatively short-term implications of change but also considering the longer-term conditions of institutionalizing the change, as well as the sustainability and viability of the organization itself. The behaviour of a trusted change leader includes flexibility, particularly under pressure, and a willingness to take measured risks. Effective change leaders also seek feedback, whether through 'management by walking around' or through more formal methods such as staff surveys – and they act on that information.

To understand how trust can be built in a positive and constructive manner, consider the example of an electrical engineer who was promoted into the role of manager in one of the GIS units at the utility company discussed earlier. When field service engineers would call him in the middle of the night for help in finding the location of a problem in an underground electrical cable, the manager did more than just answer questions and return to bed. He got in his car and drove to the location where they were working. Using the GIS on his laptop, he would quickly identify the cable, locate it and provide advice to the team so that they could dig more accurately and quickly perform the repair work to fix the outage.

In such an action-orientated work culture, the manager's efforts in going beyond the call of duty paid big dividends. He built trust from the field services staff, while at the same time establishing confidence in the accuracy of the GIS database. Actions like his can have a ripple effect throughout the organization. Even small actions to build trust can have a huge impact, as one team member in a similar situation commented when talking about his boss: 'A majority of the changes that are taking place such as reducing spending [and] streamlining process are great and will make our company very successful. But sometimes it's really the small things that make the biggest difference'.

Team leaders hold the keys to breaking complacency in Sleepy in Success

When groups are in *Sleepy in Success*, team leaders face the extra challenge of building trust and confidence in an environment of complacency. If they are not careful, they can easily become part of the complacency themselves. The very people who are there to lead others, to create accountability and to provide strong teamwork can, by their own actions, unwittingly impede progress. Unfortunately, awareness of the need for change is low in *Sleepy in Success*, and that is the issue that team leaders must tackle if they want to unlock the power for change in their teams. The issue that is difficult to grasp for those in *Sleepy in Success* is that while they wish for 'happiness', they view it as something that they need to hold on to, not realizing that the more they hold on, the more tensions they create in a fast-moving world that is constantly changing.

Maintaining happiness is an active process of keeping pace with change as well as being connected strongly to the surrounding world, not passively sitting by wishing things could be different. To break out of *Sleepy in Success*, team leaders need to take the lead in change, encouraging rather than discouraging people from taking initiative. It is easy to say that team leaders must first recognize the need to change, be willing to look at themselves in the mirror and then actively lead and engage others in the change process, but it is difficult to do. A challenge here is that there is often an underlying tension between those who want to maintain the status quo and are reluctant to 'upset the apple cart', versus those who want change but do not feel able to speak out. In a change programme, when faced with difficult choices, one team member saw the writing on the wall, commenting: 'The loss of jobs is [a] threat, but the threat of not changing is just as great'.

When leaders listen to those who are dissatisfied, to those who hold different, even radical views, and to those who want to change, they start to unlock the power to change in their teams. Trust in the team leader makes it safe for people to speak up and for them to feel confident that they can step up and start to take action to make a difference. An important thing to remember here is that the key to making progress in a change initiative often comes from unlikely sources such as conflict, which is linked to people's dissatisfaction. To paraphrase Leonard Cohen, the Canadian singer-songwriter, in his song 'Anthem', when you're focused on perfection, you don't see the cracks, but the cracks are what let the light in.

Employee engagement and organizational change

To break a pattern of complacency, many managers might think the solution is to get people more engaged with their work. Indeed, 'employee engagement' has become a popular term in recent years, encapsulating the idea that a passionate and dedicated workforce, consisting of employees who are willing to roll up their sleeves to get the job done, will achieve extraordinary results for the benefit of their organization. 'Engagement' considers complex interactions between people in the workplace, reflecting their attitudes, behaviours and feelings, and reduces that down to a single measure or small bundle of related measures. This gives the approach great appeal and is easily assimilated by those managers who seek the silver bullet: 'the one thing I need to do to turn things around'. If only life were that simple.

Many managers under pressure to improve their engagement scores will focus on doing that single thing they think will work best, only to discover to their great disappointment that their efforts have failed to achieve the desired effects. Part of the problem is that there is no clear definition of engagement, and the term is used to mean different things in different organizations and among different academics. Definitions might include motivation, employee satisfaction, trust, willingness to work, loyalty and employee commitment, but the lack of a generally accepted standard has led to much confusion about what employee engagement actually is and what drives it.

In our research, we have seen organizations with high engagement scores flounder when implementing major change programmes. High engagement, however compelling as a concept, provides no guarantee of success, as we saw in Chapter 3 on *High Performance*. Moreover, when it comes to effectively managing change, leaders have often been dissatisfied with the lack of useful and actionable information from traditional engagement surveys. As it turns out, those surveys are of limited use because:

- people don't behave in 'one way';
- people don't follow a straight line to high performance;
- people don't adhere to the principle of 'one size fits all' when it comes to change interventions.

Our research linking employee engagement measures to our data highlights the strengths in traditional engagement metrics and points towards a broader set of measures needed to effectively navigate change (see Figure 9.4). Three lessons can be derived from this work:

- Team leadership is what really drives engagement.
- Engagement viewed in three dimensions brings more insight when managing change.
- 'Engaged' and 'disengaged' employees tell only part of the story.

Lesson 1: team leadership is what really drives engagement

The first lesson comes from recognizing that engagement is very similar to what we measure as team leadership, although more accurately we should

FIGURE 9.4 Employee engagement levels linked to the change map

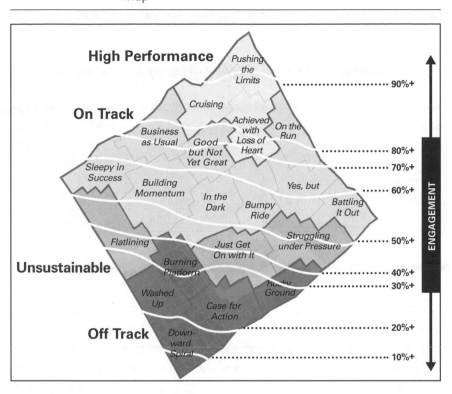

be calling it 'regard for team leadership'. When engagement survey data undergo factor analysis, the results typically yield a single factor, amounting to the quality and strength of the relationship with one's boss or supervisor. In a recent study, using a large sample of engagement data, our analysis showed that this one factor explained over 70 per cent of the variance. When traditional engagement scores are statistically matched against our 10 drivers, we find that there is almost a one-to-one relationship between what is typically measured in engagement scores and what we measure in team leadership.

Lesson 2: engagement viewed in three dimensions brings more insight when managing change

The second lesson stems from the fact that when 'engagement' scores are plotted in three dimensions on the change map, as in Figure 9.4, we see that groups with very low engagement – 30 per cent or less – are down at the bottom of the map, such as in *Case for Action*. In contrast, groups with high engagement – 80 per cent or higher – are at the top of the map, such as in *Cruising*.

In essence, 'engagement' measures the vertical 'height' on the change map, or latitude, but additional measures are needed to locate longitude on the horizontal dimensions. This is clearly illustrated when looking at the middle of the map. The lines in Figure 9.4 representing 50%+ and 60%+ engagement scores form a range that spans the higher parts of the regions in the *Unsustainable* zone and the middle regions of the *On Track* zone. There are a number of regions within this range, and they all have similar levels of engagement. Because engagement is only one of several drivers, including team leadership, the combination of drivers, each with its strengths or weaknesses, causes groups to be positioned either left or right on the change map. In *Sleepy in Success*, teamwork and accountability are low; in *In the Dark*, the level of vision and direction is low; in *Yes, but*, resources are low; and in *Battling It Out* and *Struggling under Pressure*, the level of fear and frustration is high.

We know from our research that improvement in a combination of drivers is needed to move up the change map; it is simply not a matter of improvement in any one driver in isolation. In Chapters 7 through 11 about the *On Track* zone, we discuss how different strategies are required to move up the left side, the middle or the right side of the change map. In *In the Dark*, for example, team leadership is high, and further increases in that driver will do little to help groups. Instead, improvements in vision and direction, and business leadership, are needed to reach *High Performance*.

Lesson 3: 'engaged' and 'disengaged' employees tell only part of the story

The third lesson comes from testing the many assumptions made in the employee engagement literature. These assumptions simply do not stack up when engagement data are seen in 3D on the change map. Although it may be true that highly engaged employees are seen to improve organizational performance (at the top of the change map), and disengaged employees are viewed as costly in terms of declining performance (in *Off Track*), this is not the whole story. Yes, disengaged staff do withdraw cognitively and emotionally; they do withhold discretionary effort; and they do increase employee turnover. A deeper analysis of the data, however, reveals that **engagement versus disengagement is not a black-and-white issue, nor does it behave as an either/or.**

In Chapter 3, we learned that highly engaged people and some of the best performers will often leave an organization in the *High Performance* region of *Achieved with Loss of Heart*. These employees are the very people that organizations should strive to retain. In Chapter 6, we saw that even in *Struggling under Pressure*, where team leaders and their teams feel 'disengaged', people are not thinking of leaving. Their trust in business unit and organizational leaders helps them to hang in when times are tough. In Chapter 10, we will learn that, although the performance is sound and benefits are being realized in *Building Momentum*, that region has one of the highest levels of employees who are thinking of leaving because people look at their team and business unit leaders and have reached the conclusion that those individuals are not up to the task of taking them or their careers and development further.

Team leaders and accountability

The team leader has a critical role in helping team members to develop their full potential and capabilities. In the example of the new GIS system at the utility company discussed earlier in this chapter, we asked staff specific questions about the frequency and quality of their performance discussions:

- In the last year, have you completed an individual performance review with your team leader?
- Have you had a conversation with your team leader around your development needs and opportunities?
- Do you know your learning and development targets for the next 12 months?

When we analysed the responses, we found stark differences between the 'yes' and 'no' responses. Those answering 'no' to all three questions were positioned in *Sleepy in Success*, which as we know has low accountability as one of its hallmarks. Those answering 'yes' to all three questions were positioned on the other side of the change map, in *On the Run*, located just under the *High Performance* zone. The gap between where these two groups were positioned on the change map was a difference of 76 per cent in teamwork, 52 per cent in accountability, 46 per cent in team leadership and 44 per cent in passion and drive. Additionally, for *Sleepy in Success*, business performance and benefits realization were above the norm but unspectacular. In contrast, the group in *On the Run* had business performance and benefits realization much closer to *High Performance*, indicating that having regular performance management discussions is well worth the effort.

What is more revealing, however, is that it is not simply discussions with team leaders that make the biggest difference. Staff answering 'yes' to having a conversation with their team leaders around their development needs but answering 'no' to knowing their learning and development targets had significantly less improvement than those answering 'yes' to all three questions. The message is clear. **Performance management discussions work most effectively when staff set clear learning and development targets and take responsibility for them.** Those who do so are much better positioned than those who do not. Again, this reinforces the message that the team leader's mission in *Sleepy in Success* is to enable his or her staff to change, to grow and to develop their capabilities.

A key area here is accountability. Similar to what we saw in *Struggling under Pressure*, the focus in accountability needs to be on persuading team members to want to be accountable. Motivation to do so comes from inside, not from structure or discipline imposed from the outside in. That said, the act of persuasion can provide enough impetus – tactics to use, tips and hints, and questions to ask oneself – for those who are not necessarily self-starters to conduct their own self-examination.

One important thing to bear in mind is that we have seen many times that **most team leaders believe they give more feedback, and more constructive feedback, than they actually do. Team members, on the other hand, seem to believe that they get less feedback, and more destructive feedback, than they really do** (see, for example, Zenger and Folkman, 2014). It thus becomes vital to gain the agreement of those who receive feedback that that information has in fact been given and that it has been constructive enough to lead to improved performance in the future, without more than temporary hard feelings along the way. This is a reminder that communication, accountability and building trust are not a one-way but two-way process that requires constant attention by both team members and team leaders.

Recognizing and rewarding team members

The role of the team leader is vital in having team members feel recognized and rewarded for achieving results, and in having them feel that their talents and capabilities are being utilized to the fullest extent. Performing all of those duties well is instrumental in building trust and confidence in the relationship between team members and team leader.

Helping staff to feel recognized and rewarded can be accomplished in many ways. Noticing small improvements on the way to an eventual goal

– that is, not waiting for the 'big' moments before noticing or paying attention – can make a powerful lasting impact. Addressing and maximizing rewarding aspects of the work, while minimizing the frustrating aspects of it, will keep staff focused on the things that matter. In addition, involving team members in routine problem-solving and decision-making, while at the same time applying a consistent policy of noting and recognizing improved performance and behaviour, is one of the building blocks of any high-performing team.

When people feel that their full talents and capabilities are being utilized, they contribute from their strengths and their unique talents. Equally important in today's workplace is that they also broaden their experience on the job and they see that steps are being taken to continually evaluate and develop their skills and capabilities.

According to our data, **people in *Sleepy in Success* believe that only a moderate level of their skills and talents are being utilized, compared to a very high utilization at the top of the change map in *Pushing the Limits*.** In other words, team members are sending a clear message to their leaders that a large portion of their capability is still waiting to be deployed. Ironically, leaders will often complain that they cannot get people to do what they want, and yet they have a 'free' resource they can tap into. In essence, they are failing to unlock the power to change with what they have at their disposal.

At the same time, leaders must keep in mind that not everyone needs or wants to change. People assume different roles in a change programme and all of these need to be valued. Simply put, it is not necessary for everyone to be in *High Performance*. Team leaders, especially in *Sleepy in Success*, need to find what is right for each person on a team – to work with those who want to change and to help others find what they do best and support them in those roles.

At the utility company described earlier, one GIS team member did not have the best interpersonal skills, and he had no aspirations to be a leader or to move up the management ladder. But he loved doing his job working with data, and he liked being challenged. So one day his manager walked into his office with a huge armful of design plans, field recordings and maps with as-built annotations. The process of data capture had reached a standstill for this major inner city development project because massive numbers of overlapping design plans had not been able to be sorted out, let alone recorded and mapped in the GIS database. That GIS team member was assigned to that daunting task. For three months, he focused on nothing else, hardly engaging in conversation with others on his team, and was able to finish the complex work, developing a fully integrated dataset in the GIS. He was very good at what he did, and on that team it was safe for him to concentrate on that skill. His contributions were recognized and rewarded, and he was considered a valued team member.

Seeing situations clearly

Many team leaders attempt to bring about change before having sufficient understanding of what is occurring. When their analysis of the situation is based on limited data – or no information at all, except their prejudices and faulty assumptions – their actions will produce only limited solutions. Take, for example, the following old Sufi parable, with two approaches to the same problem:

> Once upon a time, there was a traveller journeying into a new land. Walking along the road, he was met by a group of frightened people. 'What's happening?' asked the man. 'There's a monster in that field', they said, pointing, 'and each day it gets bigger and bigger, growing all the time.' The traveller looked around and saw watermelons growing. 'You fools!' he cried. 'These are only watermelons', and so saying, he took out his sword and cut one in half. The people, seeing this, turned to each other, saying 'If he kills the monster so easily, what will he do to us?' And out of fear they picked up rocks and stoned him to death.
>
> A little later another traveller ventured into this land and was met by the same group of frightened people. But this man, after seeing the watermelons in the field, gathered the people together and said, 'I've seen this monster before and I think I can teach you how to tame it'. So the story goes, he did. He lived with the people, and over time they did tame the monster. He taught them the ways of the monster, and eventually they learned how to harvest the monster, and use it as a food source.

Of course, it is far easier to implement change when one can see the situation clearly and make sense of it, but people do not always have sufficient time for that. The key is to see the situation as it is, carefully observing what is going on but without judgement – no right or wrong, no good or bad, just as things really are. The first traveller in that parable put himself at the centre of making change happen as quickly as possible. The second traveller carefully observed people's interactions and relationships, reading their feelings, the fear in their voices, listening to the words they used, trying to understand their mindsets – long before he did anything. Eventually, when he did take action, he took people along with him, not striding off alone.

Learning to accurately observe people's interactions is a critical skill that is often more difficult to acquire than it seems. It might appear counter-intuitive but **leaders can achieve some of the most powerful effects simply by making accurate statements about what is going on around them**. In the watermelon story, the second change leader accurately perceived what people were experiencing and reflected that back to them in a way that they could hear and relate to, and in terms that they could understand. We have seen over and over in our clients, and it is a rare capability, that a leader's ability to see things as they are, even in difficult times – to state the facts, often using a light touch and bringing humour to the situation – can paradoxically bring about some of the most powerful change.

Common pathways exiting *Sleepy in Success*

Twenty-six per cent of groups get stuck in *Sleepy in Success*, unable to adequately address issues with accountability, teamwork and team leadership. Let's take a closer look at some of the major pathways leading out of *Sleepy in Success* (Figure 9.5). We discuss each of those pathways below, highlighting some case examples in more depth. (Note: the examples in this section represent a composite of organizations from our research with similar experiences of change.)

Path 1: *moving to* Cruising *and* Business as Usual

On this path, 3 per cent of groups travel upward to *Business as Usual* and another 6 per cent make it to *Cruising*. A typical example of the latter is an automotive manufacturer with teams in its engine plant. Business was steady, with long-term contracts in place, and it was a desirable place to work. But a new engine model was coming soon, requiring radical new assembly methods. The new plant manager had extensive workshops conducted with all the middle managers to improve their skills for setting objectives and team-building. After 15 three-day workshops, team leaders went back to the floor, knowing that the plant manager would support them. As a result, performance and benefits increased, as did teamwork, and the plant was able to deliver new engines reliably with high quality.

FIGURE 9.5 Common pathways exiting *Sleepy in Success*

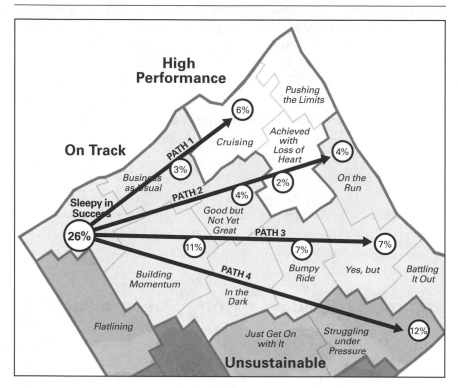

Path 2: moving to On the Run, Achieved with Loss of Heart *and* Good but Not Yet Great

On this pathway 4 per cent of groups travel to *Good but Not Yet Great*, another 2 per cent to *Achieved with Loss of Heart* and an additional 4 per cent to *On the Run*. As an example of the latter, three pharmaceutical plants initiated self-directed teams, grasping people's imagination. The pace and amount of change increased. Business leadership communicated directly about the new vision for these teams, replacing direct information from team leaders to staff. People awoke from their slumber to find their passion and drive and teamwork improved. Even given the rush to change and the pressure to form teams, people were able to manage the increased workloads.

Path 3: moving to Yes, but, Bumpy Ride *and* Building Momentum

On this path, 7 per cent of groups go to *Bumpy Ride*, 7 per cent travel to *Yes, but* and 11 per cent arrive in *Building Momentum*. An example of the latter is a start-up venture that designs and manufactures an innovative piece of hardware. The company had achieved its original goal, with production in the millions of units. The staff, however, was used to rapid growth, and when people didn't see anything new on the horizon, their level of confidence dropped; the amount of change decreased significantly and the pace of change slowed. In response, the founding partners retreated to the design centre, as the firm began planning its next product line. This helped improve vision and direction, but the biggest jumps were in teamwork, accountability, and passion and drive. Moreover, awareness of the need for change was much higher than before, and people were much more involved in planning and implementing change. Even so, although teams had mobilized for change, they did not have the right team and business leadership to get them where they wanted to go.

Path 4: *moving to* Struggling under Pressure

On this pathway 12 per cent of groups follow the path to *Struggling under Pressure*. One example is a group of employees responsible for airport facilities. Their director was a proponent of lean practices, but was unfortunately out of touch with staff needs and requirements, just expecting team leaders to deliver. Those conditions, and resistance to some of the lean practices, led to a drop in performance and benefits and the amount of change, and increases in risks and roadblocks. People lost sight of the vision and direction in the midst of their day-to-day challenges – and emotional energy declined, leaving this group *Struggling under Pressure*.

Moving away from complacency

An overriding sense of complacency is the silent enemy in *Sleepy in Success*. In this capital city in the *On Track* zone, people have embraced the vision and direction of the change programme, but they lack the discipline, teamwork and accountability to implement it successfully. We learned in this chapter that the key to overcoming these obstacles is team leadership and the ability to translate 'soft' people issues into hard measurable outcomes. In Chapter 10, we focus on another capital city in the *On Track* zone: *Building Momentum*. There, groups face a crisis of confidence as they struggle to make progress against low levels of communication and leadership buy-in. As we shall see, although groups in *Building Momentum* have some similar characteristics to those in *Sleepy in Success*, the pathways to higher performance require quite different interventions.

SUMMARY FOR CHAPTER 9: KEY INSIGHTS

- Groups in *Sleepy in Success* understand and agree with the vision for change and there is a lot of change going on, but they lack the awareness of the need to change, and the teamwork and accountability to take advantage of the opportunities to lift performance much higher. Team leadership holds the key.

- Team leaders who have inherited or have been promoted into comfortable roles with little change experience are like stockbrokers who have only ever experienced a 'bull' market, and are thrown off balance by 'bear' conditions.

- Team leaders in *Sleepy in Success* are challenged to go beyond comfortable and conventional ways of doing things. The answers often come from dissatisfied team members and from looking closely at what has failed.

- Twenty-six per cent of groups do not make it out of *Sleepy in Success* – this is because team leaders lack the skills to increase accountability, communicate better and foster strong positive emotions while combating negative feelings.

- Replacing team leaders who do not have the natural temperament or innate capacity to lead – especially in toxic work groups – can have a dramatic impact on the performance of teams.

- Trust in team leaders dramatically improves when they have well-developed capabilities to lead change, regularly conduct performance management sessions and engage in frequent face-to-face communications with their teams.

- Trust in team leaders also improves when their business unit leaders take quick remedial actions to address identified problems, and when they actively support the changes taking place.

- Employee engagement surveys typically focus on the quality and strength of the relationship with one boss or supervisor – the equivalent of team leadership in our drivers. However, this is only one of the many critical factors that are needed to reach high performance and high levels of engagement.

- Performance management discussions work most effectively when staffers not only have conversations with their managers but, more importantly, when they set clear learning and development targets and take responsibility for them.

- Team leaders typically act as gatekeepers between their managers and their staff – they can either help or hinder change. Getting the right team leaders in place with the right skills and knowledge is one of the wisest investments that an organization can make.

- Strong business leadership plays an enormous part in transforming low levels of team leadership; the engine for change comes when team and business leaders work together synergistically.

Building Momentum
When good is not good enough to jump to the next level

10

> *Man is not the sum of what he has already, but rather the sum of what he does not yet have, of what he could have.*
> **JEAN-PAUL SARTRE**

Change at the financial services firm had been constant for three years, but midway into its transformation programme the company could not make the jump to the next level of performance. Initially, the firm had commenced its change journey because it was losing millions of dollars a year. At the time, transformation was necessary just to survive. Now, the business had not just survived but thrived. The business was profitable and staff had reason to feel excited about the new product streams and technologies that were coming on line for the first time. Moreover, the company had made fundamental changes to its communication strategy, focusing on direct face-to-face communication from people's managers, and had linked its bonus scheme to achieving engagement objectives as well as business targets. Consequently, morale had surged to a new high. Now, though, people were pushing back on further change. As one employee commented, 'We've been through the change... We've achieved what we aimed for... We've got performance up; we've got our profitability up... Isn't that enough?'

That feeling of having run out of steam and lacking the drive to continue pursuing aggressive targets is common for those in *Building Momentum*, a capital city of the *On Track* zone. For the 11 per cent of groups that find themselves there, a lack of leadership is the crucial issue as the change programme begins to stall. We first discussed the above financial services firm in Chapter 3, where we described how the company was eventually able to make it to the *High Performance* zone. In this chapter, we explain the various challenges the firm faced as it made its way along that difficult journey.

After a new CEO took over the reins at the company, good was simply not good enough. The board wanted a larger return on its investment in the transformation by strengthening the balance sheet and by managing the capital base. As such, executives pushed harder for results, but the organization responded by asking the senior leadership for more guidance, reassurance and direction. One frustrated business unit leader had this to say: 'You know, I'm not a messiah. You need to come up with the answers'. A standoff developed, with staffers looking to leaders and leaders looking to staffers for answers. There is an old Sufi expression that says, 'You can see the world in a grain of sand – if you know how to look'. Indeed, as so often happens with change programmes, the answers were there in front of the firm's leaders, but they failed to see them. In a survey of employees, one perceptive staff member at the company clearly stated what needed to be done, but her words were lost in the day-to-day urgency of getting things done. As she so accurately summarized, 'I have been encouraged by the clear efforts being made by the leadership team on this transformation to improve the working atmosphere. My view is that these actions are taking effect but there is still some way to go to fully regain trust, and in some instances a change in people's attitude is needed'.

Building Momentum insights

As we have seen in other regions in the *On Track* zone, leaders need to shift gears and motivate staffers with a sense of excitement for growth, rather than motivating them using fear. **Strong trust makes it safe for people to move forward with a sense of excitement**. It is important to note that leaders who push for results without recognizing the need to invest in building trust are simply spending the currency that has been saved in the 'trust bank'. Like any finite resource, trust can quickly become depleted and, when it has silently run out, leaders are left having to push harder and harder for results, ultimately getting less and less in return.

In our research, we have studied the drivers and impact of trust in organizations, and we have investigated the relationship between trust and leadership, specifically as it pertains to groups in *Building Momentum*. That analysis has led us to two key insights, the first having to do with leadership and the second relating to trust.

Insight 1: the linchpin of change is business unit leadership, not corporate or team leadership

Corporate executives often get the most publicity, while team leadership is typically lauded as the foundation for getting work done. Our research, however, clearly shows that the role that is the most important in implementing change lies elsewhere, with the business unit leaders, or divisional heads. These individuals, often sitting unnoticed between the corporate and team leadership, are the ones who have the most impact in delivering business benefits and ongoing improvements in performance. **Of all the drivers of change, business leadership has by far the most significant impact on benefits realization and business performance.** It has a major influence on almost all drivers, the exceptions being teamwork, accountability, and passion and drive. As it turns out, those three drivers are the primary responsibility of team leadership, which itself is driven by business leadership. Thus, in summary, nothing budges without first being pushed, even if indirectly, by business leadership.

In essence, business leaders act as the linchpin that brings into action those who are both 'above' and 'below' their level in the organization. As such, they require a complex set of skills for working with team leaders at one level, with entire teams at another level, and with senior executives at still another level where they must negotiate to get people the resources they need to implement the change programme effectively. This is squarely their responsibility. From the top down, business leaders must also translate the vision into terms that staffers can understand and, more importantly, embrace. If teams do not have the resources they need to do their job well, then that is a failure of leadership, especially at the business unit level. To be successful in these various roles, business leaders need a strong foundation of trust, particularly in times of change. This brings us to the second insight.

Insight 2: trust is important in one-to-one relationships, but that is only a portion of the overall trust picture

In organizations, trust is typically considered in one-to-one relationships, between leaders (trustees) and followers (trusters). Our research, however, has found that view of trust to be much too narrow. Our data indicates that the leader–follower relationship is only part of a much larger pattern of 'trust alignment' that successful organizations build, with very strong interdependencies and interconnectedness across and between all levels of leadership. Of course, the building of trust in one-to-one relationships is still important, but it is just a portion of the overall trust picture.

Our research shows that two of the most influential factors of trust for each level of leadership – corporate, business unit or team – are trust in the other two levels of leadership. In other words, trust begets trust begets trust, and change is successful when leaders across *all* levels of the organization focus their efforts and energies to achieve a common goal. The collective power of such trust alignment on business outcomes goes far beyond the power of what any single individual can achieve, regardless of how good a leader that person might be. Furthermore, to build such a 'trust grid', the most effective actions are different than those used to establish trust in individual relationships. That is, the trust grid does not arise from a series of specific actions between two individuals. Instead it is constructed from people primarily doing their jobs well: leaders (and followers) doing what they are supposed to be doing as part of their day-to-day business, at the same time as being deeply connected with the organization's core values.

Building, supporting and sustaining the invisible trust grid through all communications, actions and deeds are the real tasks of leaders in the most successful organizations. This involves not just focusing on leader–follower relationships but also on building trust across and between the different levels of leadership they interact with. Trust enables potential to be realized, both for individual staffers and for the company. The classic saying – 'the whole is more than the sum of the parts' – is applicable here.

Building momentum for change

For groups in *Building Momentum*, the vision is clear. People see the need for change; they know where they need to go; and they push to achieve benefits. But **groups in *Building Momentum* are held back by a lack of communication**

FIGURE 10.1   Change map and driver profile for *Building Momentum* region

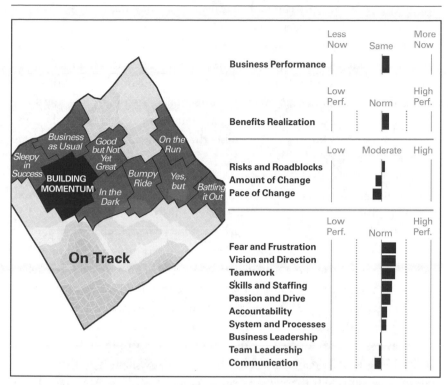

and low business and team leadership (see Figure 10.1). Systems and processes are close behind, but the crucial issue is the absence of leadership. That deficiency in the face of teams' high positive emotional energy and drive to succeed is a recipe for frustration, resulting in many staffers, including some of the best employees, thinking of leaving.

In *Building Momentum*, the pace and amount of change taking place are low. In fact, they are the lowest for any region in the *On Track* zone, particularly with respect to growth and new ways of working. This confirms people's perceptions that not much is happening. Over time, staffers start to wonder if the organization will provide the resources they need to succeed, or if they are simply going to be asked to do more with less. People want to succeed but are often stuck in roles that have become unsatisfying. To make matters worse, staffers are not getting the necessary support from above or the communication from their managers that is required to do their job. People in this region use language based on the present and future, with a strong focus on business and project objectives. Words such as 'targets', 'delivering', 'strengths', 'useful' and 'potential' are commonly used.

The danger here is that pressure can build up quickly and staffers can become critical of management. When that happens, the response from leaders is often to view the criticism as being negative. They miss seeing the staff wanting to be part of a larger agenda, and they are frustrated that team leaders are not doing their part to make that happen. The lack of information coming from face-to-face interactions with immediate supervisors doesn't help, as people are forced to rely on rumours. There is insufficient performance management and not enough managerial feedback. In addition, while some staffers are content doing a good job and want to leave things as they are, others aspire to reach towards becoming the best in class, possibly resulting in tension in the workplace.

Not surprisingly, **Building Momentum is the region in the *On Track* zone with the highest number of people who are thinking of leaving the organization.** This is not because the business is doing terribly – in fact, things are okay although not great. Instead, people are thinking of leaving because they just don't see that they can go any further in the company and they feel that their talents are going to waste. Questions that staffers frequently ask themselves include: 'Is this company doing things that are worthy of my staying here?' and 'Do our leaders have what it takes to get us where we're going?'

To better understand those dynamics, we analysed data from a human capital assessment conducted for one company in more than 50 countries. Of the 154,800 staff responses, 10,800 people subsequently left the organization. We found that there were distinct categories of the 'leavers' and we developed different risk profiles that organizations can use to predict the percentage of people at risk of jumping ship. Of the leavers in our dataset, 41 per cent quit because of poor relationships with their supervisors. This included three major categories. The first included younger staffers who were committed to the company's employee value proposition but had hit roadblocks in their career path. The second included experienced staffers with good performance ratings who were dissatisfied with their working conditions, job design and work–life balance. The third category included employees who clearly had mismatched expectations, feeling unsupported in their career and skill development, and were generally very negative across the board. In all three cases, people had strained relationships with their supervisors, of whom they were very critical.

From the total group of leavers, 38 per cent had received poor performance ratings, while the remaining 62 per cent had either been reviewed as having good performance or better. In fact, 23 per cent of the leavers had been rated highly. In other words, in an increasingly tight labour market with growing competition for talent, organizations are losing their most valuable assets – highly talented employees with great promise. Furthermore, when we look at where these leavers typically tend to be positioned on the change map, we found that many were in *Building Momentum*.

For their part, **team leaders in *Building Momentum* have difficulties with managing pressure and workload, and are often underskilled**. Many feel that their hands are tied by top management because of a lack of resources and scarcity of new opportunities. Without support from above, they find it increasingly difficult to make things happen. As we have seen in previous chapters, when business leaders recognize this dynamic and invest in coaching, training and performance management, they can provide the necessary stimulus for moving everyone forward. Given that passion and drive is well above the norm within teams in *Building Momentum*, the ongoing support from the business leadership for the team leader can be an extraordinarily powerful factor. To understand that dynamic, let's return to our example of the financial services firm.

How business leadership mobilized commitment to change

For that organization of close to 1,000 staff, it took about a year and a half to move from *Building Momentum* to *Cruising*. Looking at that business from the outside, we might think that not much happened during that time frame, but Figure 10.2 provides clues to indicate otherwise. The figure shows the positions of the five organizational levels – from the executive level (6 per cent of total staff), through business unit and team leaders (22 per cent) to team members (72 per cent) – on the change map across this phase of the transformation, from tracking periods 7 through 11. Note that all levels of leadership, for the most part, tended to align in *High Performance* (*Pushing the Limits*, *Cruising* and *Achieved with Loss of Heart*) during that time frame. In contrast, team members were stuck in *Building Momentum* until finally making it to *High Performance* (*Cruising*) in period 11.

These results were far from random or accidental. Behind the scenes, significant work had taken place to mobilize commitment and gain alignment across all levels of leadership, ultimately resulting in the entire business making it to the *High Performance* zone. Based on a further analysis of our database, the lesson was clear: **without strong alignment between leaders at all levels, the organization as a whole will fail to make the jump to the highest regions of the change map.**

FIGURE 10.2   Journey on the change map for a financial services firm and its various levels

	Period 7	Period 8	Period 9	Period 10	Period 11
Overall Organization	Building Momentum	Bumpy Ride	Building Momentum	Building Momentum	Cruising
Executive Team	Pushing the Limits	Cruising	Cruising	Cruising	Pushing the Limits
Divisional Heads	Cruising	Cruising	Yes, but	Cruising	Cruising
Business Unit Leaders	Achieved with Loss of Heart	Yes, but	Cruising	Cruising	Cruising
Team Leaders	Achieved with Loss of Heart	Yes, but	Cruising	Cruising	Cruising
Team Members	Building Momentum	Just Get On with It	Building Momentum	Building Momentum	Cruising

The financial services firm was among the select few – only 12 per cent – of all groups in *Building Momentum* that were able to make the jump to *High Performance*. That transition is perhaps one of the most difficult and least understood challenges of change leadership. Let's take a closer look at the role that each leadership level played in that successful transformation.

Different leadership roles

Team members, who made up the critical mass of the financial services firm, were initially positioned in *Building Momentum*, but then the top leadership mandated a worldwide cost-reduction programme to be implemented over a short time frame, with the local subsidiary having to reduce staff by 15 per cent. In Figure 10.2, the measurement at period 8 was taken a month after this was announced. Not surprisingly, team members had dropped into *Just Get On with It*, revealing an immediate negative hit on nearly all performance indicators. Specifically, the level of vision and direction had plunged, and people were no longer as confident in the business leadership as they had been. At the same time, the level of fear and frustration had risen.

Fortunately, the executive team's response helped turn that tide. As we have seen in earlier chapters, downsizing usually prompts much blame and anger among staff, and at such times leaders often become silent on the matter or they attempt to shift the blame: 'It's not our fault; it was industry and global pressures beyond our control'. The financial services firm, however, had realized the importance of keeping the communication channels open in order to maintain high trust levels. Among the measures undertaken to accomplish that, the executive team began to hold monthly lunchtime sessions called 'Let's Talk', which were open to the entire organization. During those meetings, people could ask questions about any issue and get answers. Emotions were running very high then and it would have been easy to avoid such difficult conversations, but the leadership resisted that temptation. In addition, senior executives directed their divisional and business unit leaders to conduct numerous face-to-face discussions. Thanks to management's eagerness to work through these staff issues, leaders were not only able to sustain employee trust but build on it. As a result, team members as a group bounced back quickly, returning to *Building Momentum*.

During this period, senior executives maintained their position in *High Performance*. They held their nerve and didn't panic, enabling them to take effective actions to keep the change programme on course. Specifically, they continued to invest in systems and processes and in building capability through leadership and management development programmes. Executives knew they needed to keep people focused and they took action to recommunicate the vision so that others would not lose sight of where they were headed. In addition, they pushed their recently trained managers and team leaders to deliver results in return for the investment they had made in coaching and training them.

Business unit and team leaders had a tougher task. At the start of period 7, these two levels of leaders were positioned in *Achieved with Loss of Heart*, after having expended considerable effort in the earlier phases of the transformation only to arrive feeling tired and undervalued. When the downsizing occurred, the business unit and team leaders were hit hard, losing staff with critical skills and knowledge. Consequently, they dropped down the change map into *Yes, but*.

To keep the change initiative from stalling, the divisional heads and business unit leaders replaced any underperforming team leaders. If a team had had three consecutive periods of poor results in positioning on the change map, and did not respond to the coaching they received, then serious questions were asked about its leader's capabilities. In that assessment, people management was considered to be equally important as achieving business targets. The result was that the business unit and team leaders quickly bounced back into *High Performance*, maintaining a position in *Cruising* for the next three periods.

The ripple effect of these actions can be seen in period 9 of Figure 10.2, when the divisional heads dropped into *Yes, but*. At this point, the divisional heads needed to recognize that, while they had been part of the solution, they had also become part of the problem. They realized that they had been micromanaging and usurping the authority of their direct reports and team leaders – behaviour that was antithetical to building capability. When they stopped doing that and became more confident in the trust they had built up, they bounced back into *Cruising* and sustained that level for the next two periods.

The crucial lesson here is that each leadership level had to face and resolve unique challenges to find the best way forward. In particular, the divisional heads and business unit leaders – denoted by the driver we refer to as 'business leadership' – played a critical role. Without their support for change and alignment across all levels, the team members would have found it impossible to make the jump to *High Performance*.

The vital role of business leadership in change initiatives

When implementing change, business leaders need to have the capacity to learn fast and make adjustments on the fly. They must also have the leadership agility to persevere under the pressure and the fast-moving actions required by the changes taking place. To measure business leadership, we ask everyone in a business unit leader's areas of responsibility to assess his or her capabilities in the following way:

- Does the business unit leader actively demonstrate support and commitment for the change process?
- Does he or she provide the appropriate levels of time and resources needed to ensure the change is successful?
- How confident and trusting are you in his or her leadership?
- How well is the change being managed?
- How responsive (quick and efficient) is the remedial action taken to address identified problems?

We then use these perceptions much like 360-degree feedback to build a clear picture of the business leadership.

After analysing that data, we found that **the main drivers of business leadership highlight that position's responsibilities both above and below in the organization. Overall, the top drivers of business leadership are vision and direction (which are the responsibility of top management), closely followed by team leadership.** In other words, to be successful, business leaders must help both the executives above in the organization as well as the team leaders below. Three other drivers follow with less impact: systems and processes, communication and the lowering of fear and frustration:

- *Vision and direction.* Some people see vision and direction merely as a fine collection of words, printed and placed in the reception foyer of large corporations, typically attributed to top management. Yet, **although it is the role of top management to formulate, communicate and hold true to the vision for change, it is the business leader's role to successfully implement that vision.** As we have seen in earlier chapters, when leaders and staff are aligned, there is an emotional commitment. Business leaders need to explain the vision to many audiences, in many different forums, and in myriad ways, constantly keeping the communication about the vision and direction up to date to gain buy-in. It also falls on them to communicate the benefits of the change to the audiences under their responsibility – especially the team leadership – continually refreshing and reinforcing that message and answering the key question, 'How will everyone be better off after all this?'

- *Team leadership.* The next-most powerful driver is team leadership, in which the business leader plays a key role. This highlights the fact that business and team leadership is the engine for effective change. Indeed, those business leaders who work closely with team leaders, united in action by the vision and direction, will be vastly more effective than those who lack such collaboration. It is the responsibility of business leaders to align teams so that everyone is pointed in the same direction, all headed towards a common purpose. When business leadership is strong, team roles, goals and outputs can all be in synch with the overall organizational vision and direction.

- *Systems and processes.* The business leadership is responsible for the higher-level systems and processes, including knowledge management tools, customer feedback mechanisms and so on. It is the job of business leadership to ensure that those systems and processes are functional and, when there is a problem, to implement fixes with minimal delay. Failure to do so could be viewed by staffers as a lack of support from the business leadership, which could adversely affect people's trust and confidence in management. Effective business leaders help remove risks and roadblocks, especially in situations where the team leader does not have the power to do so. In particular, allocating task forces and resources to resolve issues that are inter-team rather than intra-team is a necessary but often neglected part of that role.

- *Communication.* We have discussed in previous chapters how communication is typically a standalone driver that has little impact on other drivers. In the case of business leadership, though, communication is the fourth most powerful influence because of the linkages between business leadership, team leadership, systems and processes, and vision and direction. These linkages are supported by huge amounts of written and in-person information, presented through many different channels, and to a wide variety of audiences. **Effective business leadership plays a role that is essentially about networks, linkages and connections – how much teams rely on one another, and how each team's outcome affects other teams' outcomes**. The role of business leadership is to ensure that teams understand those connections, including the overall link to the big picture that is painted by the vision and direction.

- *Fear and frustration.* Finally, business leadership must constantly monitor the emotional climate for signs of unchecked fear and frustration. This is particularly vital in groups and teams at the lower levels of performance, because negative emotions tend to block people from embracing the vision. Even at the higher levels of performance, the managing of fear and frustration cannot be taken for granted, and the business leadership must always foster a climate of support. Staffers should not have to fight processes or systems in order to do their jobs. Nor should they have to risk safety, quality or the organization's reputation to meet their performance goals.

On a more strategic level, **business leadership has three interrelated and interacting roles: to align and gain commitment to the vision; to mobilize the power of teams in making change happen; and to link and join across and between groups,** building strong value chains that connect people and systems and processes to business outcomes. When performed effectively,

FIGURE 10.3 Effect of business leadership on benefits realization

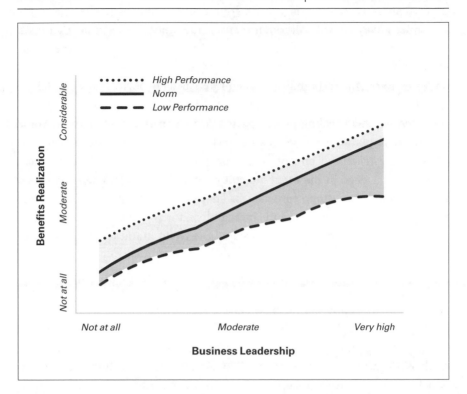

the role of business leadership can have a significant impact on benefits realization for both the norm and high-performing groups (Figure 10.3). The impact for low-performing groups is less, but still significant. As we saw in Chapters 4 through 6, it is the team leadership that makes the most significant impact in low-performing groups and the business leader's role is to enable that to happen through effective policies and procedures.

Building business leadership capability

Given the crucial importance of business leadership, how should organizations go about building that capability? In our research, we have found that one of the most important ingredients is building trust. Trust and improved performance follow from the perception that leadership is taking quick remedial action and addressing risks and roadblocks in implementing the change. As a result, business performance improves and benefits realization increases. People connect the decisive leadership action to these improved outcomes, and trust builds. This begins a virtuous cycle of action–performance–trust. This is reflected in other research studies (see, for example, Covey, 2008). Although many leaders understand that there is a clear linkage between building trust and achieving sustainable business outcomes, they are much less certain on how to build trust in the first place, and how to regain and rebuild it when it has been broken.

When leaders receive feedback from their organization that trust is low, we often see them feeling powerless in the face of that information. Some will try to explain away the lack of trust with blanket statements such as, 'Well, we restructured and of course people didn't like it'. We have seen, however, that **even in the most difficult downsizings leaders can still retain trust and even strengthen core values**. That said, trust is perhaps one of the toughest issues to discuss, and the intangible nature of trust makes it difficult to take action on. Knowing what to do, how to do it and when to do it are among the least understood – yet potentially most powerful – interventions that organizations can make.

The literature offers some guidance. According to one model (Hurley, 2006), trust depends on various factors, including the risk-tolerance and relative power of the 'truster'. Another framework (Covey, 2008) lists the specific behaviours of leaders who typically inspire trust in followers, such as demonstrating respect, displaying loyalty, delivering results, and so on. Much of the literature focuses on teaching people how to build trust in one-to-one relationships. That capability is certainly essential as trust ultimately resides within the relationships between people. The danger, though, is that it can lead to a myopic view that fails to consider how organizations also need to establish a 'trust grid' by building trust across and between the different levels of leadership.

The drivers of trust at each level of leadership

In our research, we ask three questions that directly examine the question of trust at different levels of the organization:

- Corporate leadership: *How confident and trusting are you in the leadership of the executive team?*
- Business unit leadership: *How confident and trusting are you in the leadership of your business unit manager?*
- Team leadership: *How confident and trusting are you in your immediate supervisor's/boss's leadership?*

Using that data, we can test our assumptions about trust, and investigate how it might differ between the three hierarchical levels, how the relationship between the leadership levels tends to play out, and how one level of leadership can help other levels in building trust.

Trust in corporate leadership

Taking the highest level first, we find that trust in corporate leaders is primarily driven by emotional agreement with the vision, evident realization of the change benefits, and people's confidence that changes will lead to improvement in business performance in the future. This is the core responsibility of top management. Furthermore, corporate leadership is equally driven by trust and confidence in the business unit leadership. This means that senior executives cannot simply focus on individual actions to build others' trust in them; they must also consider how they can help business unit leaders to build strong trust and confidence with their respective staffs. In other words, if trust is low in the business leadership, then corporate executives will also get tarred with the same brush.

In addition, our analysis shows that the next most important set of drivers of trust in corporate leadership are, in fact, the same actions that need to be taken primarily by business unit leaders to build trust. Specifically, **senior executives help build trust through ensuring that the leaders reporting to them effectively manage change by visibly providing time and resources to support the change, by actively demonstrating support and commitment for the change and, most importantly, by taking quick remedial actions to solve problems**. On an organization-wide basis, corporate leadership holds the responsibility for staff reward and recognition, for nurturing passion and drive, and for supporting the change effort with written information. As we have seen, passion and drive are intimately linked to the strength of core organizational values – which are also the responsibility of senior executives who must nurture and build those values. Trust in corporate leaders is high when the level of risks, roadblocks and rumours are low, indicating that it is their job to address those issues. Any failure to do so will have a negative impact on how the broader organization will view their leadership.

Trust in business unit leadership

Moving to the next level, we find that **the number one driver of trust in business unit leadership is trust in corporate leadership. This highlights the fact that the top two trust levels are intimately connected.** Business unit leadership can reinforce trust in corporate leadership by doing its part to ensure that staffers understand and, more importantly, emotionally agree with the vision; that they recognize the importance of realizing the benefits of change; and that they are confident that the change will improve the performance of their business. The next drivers of trust in business unit leaders are actions that are primarily within their control. Business unit leaders build trust by visibly providing support, time and resources, and by taking quick remedial actions to solve identified problems.

Our analysis also shows that **trust and confidence in team leadership is a key driver of trust in business leadership**. Just as corporate leaders need to help business unit leaders be successful and vice versa, the same dynamic plays out between business unit leaders and team leaders. Moreover, business unit leaders have an important responsibility for reward and recognition in the areas that they oversee, in much the same way as corporate leaders are responsible for organization-wide recognition and reward. Every level, including team leadership, must manage a portion of this responsibility according to its span of control.

Trust in team leadership

When it comes to team leaders, our analysis shows that they can build others' trust and confidence in them by setting the example in implementing change. First and foremost, **team leaders need to effectively lead change by building and mobilizing people's commitment, by carrying out performance management with staffers on a regular basis, and by ensuring that their teams receive high levels of face-to-face communication**. Team leaders are ideally placed to clarify the roles of each staff member, especially as those roles evolve throughout the change initiative. Utilizing the talents of team members, often in adapting to new roles, not only lowers the level of distress and fear, it also helps build trust. In addition, trust is built through good teamwork, which is also the responsibility of team leaders.

Our analysis also shows that an important driver of trust in team leaders is trust and confidence in the business unit leadership and, to a much lesser extent, the corporate leadership. In turn, team leaders can support trust in leaders at other levels by acting quickly to solve problems and by demonstrating support and commitment for the change programme. These complex interdependencies are reflected in our leadership trust grid.

The leadership trust grid

One of our most important findings is the degree to which organizational trust is interconnected, with each level of leadership highly interactive with – and dependent on – the other two. As such, trust levels cannot be considered in isolation from one another. From a regression tree analysis of our data, confirmed by SEM, we were able to detect the pattern of interactions and interdependencies that we have labelled the 'leadership trust grid' (Figure 10.4).

In the grid, the overall trust in an organization is held together in an interrelated series of actions. In combination, those actions develop confidence in staffers that management knows what it is doing, is responsive to their needs, and is willing and ready to provide support to help every person bring about change. The synergistic effect of such collective actions goes well beyond what is possible from any single level of leadership working in isolation from the others.

FIGURE 10.4   The leadership trust grid

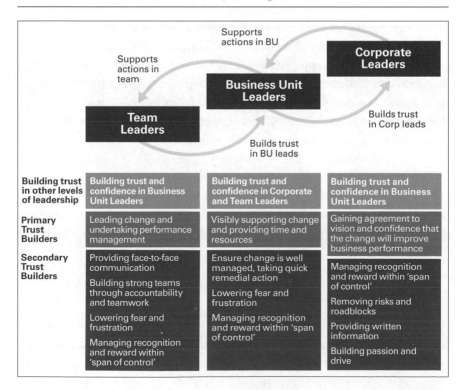

Moreover, our research shows that leadership trust flourishes when leaders go beyond their own duties and help other leaders around them. This is where organizations can tap into the real power and synergy of the trust grid. It is also important to note the mutual nature of different relationships. For instance, when a team leader does his or her job well, the staff confidence and trust in that person will grow. When staffers do their jobs well, the team leader is able to delegate with confidence and can trust that work will get done well without the need to micromanage.

For the most part, the trust grid remains invisible to staffers, yet it is the glue that holds everything together, enabling the organization to run smoothly. In the example of the financial services firm, we saw the importance of leaders leading from the front, not from behind. In remaining calmly strategic, those leaders were able to establish the conditions for others to take charge of their own destiny, much like creating a low-pressure area on the top of an aircraft's wings, such that the plane is 'pulled up' by the resulting lift rather than 'pushed up'. In Chapter 8, we saw how the most successful organizations are able to gain high emotional agreement to the vision, which equates to considerable trust in top management, before people have a full understanding of where they are going or how they are going to get there. Only an environment of high trust can enable that kind of uplift.

Unfortunately, the trust grid is often taken for granted until it disappears. When that happens, the results can be devastating. Vision evaporates, leaving people with no sense of purpose and direction coming from top management. Business unit leaders ignore problems in their operations while the change initiative slides completely off the agenda. Team leaders flounder without the skills to build strong teams, and accountability in any shape or form is non-existent. When it comes to reward and recognition, the overriding goal is simply to get ahead in the organization, as any collective effort to accomplish a non-existent vision is now meaningless. Barriers go up where there is no logical reason for them to be there. Across the organization as a whole, self-entitlement and political interests dominate the change agenda. In such an environment, competent leaders struggle to function, as the alignment between leadership levels collapses or is distorted by strong factional interests.

Patterns of leadership trust

As groups move around the change map, they experience different patterns of trust interplay among the three leadership levels. Figure 10.5 shows the benchmarked trust patterns – for the corporate, business unit and team leadership levels – for each of the capital cities along with their corresponding strength in benefits realization and business performance. The patterns indicate

FIGURE 10.5 Trust in the capital cities across the three leadership levels

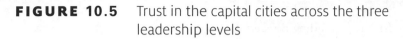

	Trust across different levels	Benefits Realization	Business Performance
	Norm	Norm	Same
Cruising	■ Trust in corporate leaders ■ Trust in business unit leaders ■ Trust in team leaders		
On the Run			
Building Momentum			
Sleepy in Success			
In the Dark			
Yes, but			
Struggling under Pressure			
Just Get On with It			
Case for Action			

varying trust levels that have different impacts on various aspects of a change initiative, including the people who are both involved in the change and are trying to deliver performance for the daily business as well.

When all trust levels are low, as in *Case for Action*, the impact can be measured in terms of unrealized benefits and the loss of business performance due to the disruption from poorly implemented change. In this case, not only has the change failed to materialize as intended, it has also caused significant collateral damage to the existing business. In *Just Get On with It*, corporate and business unit trust levels are much lower than trust in team leaders. As we discussed in Chapter 5, effective interventions involve restoring trust in corporate and business leaders, as well as working with core values to generate strong passion and drive. In *Struggling under Pressure*, team leadership suffers, as its trust level is out of alignment with the other two levels, requiring support from upper management to rebuild the capability and trust in team leaders.

Throughout the regions of *On Track*, differences across levels are most pronounced. In *Yes, but*, alignment across all levels is high but, as we saw in Chapter 7, trust is not the issue – it is the lack of resources that is the issue. For *In the Dark* groups, low trust in corporate leadership is connected directly with a low agreement to the vision, adversely affecting benefits realization. In *Sleepy in Success*, low trust in team leaders prevents team members from really grasping the opportunities for change. As we outlined in Chapter 9, corporate and business leaders need to step in and help out by building trust in the team leader's capability to make change happen.

Making the move into *High Performance* requires an alignment of high trust at all levels. In the example of the financial services firm that we discussed earlier in this chapter, business unit leaders' trust in corporate leadership leapt nearly 50 per cent, and team leaders' trust in corporate leaders jumped 30 per cent across the transition period. The trust of team leaders in their bosses also increased, while team members' trust in corporate leaders increased 23 per cent. Collectively, this greater trust and alignment among leadership levels helped create the 'lift' that pulled the firm into *High Performance*.

Recognizing these patterns of trust and taking actions to correct any misalignments are the keys to tapping into some of the deepest and most powerful insights in organizational change. This responsibility is the mandate of leaders and, with the right actions, they can rebuild and strengthen the trust grid across and between different levels. Successfully accomplishing that trust will lead to a flow of benefits, not just to the individuals involved – whether they are leaders or followers – but also to the organization and change programme as a whole.

Unlocking the trust dynamic in *Building Momentum*

The big question, then, is how can groups in *Building Momentum* use these findings to move into higher regions on the change map? At the start of the chapter, we mentioned that staffers in this region are more than ready to deploy their skills, knowledge and experience, and they are aware of the need for change. The problem, though, is that they feel that their talents and capabilities are not being fully utilized. From the leaders' perspective, this is essentially a 'free' resource just waiting to be tapped, if only they knew how.

As we have seen from our analysis, trust is a powerful enabler because it improves not just the quality of a single one-to-one relationship. **When leadership trust across a company is aligned at high levels, the resulting grid of relationships can provide a single individual with access to the resources, expertise and experience of potentially thousands of people throughout the organization,** opening up enormous opportunities for that person to realize his or her full potential. It is the responsibility of leaders to create that environment.

In *Building Momentum*, the strength of trust in business unit leadership is insufficient to establish such optimal conditions, and the relatively low level of team leadership does not help matters. Rebuilding alignment in the trust grid is the responsibility of all leaders. In the best-case scenario, business unit leaders in *Building Momentum* are aware of the challenges involved and seize the opportunity to make change happen. When that doesn't happen, though, it will fall on the senior executives to take action. Ideally, business unit leaders would be working with corporate execs to build trust, while team leaders also do their part in building the trust and confidence of their team members.

From the example earlier in this chapter, we saw how senior executives can take the lead in rebuilding trust alignment. Those executives worked closely with divisional heads, which then helped business unit leaders to manage change more effectively. This, in turn, helped team leaders to build strength in their teams. In other words, if a leader wants his or her managers to build trust with their staffers, he or she must first invest in building trust with those managers.

At the financial services firm in our example, the senior executives were initially the only level that looked to the longer-term sustainability and viability of the organization itself. Along with their divisional heads, the first step they took was to work closely with business unit leaders to establish a mindset for which institutionalizing the change was just as important as fixing immediate problems. Then, after supporting that mindset shift with the necessary capability-building and resourcing, they ensured that the business unit leaders had the competence in the critical skills required to instill confidence across the teams. The goal was to establish that leaders understood what had to be done, and that they had a viable plan for moving the organization forward.

All of this required a good deal of empathy, first on the part of senior leaders. Because trust is a reciprocal quality – 'I can't trust you if you don't trust me' – the top execs had to trust their business leaders to get on with their jobs, and in doing so they broadened the trust grid to include lower levels of the organizational hierarchy. This, however, was not blind trust. The senior leaders sought and acted on feedback, whether through 'management by walking around' or through more formal methods such as staff surveys and organizational climate questionnaires. Poor performance was not tolerated, and leaders who consistently demonstrated a bad track record were replaced. **When it comes to trust, people are always watching what leaders and supervisors do with underperforming employees. If they say one thing but then do something else, the trust grid will suffer.** As such, leaders need to act predictably and consistently, especially when applying policies, procedures and rules.

Common pathways exiting *Building Momentum*

Nineteen per cent of groups get stuck in *Building Momentum*, unable to adequately address issues of lack of communication and, most importantly, business and team leadership. Let's take a closer look at the common pathways leading out of *Building Momentum* (Figure 10.6). We discuss each of those pathways below, highlighting some case examples in more depth. (Note: most of the examples in this section represent a composite of organizations from our research with similar experiences of change.)

Path 1: moving to Cruising and Good but Not Yet Great

On this path 5 per cent of groups move from *Building Momentum* to *Good but Not Yet Great* and another 7 per cent travel to *Cruising*. For the financial services firm discussed in this chapter, the move to *High Performance* was

FIGURE 10.6   Common pathways exiting *Building Momentum*

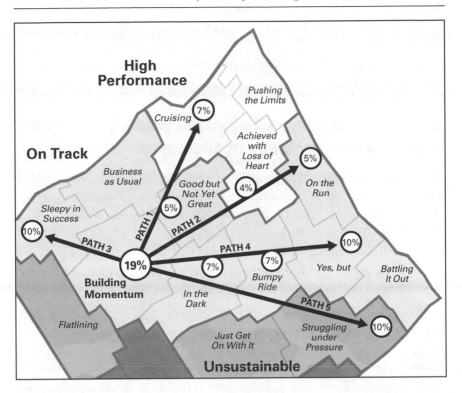

achieved through a huge jump in communication, and team and business leadership. In addition, fear and frustration dropped, and risks and roadblocks were eliminated, even while the amount and pace of change increased. People wanted to be part of a more dynamic and progressive organization – and got it. The key was greater alignment and increased trust across the levels of leadership, resulting in a significant boost in performance and benefits.

Path 2: moving to Achieved with Loss of Heart *and* On the Run

On this pathway 9 per cent of groups in *Building Momentum* move upward and to the right of the change map, with 4 per cent moving to *Achieved with Loss of Heart* and 5 per cent ending up in *On the Run*. As we discuss in Chapter 11, when groups move along this path, things start to heat up. For example, a worldwide reorganization at a global paper and packaging firm had been going on for 18 months when the company picked up the amount and pace of change dramatically. The firm chose its best managers to drive the change, improving business leadership. Passion and drive bubbled throughout the renewed organization, and fear and frustration levels dropped. However, the benefits of growth and improved performance were at risk, as groups lacked adequate resources. Additionally, discipline was needed to maintain the cohesion among team members and, in the rush to cross the finish line, leaders forgot that they needed to keep communicating, landing the firm in *On the Run*.

Path 3: *moving to* Sleepy in Success

On this path, 10 per cent of groups move to the adjacent region *Sleepy in Success*. For example, an agricultural organization formed through a number of small cooperatives caused substantial disruption. Teamwork and accountability dropped substantially, leading to a loss of passion and drive. In addition, the former cooperatives were less involved in the change as the greater amount and pace of change outran them. While performance and benefits were maintained, people could no longer make change happen fast and flexibly.

Path 4: *moving to* Yes, but, Bumpy Ride *and* In the Dark

On this pathway 7 per cent of groups land in *In the Dark*, another 7 per cent in *Bumpy Ride* and 10 per cent wind up in *Yes, but*. A national betting organization undertook the latter path, experiencing rapid growth due to its early adoption of internet betting. Executive leadership, highly savvy in new technology, boosted communication and chose the right team leaders and business leaders for the job. The vision had become clearer, and promised benefits were being delivered. However, groups were challenged with a lack of resources to implement all the refurbishments from manual systems. Staffers struggled to keep delivering results, while business and team leaders managed as best they could, but everyone found it increasingly difficult to make headway.

Path 5: *moving to* Struggling Under Pressure

On this path, 10 per cent of groups drop down to *Struggling under Pressure*. Such was the case for a consortium of real-estate developers that switched from face-to-face customer contact to more online transactions. Even as the new technology was being implemented, the vision and direction for doing so was not clear to teams. Consequently, teamwork plunged and accountability decreased, and people struggled to hold things together. The pressure was on the business unit leaders to stabilize the situation and build team leadership capabilities.

The trust grid and organizational flexibility

In this chapter we focused on *Building Momentum*, a capital city of the *On Track* zone, where groups struggle with a lack of both business unit and team leadership. For a better understanding of such issues, we introduced the 'trust grid', which describes the interdependencies of the three major hierarchical levels of leadership in an organization: corporate, business unit and team. In the next chapter, we turn our attention to *On the Run* and discuss the drivers of growth and new ways of working. We see from our research that having a strong trust grid enables flexibility and greater control in a rapidly changing environment, dramatically improving the quality of decision-making. This is especially important when the pace of change dramatically increases the speed of decision-making and the corporate vision becomes much more obscure, forcing groups to pilot through a thick cloud rather than clear skies.

SUMMARY FOR CHAPTER 10: KEY INSIGHTS

- In *Building Momentum*, the lack of communication and low business and team leadership in the face of highly motivated teams is a recipe for frustration. They risk losing their most valuable assets – highly talented employees with great potential. Focusing on these areas will unlock this dynamic.

- Leaders who push for results without recognizing the need to invest in building trust to take the organization further are simply wasting the 'trust currency' they already had 'saved in the bank'.

- Business leadership has by far the most significant impact on benefits realization and business performance. It has a major influence on almost all drivers, the exceptions being teamwork, accountability, and passion and drive. Those three drivers are the primary responsibility of team leadership, which itself is driven by business leadership.

▶

- One of our most important findings is the degree to which organizational trust is interconnected, with each level of leadership – corporate, business unit and team – highly interactive with and dependent on the other two. Trust begets trust begets trust – and the synergistic effect of collective leadership action goes well beyond what is possible from a single level of leadership acting in isolation from the others.

- The trust grid does not arise from a series of specific actions between two individuals. Instead, it is constructed from people primarily doing their day-to-day jobs well while remaining deeply connected with the organization's core values.

- Trust in corporate leaders is primarily driven by emotional agreement with the vision and evident benefits realization, followed by trust in business unit leaders.

- Trust in business unit leaders is driven by trust in corporate leadership, as well as actions that are primarily within their control – visibly providing support and taking quick remedial actions. Trust in team leaders is also an important driver.

- Trust in team leaders is driven by the need to build skills and capabilities, effectively lead change, and lower fear and anger in their teams. Managing upwards, trust and confidence in business unit leaders are an important driver of trust in team leaders.

- Unfortunately, the trust grid is often taken for granted until it disappears, but successful organizations are able to spot misalignments well in advance and 'self-correct', mobilizing other levels of leadership to build alignment where trust in one level is low. Correcting such misalignments is one of the most difficult things to do, but doing so will reap substantial dividends when implementing change.

- When leadership trust across an organization is aligned at high levels, the resulting grid of relationships can provide a single individual with access to the resources, expertise and experience of potentially thousands of people throughout the organization, opening up enormous opportunities for that person to realize his or her full potential.

On the Run
Keep it together when the goal is rapid growth

... mental health is based on a certain degree of tension, the tension between what one has already achieved and what one still ought to accomplish, or the gap between what one is and what one should become. Such a tension is inherent in the human being and therefore is indispensable to mental well-being. We should not, then, be hesitant about challenging man with a potential meaning for him to fulfill.

VIKTOR E FRANKL

In the fast-paced environment of this biotechnology startup, the fundamental challenge for the new directors was to manage rapid growth. Since its founding, the firm had hit the ground running: 14 colleagues had made the move from the academic world; researchers had discovered new biomolecular techniques that held great promise; and initial funding allowed the scientific projects to be undertaken. Within the first year, the startup had 35 staff spread across various cities and countries but, as the firm continued its rapid growth, it began to encounter a number of challenges. The major stakeholder that was funding research required adherence to tight commercial milestones, and greater accountability and control were needed to integrate work practices across newly acquired research groups. Moreover, the directors needed to build a culture where innovation could blossom and grow, all while managing everything else that needed to get done, including recruiting top talent and structuring and organizing the startup for its planned initial public offering (IPO).

When we tracked the biotech startup at the end of its first year, we found that the firm was positioned in *On the Run*, the last of five capital cities in the *On Track* zone. This region is characterized by fast-paced change and rapid growth. In fact, with the exception of groups in *Pushing the Limits*, those in *On the Run* have the highest amounts of change taking place – in particular, with respect to growth and new ways of working. In *On the Run*, people understand and agree with the company direction; they have high confidence in leadership; they feel valued and are not thinking of leaving; and they are very involved in making change happen. In short, change is exciting and everything seems to be headed in the right direction. Yet, in the rush to reach ambitious targets, groups have much to accomplish and it can be difficult for everyone to hold things together.

At the biotech startup, the director found himself asking the same question that the CEOs and programme managers in much larger organizations often struggle with: 'How much change can my organization absorb without falling apart, and what happens when we ramp up the pace?' These leaders are torn between the desire to meet marketplace expectations as quickly as possible, and the need to ensure that staffers do not become overwhelmed or simply burnt out from too much change, too quickly. In juggling these conflicting demands, they wonder how close to the edge they can go without the organization plunging off the cliff. Although only 4 per cent of groups reside in *On the Run*, the region holds the keys to understanding how to manage high amounts of change at a fast pace – a vital capability for any agile organization.

On the Run insights

Our research clearly shows that organizations with the best business performance and benefits realization are also the ones that have the greatest amount of change taking place at a fast pace. This, however, does not simply mean that leaders should ramp up the volume and pace of change to attain better outcomes. Indeed, our research results have shown that change affects different groups in vastly different ways, leading us to two important insights about the very nature of change, the first comparing high-performing versus low-performing groups and the second concerning the capacity to increase the amount and pace of change.

Insight 1: high-performing groups thrive on change; low-performing groups stumble on it

When comparing high-performing and low-performing organizations the former have more change taking place, they manage it better and they gain greater benefits from it. In fact, our research shows that high-performing groups have 30–50 per cent more change taking place than lower-performing groups, and they continually improve their capacity to manage change as the amount of it ramps up. By contrast, low-performing groups initially improve their capacity to manage change with an increased amount of change, but then this trend quickly levels off and rapidly declines in the face of more and more change.

When the amount of change is plotted against benefits realization, that relationship follows very similar patterns (see Figure 11.1). This is not surprising, given that these two factors are highly correlated. In high-performing groups, benefits start from a high base, even with little change taking place, and they keep increasing as the amount of change rises. In

FIGURE 11.1   Well-managed change versus the amount of change

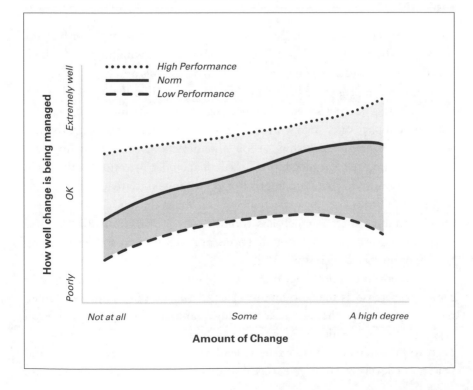

contrast, low-performing groups start from a low base of benefits that ramps up when change starts to happen but then quickly levels off and drops away.

When it comes to increasing the pace of change, again the same patterns repeat themselves. Instinctively, one would think that staffers would be worse off with an increased pace of change, yet our research shows that this is not the case for high-performing groups. Like well-trained athletes, they build up the capacity to run faster and longer without being rendered breathless and incapacitated. As we saw in Chapter 3, their ability to manage change peaks not when the pace of change is 'just faster than okay' but when it is 'too fast'. Business leadership, clear vision and direction, and low levels of fear and frustration hold the keys to remaining on track when things speed up. All the evidence shows that the ability to manage change in low-performing groups starts dropping when the pace gets faster than 'okay'. **Low performers simply cannot support or sustain high amounts of change taking place at a fast pace**.

Insight 2: a sufficient capacity to manage change is required before increasing the amount and pace of change

An accelerated amount and pace of change will deliver business benefits more quickly, but the process is like racing a car on a winding road at high speed. The negative consequences of poor driving skills and capabilities will be all the more pronounced, and evidenced faster, than if the vehicle were travelling at a slower speed. Similarly, when organizations ramp up the amount and pace of change without also building the necessary capabilities – stronger business leadership, vision and direction, communication and teamwork (and team leadership to lower fear and frustration) – they will lack the stability to maintain control of the change initiative and will consequently fail to realize the expected benefits. When the amount and pace of change are high there is much less room for error, and it falls on business leaders to ensure that their organizations are well prepared *before* putting their foot on the accelerator.

It is important to note that our research shows that fear and frustration typically increase as the amount and pace of change ramps up. Even when people agree with the vision for change, apprehension and disruption typically become widespread among staffers, presenting difficulties that need to be overcome. Wise business leaders keep a close eye on fear and frustration levels when they venture into this territory. Even when things are going well, as we will see later in this chapter, they prepare far in advance for what could potentially go wrong and are prepared to take action on small signs and symptoms, long before big problems occur.

On the Run – a lot of change at a fast pace

Groups in *On the Run* have the capacity to manage a great amount of change at a fast pace, thanks to low levels of fear and frustration and high levels of business leadership, vision and direction, teamwork, passion and drive, team leadership and accountability (see Figure 11.2). In this capital city, people want to be challenged and they strive to do their best. As one staffer remarked, 'We need more challenge to keep our sharp edge from dulling'.

For those in *On the Run*, trust in organizational leadership is very high, with trust in business unit leadership and team leadership following close behind. This trust across all levels enables the organization the flexibility to

FIGURE 11.2   Change map and driver profile for *On the Run* region

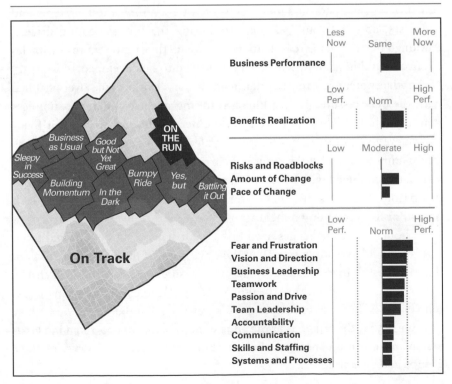

change direction quickly, and this is where the real power to change comes from for groups in *On the Run*.

Another key strength in this region is that people are able to maintain low levels of anger, distress and fear, even given the amount and pace of change taking place. In fact, the levels of those negative emotions are among the lowest compared with other regions on the change map, defying the assumption that fear and frustration must necessarily increase as the amount of change and pace ramp up. This, along with high vision and direction, and strong business leadership, is the reason why groups can improve business performance and realize significant benefits from their change initiatives.

In *On the Run*, people are quite passionate about the change programme, binding together in good teamwork. They talk about 'cooperation', 'collaboration' and 'sharing', but in the same sentence they refer to 'achieving', 'increasing' and the fear of 'losing' or 'missing deadlines'. In terms of a psychological mindset, people are ready for more change. They see that the vision just ahead of them is almost in their grasp, and they want to get there, although they may lack the necessary operational skills and resources. Leaders expect much from team members, and they in return have high expectations of their leaders.

The downside in these situations is that role clarity and accountability can suffer. In fact, accountability along with communication, systems and processes, and skills and staffing are among the lowest scoring drivers. Although these drivers are well above the norm, they represent the obstacles to success and indicate where capabilities need to be developed.

Another potential danger is that team leaders can become overwhelmed with the job pressure and workload, resulting in their communicating less than they should. This can leave teams vulnerable to narrowing their focus to achieve only short-term objectives. Indeed, the connection between the 'big picture' vision and the reality of carrying out daily tasks can easily be lost. This, combined with a lack of role clarity, can fuel conflict, rivalries and turf battles. Team members might, for example, blame each other for a lack of skill or for letting down the team.

Although these challenges need to be dealt with at an operational level, leaders should avoid focusing all of their attention in that direction. Instead, their real task is to maintain a crystal-clear business strategy that will ensure the organization remains in a 'healthy state' – able to continually renew and reinvent itself in order to sustain ongoing growth. **On the Run is somewhat unusual in that the region is at the edge of high performance, requiring leaders to make more conscious choices about the future pathways of their groups and organizations.**

Making choices

In our discussion of the other capital cities, we considered upward movement on the change map as generally good, but that is not necessarily the case for those in *On the Run*. When organizations like the biotech startup are investing in rapid growth, simply maintaining their position in *On the Run* can be the optimal goal. After all, the only way to move higher on the change map is to journey into *Pushing the Limits* and, as we have seen in Chapter 3, this brings the challenge of staying on top of Everest – a very difficult position to maintain. On the other hand, moving sideways on the change map has other drawbacks. In *Cruising*, life becomes more comfortable – a stronger overall driver strength with a decrease in the amount and pace of change – but performance and benefits drop. In *Achieved with Loss of Heart*, groups run the risk of burning out good employees. Lastly, going down the change map might be an option for some business leaders but not for those with aggressive growth targets. Yet even simply maintaining a position in *On the Run* has its fair share of challenges, not the least of which is the difficulty for staffers to keep up with a high level and pace of change over a long period of time.

When we revisited the biotech startup towards the end of the second year of its operations, staying in *On the Run* had become the goal. With a staff of 64, the company had grown and continued to flourish. Thanks to additional funding, it had launched its first product, and leaders had continued to focus on building a culture of innovation. Performance and benefits showed improvements, and the startup had consolidated its position higher up in the region. People were managing many different types of change inside and outside the company as they worked collaboratively with other larger organizations in different countries, resulting in a dramatic increase in the pace of change.

Meanwhile, new funding had enabled the company to improve much-needed systems and processes and to recruit additional staff. A performance management system was also put in place, which helped increase the level of accountability – something that the startup had struggled with from the beginning. All in all, people were excited about what they were doing and where they were headed, resulting in a rise in passion and drive and a decrease in fear and frustration to very low levels.

There were, however, some rough spots. While the levels of business leadership slightly improved, vision and direction dropped (although the level was still very high) and communication fell much further. It seemed that managers and team leaders were too busy to sit down with their staffers to keep them regularly informed, making the classic mistake of assuming that everyone already knew what was going on. This lack of communication posed a significant challenge to future growth. 'Changing too fast may mean we can miss a potential problem', noted one staffer. 'Some people think we are still in a university and unless we become a service-orientated business, keeping our commitments and deadlines, we will miss the opportunities we have.'

The overall strategy at the biotech startup was to list the company in an IPO and then, at a later point when the business had proven its worth, to divest it to a larger player in the market. As such, rapid growth was clearly a vital component of the strategy. Inside large organizations, with many moving parts all undergoing various types of change at different stages, the reasons for amplifying the volume and pace of change are not always as clear-cut. Indeed, surprisingly very little is understood about how business outcomes are delivered from the standpoint of increased change, and the impact it has on people. This leads us to the tale below of two organizations that dealt with rapid change in strikingly different ways.

Two organizations, two trajectories

Although groups arrive in *On the Run* with a great deal of change already taking place at a fast pace, they typically start their acceleration in other regions. Understanding how and why some groups make it to *On the Run* while others don't provides key insights into the capacities needed to successfully manage considerable change. To that end, we analysed the change programmes at two organizations as they ramped up the volume of change, in order to see how the decisions leaders made sent them on different trajectories. What is interesting in the two cases – both inside large organizations – is that they each started their acceleration in the same region on the change map, both experienced a similar ramp up in the overall amount and pace of change (within 10 per cent of each other on average scores), and yet they each ended in very different regions on the change map.

The first change programme was a major business transformation in the retail arm of a government services organization. With more than 1,000 branches serving more than 300,000 clients daily, the retail arm was losing money and the business objectives for the change programme included increased revenues, decreased costs and the better management of both. In addition, customer satisfaction and service quality levels had to be improved, all while introducing a product range and services more relevant to the customer base. The new initiative would affect a staff of 6,500, many of whom had a history of civil service and were used to the perks that came from working for the government. Organizational leaders faced the challenge of managing an ageing workforce, where middle management had a track record of resisting change and not taking full responsibility for the business outcomes. The change programme would introduce a new organizational structure and commercial model, offering new opening hours that better fitted the customers' needs, and improved career paths for each employee. As a result of the transformation, some agencies would be closed; staff transfers would take place; and, for the first time, managers would be given the authority to assign personnel to achieve optimal staffing ratios.

The second programme was a supply chain reconfiguration at a large pharmaceutical company. That initiative called for the introduction of new technologies and ways of working in order to enable more effective process management and warehouse consolidation across the firm's massive supply chain, which spanned 35 countries with different regulatory requirements. Changes in staff roles and responsibilities were designed to improve forecasting, demand management and sales and operations planning. For the programme to be successful, changes in mindsets and behaviours would be needed to attain the full benefits realization. The company had a strong track record of change and had been through many restructurings before, although it had not experienced the size and scale of this type of initiative.

Different strategies, different results

We first tracked the retail group just after an initial pilot programme had been rolled out. We then returned six months later and found that the group had moved from *Struggling under Pressure* to *Bumpy Ride*, following a path that 5 per cent of organizations take. For the supply chain transformation, we first tracked that firm coming out of the design phase and then conducted a second measurement point eight months later. We found that the programme had moved from *Struggling under Pressure* to *On the Run*, a less common and more difficult path that only 2 per cent of organizations take. Figure 11.3, which shows the percentage changes in the driver profile for both change initiatives, tells the story of where each focused its attention and the resulting capacities that were built along the way.

Clearly the retail group had focused its efforts and energy on improving the levels of teamwork, accountability, communication, and vision and direction. It neglected, however, to address issues with systems and processes, and skills and staffing, and people did not pay sufficient attention to building team and business leadership, nor to managing employee emotions.

FIGURE 11.3 Percentage changes in the driver strength as two change programmes moved up the change map

Business Transformation (Retail Group)		Supply Chain Reconfiguration (Pharmaceutical Company)	
Driver	% change	Driver	% change
Teamwork	**+47%**	**Fear and Frustration**	**+79%**
Accountability	**+32%**	**Teamwork**	**+70%**
Communication	**+31%**	**Vision and Direction**	**+62%**
Vision and Direction	**+20%**	**Passion and Drive**	**+55%**
Business Leadership	+6%	**Business Leadership**	**+51%**
Team Leadership	+6%	**Accountability**	**+48%**
Passion and Drive	+3%	**Team Leadership**	**+47%**
Fear and Frustration	*–7%*	**Communication**	**+43%**
Skills and Staffing	*–21%*	Skills and Staffing	+10%
Systems and Processes	*–23%*	Systems and Processes	+10%

Nevertheless, by improving accountability and teamwork, the group tackled the main issues needed to move out of *Struggling under Pressure* and upward into *Bumpy Ride*.

The supply chain reconfiguration also focused on improving teamwork, accountability, communication, and vision and direction, achieving significant improvements in these drivers. In addition, the firm invested heavily in improving the underlying emotional climate by reducing fear and frustration while increasing passion and drive. Moreover, attention was paid to building business and team leaders' capabilities. The strategy was to do what was needed to move out of *Struggling under Pressure* and well up the change map, with the programme eventually making its way to *On the Run*.

The two change programmes were both successful in moving upward from *Struggling under Pressure*, but each faced a significantly different future. Although it may appear that *Bumpy Ride* and *On the Run* are at somewhat similar levels of latitude on the change map, their prospects for growth are quite different. The supply chain group in pharmaceuticals is much better equipped to manage and sustain high growth, because it has a much stronger and better-targeted driver profile. We know from our path analysis that 21 per cent of groups make it to *High Performance* from *On the Run*, whereas only 11 per cent make it from *Bumpy Ride*. Furthermore, only 5 per cent of groups drop down from *On the Run* to the *Unsustainable* or *Off Track* zones, whereas 17 per cent follow that path from *Bumpy Ride*.

The different types and key drivers of change

Although we use the term 'amount of change' to describe the total volume of change occurring in an organization, we recognized early on in our research that there were different categories involved. Initially, we asked staffers about 15 different types of change, including restructures, systems implementations, changes in top management, joint ventures, downsizings, mergers, process changes, changes to staff benefits, changes in culture, and so on. Our analysis narrowed these down to four broad types of change that we now measure and track:

- **When organizations change their shape and size:** this category includes joint ventures, acquisitions and mergers that change the boundaries of the organization. When downsizing occurs, the organization's size is also reduced.

- **When organizations grow their business:** change here consists of the introduction of new products or technology to customers, including diversification of a company's offerings. It can also involve providing new benefits to staff. This type of change creates a sense of growth for the organization, its customers and staff.

- **When organizations reorganize their internal functions:** without changing their boundaries or growing their business, organizations will sometimes restructure and reorganize their internal capabilities. This could include changes in structure, functions, systems and processes. It might also involve a reorientation of business direction, changes in top management, process improvements and IT systems changes. For employees, the resulting impact might consist of different roles, relationships and values, including cultural changes and new ways of working.

- **When organizations change the ways that people work:** this category is actually a subcategory of restructurings but we separate it out to cover cases in which organizations merely 'shuffle the deckchairs'. That is, they will restructure their businesses without producing a change in people's mindsets, a shift in culture, or genuinely novel ways for people to do their jobs.

Obviously, if all categories of change occur at the same time, then the organization will have a major transformation on its hands, and staff will experience a tremendous amount of change. Even then, lots of change is not inherently a bad thing. As we discussed earlier, high-performing organizations tend to thrive on change because they have the right capabilities in place. But what exactly are those capabilities?

Our research tells us that business leadership, vision and direction, teamwork and communication are the key drivers that support and sustain high amounts of change. The results also indicate that the levels of fear and frustration, and risks and roadblocks, typically increase when the amount of change ramps up, while the effects of systems and staffing, skills and processes, accountability and team leadership are not significant. Furthermore, these driver combinations play out differently for each of the four types of change.

Business leadership is the number one driver for organizations altering their size and shape, driving growth and changing the way that people work. It is also an important driver for internal restructurings, but in this type of change other drivers – low fear and frustration, clear vision and direction, and strong teamwork – are much more important. Vision and direction is the second most important driver for growth, restructurings and changing the way that people work, but it is not as important for organizations changing their size and shape. In mergers, for example, the most significant drivers are strong business leadership, low fear and frustration, and strong teamwork. Looking deeper into the drivers of growth, we find that passion and drive, teamwork, and systems and processes come into play along with lowering the levels of fear and frustration. When organizations are changing the ways that people work, teamwork and communication along with lowering fear and frustration take precedence.

These findings help us to understand what we saw in Chapter 3, specifically, what is needed to stop the fall from *Cruising* when the level of growth drops away. In *Cruising*, groups risk becoming 'addicted' to change – the relentless focus and the stimulation – and it is only through strong business leadership, clear vision and direction, high passion and drive, and good teamwork that people can counter this effect and maintain stability when the withdrawal symptoms set in.

Managing change at a fast pace

When we look at the critical capabilities for handling change at a fast pace, we find that the results are unambiguous. Strong business leadership wins by a mile, followed by good communication, highly engaged teamwork and, to a much lesser extent, effective systems and processes. We also find that the level of fear and frustration rises during a period of rapid change and, as we have just mentioned, this needs to be managed as a source of 'increasing adrenaline' rather than an obstacle that eventually derails an initiative. The driver profile for the pace of change is similar to the profile for the amount of change, the difference being that vision is not a requirement for fast pace, but communication plays an even more prominent role.

A syndrome in modern organizations that probably was not so prevalent decades ago is people's absolute level of busyness. This is particularly so for executives and managers, who are often under enormous pressures. When it comes to communications, staffers struggle to schedule prolonged sessions with their supervisors, because management just doesn't seem to have the time for that essential function. High-performing organizations, however, avoid falling into that trap. They recognize that social media might help broaden the channels of communication, enabling more information to circulate more freely, but they are also aware that such technologies cannot replace the quality and effectiveness of face-to-face communications.

In Chapter 3 we saw that, typically speaking, the optimal pace of change for groups was slightly faster than 'okay', but when the pace increases to the highest end of the scale – perceived as 'too fast' by most people – only high-performing groups are able to keep improving their benefits realization and business performance. Other groups that lack any core capability, especially business leadership, will typically unravel when the amount and pace of change increase. We can apply these insights to the two groups that we compared earlier in this chapter.

The pharmaceutical company built up significant capability in the drivers that matter most when it comes to managing a lot of change at a fast pace, namely, business leadership, vision and direction, teamwork and a lower level of fear and frustration. Passion and drive are also important in growth, and the firm paid much more attention to managing that emotional dimension than did the government retail organization. For its part, the government retail group built capacity in the drivers that had some impact on supporting and sustaining large amounts of change – teamwork, communication and, to some extent, vision and direction – but it needed to focus more attention on the main drivers – specifically, building business leadership and reducing fear and frustration – to move higher up the change map.

The result was that the pharmaceutical firm ended up in *On the Run*, where it was positioned near the border of *High Performance*, while the government retail group found itself in *Bumpy Ride*, where it struggled to maintain the positive gains it had made, given the great amount of change that continued to take place at a fast pace. The two regions have considerable differences. In *On the Run*, around 25 per cent of teams experience negative feelings, whereas in *Bumpy Ride* that figure is 50 per cent, reaching the 'tipping point' that we described in Chapter 4. When it comes to positive feelings, around 90 per cent of groups in *On the Run* have them, whereas the corresponding figure for *Bumpy Ride* is about 70 per cent. These results reinforce the importance of monitoring positive and negative feelings as lead indicators, as we discussed in Chapter 5.

Knowing where and when to take action

Traditionally, the 'mystique' of skilful change management was locked up in a lifetime of change expertise. We are reminded of the story of the factory owner whose boiler had broken. He called an experienced engineer who walked around the boiler, listening to the sounds it was emitting, and then took out his hammer and firmly hit a part of the equipment. The boiler then quickly started up, returning to operation. For that work, the engineer charged $1,000, a fee that infuriated the factory owner. 'You were barely here for 30 minutes!' the owner exclaimed. The engineer replied, 'Well, my fee was $100 for the 30 minutes of my time, and the remaining $900 was for knowing exactly where to strike the boiler'.

When it comes to organizational change, 'knowing exactly where to strike the boiler' is not some arcane secret known to just a select few. Indeed, as we have seen throughout this book, our driver analysis helps unlock the dynamics of each capital city, revealing the underlying patterns so that leaders can accurately assess what actions are required, and then systematically work with different combinations of drivers to move up the change map.

We have seen with our 10 drivers that some actions are easier to implement, while others are more difficult and require a greater commitment of resources, time and effort. A discussion around staff roles and relationships, for example, is one of the least threatening interventions and can become part of a person's regular job performance review. Following up those discussions by putting accountability in place can be a relatively simple process when organizations have effective performance management systems and have systematically trained their leaders for that task.

When it comes to teamwork, communication, and even vision and direction, most organizations have a standard vocabulary of actions and predefined tools and methodologies for use across the organization. In the case of the government retail group, for example, managers effectively used such resources to move further up the change map, but this only got them so far. They had improved team leadership by 15 per cent, yet trust in organizational and business unit leaders had dropped by 10–15 per cent. In fact, all levels of trust were below the norm, which meant that the group lacked the leadership strength to move any further up the change map. People were in new territory and were not equipped to work with deeper-level emotions, nor had leaders ever talked openly about what was needed to build trust and gain greater alignment.

Managing deep emotions

To be sure, working with deep emotions and building trust requires time and patience, and the process depends heavily on leaders' skills and knowledge. Some of the most difficult interventions involve bringing personal feelings and the underlying interpersonal dynamics into the open for personal reflection or for team discussion. Although many leadership teams shy away from these kinds of discussions, because they are typically uncomfortable or unfamiliar with them, our analysis tells us that the process cannot be avoided if groups want to make progress towards high performance.

Tim Dalmau, who writes about organizational growth and decline (Dalmau, 2014), sees decline as the enemy of growth and stresses the importance of leaders being able firstly to spot when decline starts to take place and secondly to assess the correct level at which the problems exist so that they can take the appropriate actions at that level or deeper. Only by doing so can leaders recycle decline back into growth. Dalmau also states that actions taken at a higher level will be ineffective, and in fact they may further accelerate the problems to burrow deeper and deeper into the organization.

From our research we have seen that as people become more fearful, losing both a sense of where they are headed and the capability to keep moving forward, they tend to fall further and further down the change map. First they question operational practices, then the rational purposes of what the organization is doing and why. Eventually the questions become more emotional than logical, corrupting the very foundations of the change programme. Moreover, as the fear becomes more widespread and pervasive, people could begin to question why the organization as a whole even exists. Skilled leaders know how to turn these situations around by, as Dalmau asserts, taking the appropriate actions at the right level or deeper. Unfortunately, though, many executives end up focusing their attention at the wrong level.

The leaders in the government retail group discussed in this chapter, for example, concentrated on improving teamwork, accountability, communications, and vision and direction. Those actions helped move people out of *Struggling under Pressure* but then the group ran into much deeper issues when it landed in *Bumpy Ride* – namely, high fear and frustration, and low levels of trust, particularly with respect to business unit and organizational leaders. If leaders had continued to focus on teamwork, communication and vision – and even if they had executed their plan brilliantly – they would not have been able to move the organization further up the change map because the real problems were elsewhere. Moreover, staff would see these actions as 'missing the main point' and, until the actual issues were addressed, people would feel that they had not been listened to, which would then erode their confidence in leadership.

The lesson here is that interventions need to be made at sufficient depth to resolve critical issues. If, for example, they are made without first creating a safe and trusting environment, they may lead to more problems than people can deal with in the time available, potentially causing more damage than good. We saw this previously in Chapter 9 with the watermelon story, where out of the people's fear they 'killed the messenger'. On the other hand, if actions are taken too superficially, they will bounce off the organization, having little or no impact. Furthermore, when working at the deepest levels of organizational culture and values, leaders should not focus their attention on only logical and rational matters. Instead they also need to concentrate on deep emotions and trust, even if such issues are among the most difficult types to resolve.

Supporting and sustaining high levels of growth

The leader's task in *On the Run* is to ensure that teams at all levels have the capabilities to support and sustain high performance, that is, to ensure the organization constantly remains in a 'healthy state', one that enables people to thrive on growth. People should feel invigorated (rather than becoming exhausted or addicted) to the fast pace, as this is ultimately what fuels innovation and provides the greatest benefits.

In *On the Run*, the highest risk to continual growth is that the organization becomes fragmented under the constant pressure for change, and people start to doubt where they are heading. To avoid that, leaders need to gather staff together for open discussions in order to regroup and rebuild team cohesion, especially before launching new stages of an initiative. Staffers who might see themselves as not having influence or control over their workloads and outcomes become empowered when they feel a stronger sense of connection with others on their teams. This can also give everyone a renewed sense of purpose.

In such discussions, leaders, managers and staffers tend to engage mainly in the obvious conversations, focusing on solving operational problems: 'How do we obtain the necessary resources to manage the workload?' and 'How do we gain greater role clarity to enable day-to-day operations to run more smoothly?' But if the talk is only about operational matters, leaders miss the most important levels of communication needed to maintain peak performance.

Since the earliest times, people sitting around the campfire and telling stories have been an essential part of any journey. Such conversations are a valuable way for people to connect and share their experiences, and change travellers are no different. Even in work environments that have become increasingly virtual, this age-old ritual remains one of the most powerful mechanisms for leaders to bring stability and cohesion in times of rapid change and growth.

In the workplace, storytelling is most effective when it speaks to the deepest levels of corporate culture and values – when it renews people's sense of 'who we are' and 'why we are here', both with respect to individuals as well as the organization as a whole. When people's questions are answered emotionally, not intellectually, they walk away with a renewed sense of purpose that enables them to tackle day-to-day difficulties without becoming overwhelmed or losing track of the details of what they are doing. Open and honest storytelling creates shared meaning, breaks down barriers, overcomes entrenched positions and makes more energy available to focus on the tasks at hand.

To master company growth, leaders must accept that setbacks and doubt are a natural part of the process. They will encounter new situations and must understand that innovation comes with risk. Instead of avoiding the unknown, they need to take advantage of the promising opportunities that might arise. Discussions 'around the campfire' can be very effective in such circumstances to help people deal with the bumps and bruises that will inevitably occur along the way. Through such conversations, leaders can answer the most pressing staff questions: 'Why are we afraid of this change?' 'What weaknesses do we need to shore up?' 'What doubts does the leadership have, and what doubts do staffers have?' Here, leaders should avoid manipulating the discussion to arrive at a predetermined outcome. Instead they should lead with a genuine desire to open the conversation to the very issues that need the most attention, especially those that might have previously been deemed 'undiscussable'. Our ability to imagine the worst only becomes a problem when it enables fear to take over, impairing people's ability to perform their jobs. Highly disciplined teamwork, good leadership and a strong sense of purpose can help to control and contain our fears so that they do not become overwhelming.

The value of early warning systems

Early warning systems can be an effective mechanism to battle fear. When venturing into territory where lots of change is occurring at a fast pace, savvy leaders are always keenly aware of staff stress levels. They are constantly monitoring the questions people ask and checking that these are addressed at all levels of the organization. Such leaders also ensure that mechanisms are in place to quickly detect any operational lapses – declines in the quality of products, service, delivery, and so on. In fact, leaders in this situation constantly ask the question, even when things are going well, 'If this initiative were to derail right now, where would the failure come from?' From the outside looking in, it might seem like these leaders are not doing much because everything appears to be running smoothly, but this is the mark of true change leaders – they are adept at anticipating problems in advance and taking action long before things go awry.

At the pharmaceutical company discussed earlier, the main reason why the supply chain reconfiguration managed to position itself strongly for growth in *On the Run* is because leaders took action not only to address the stated problems at the operational levels of 'what do we do?' and 'how do we do it?' but, more importantly, they also focused on addressing the deeper questions of 'why are we here?' and 'who are we?' Through that process, they were able to lower people's fear and frustration while building passion and drive, business leadership, and vision and direction. Moreover, they were able to realign the trust levels among different leaders so that they were all working for a common purpose, reaffirming the staff's belief that the entire organization was on the right path.

Common pathways exiting *On the Run*

On the Run is one of the most common destinations for groups on the change map: 22 per cent of groups remain there, either content to stay in the region or unable to adequately address issues of communication, and business and team leadership. Let's take a closer look at some of the main pathways leading out of *On the Run* (Figure 11.4). We discuss each of those pathways below, highlighting some case examples in more depth. (Note: the examples in this section represent a composite of organizations from our research with similar experiences of change.)

FIGURE 11.4   Pathways exiting *On the Run*

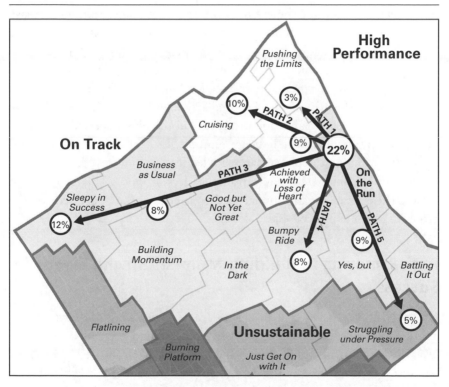

Path 1: *moving to* Pushing the Limits

On this path, 3 per cent of groups are able to move from *On the Run* to the very top of the change map, reaching *Pushing the Limits*, and we have only seen smaller groups make it, never entire organizations. The interesting feature is that no further increases in the amount and pace of change are needed – the trajectory is set – but significant increases in most drivers are needed. This leads to substantial increases in benefits and performance, particularly customer service levels, demonstrating the service excellence mindset that these groups possess.

Path 2: moving to Cruising and Achieved with Loss of Heart

Another 19 per cent of groups make it to *High Performance* but 10 per cent of those groups wind up in *Cruising* and another 9 per cent land in *Achieved with Loss of Heart*. Consider the example of a private equity firm that sold its building and construction business in piecemeal fashion. That decision was a huge shock to the cement division, resulting in a significant increase in fear and frustration levels. As rumours swirled, risks and roadblocks increased while morale dropped, with people feeling unappreciated. Employees soon became less confident that the change would improve performance, and the number of people thinking of leaving increased. Fortunately, performance stayed at similarly high levels to those in *On the Run*, though benefits realization dropped. On the plus side, under the new management, all units were held accountable for achieving objectives, and communication increased. Trust in team leaders also improved, but trust in the mix of old and new organizational leaders dropped. This gap in trust between team and organizational leaders needed to be addressed for the group to retain its best people.

Path 3: moving to Building Momentum and Sleepy in Success

On this pathway, 8 per cent of groups travel to *Building Momentum* and another 12 per cent to *Sleepy in Success*. The sand and gravel division of the private equity firm discussed above experienced the latter move. The business had previously operated across a number of international borders, but now each country operated in isolation, no longer concerned with the organization as a whole and effectively ignoring the change. In this situation, all drivers, business performance and benefits realization declined substantially. The root of the problem was a loss of trust in the groups across borders, resulting in a collapse in the very dynamics that had held together this large, unified, international team.

Path 4: moving to Bumpy Ride

On this pathway 8 per cent of groups travel to *Bumpy Ride*. An example of this was the specialized demolitions division of the private equity firm mentioned above. That business was divested, leading to an increased amount of change – with new customers and new technical demands and challenges. This led to considerable stress and strain for the commercial and sales groups. The business had, for instance, taken on a technically difficult and extensive project that required new techniques and much higher safety precautions. The organization struggled to meet these needs as key staff had left and were replaced with inexperienced operators. Fear and frustration took over and trust in top management plummeted. Business and team leadership also declined significantly. Benefits and performance likewise dropped, and the number of people thinking of leaving increased. As people left, the loss of knowledgeable and specialized talent became crippling, and the *Bumpy Ride* was in full effect.

Path 5: moving to Struggling under Pressure and Yes, but

On this path, 9 per cent of groups fall to the adjacent region of *Yes, but* and another 5 per cent move further down to *Struggling under Pressure*. The former design centre of the private equity firm discussed earlier followed the latter path. A building industry association bought the design centre and expected it to become its flagship innovation centre. Staff received this news badly, however, and the inept handling of the transformation led to a plunge in all drivers, except systems and processes, and skills and staffing, which remained about the same. However, the resources now at people's disposal did not make up for the lack of leadership and vision. Emotional energy swung to the negative as people were *Struggling under Pressure*.

Building organizational agility

In this chapter, we focused on *On the Run*, the last of the nine capital cities on the change map. This region is characterized by tremendous change, both in terms of the overall amount of change as well as its pace. Here leaders struggle to meet ambitious growth expectations, and the danger is that they might overwhelm staffers and burn them out with too much change, too quickly. Yet those organizations that can build the necessary capabilities to handle lots of change at a fast pace will gain the competitive advantage of agility. As we will see in Chapter 12, the core competency of agility has become all the more important in today's increasingly turbulent business environment.

SUMMARY FOR CHAPTER 11: KEY INSIGHTS

- *On the Run* holds the key to understanding how best to manage high amounts of change at a fast pace.

- High-performing groups have 30–50 per cent more change taking place than low-performing groups.

- Under conditions of considerable change, business leadership, vision and direction, teamwork and communication are critical foundations that bring stability to the organization.

- Strong levels of trust between leaders, and clear vision and direction, enable organizations to improve business performance and realize significant benefits while the amount and pace of change ramp up.

- Ramping up the amount and pace of change without first building the capabilities needed to remain on course is a very risky change strategy.

- Typically, when the amount and pace of change increase, fear and frustration increases, and risks and roadblocks become greater, but groups in *On the Run* defy this trend and keep them low. They build individual and organizational resilience in the face of high uncertainty in order to increase the likelihood of riding out each wave of change.

- In high-performing groups, benefits increase as the amount of change goes up. In low-performing groups, benefits quickly level out and drop away.

- Benefits arrive more quickly when the pace of change is ramped up but so do the consequences of poor decision-making. When there is less room for error, well-managed change is the secret to maintaining stability and control.

- Organizations can go at a fast pace if they have strong business leadership, good communication and highly engaged teamwork.

- When the pace moves to 'too fast' for most people, it is only high-performing groups that can maintain cohesion at this speed and keep improving business performance and benefits.

- It is hard to sustain high levels of change and a fast pace over a long period of time. Groups do not stay in *On the Run* for very long. Conscious choices must be made whether to stay the course by building stronger capabilities and pushing harder, which risks burning people out, or to reduce the amount and pace of change.

- Wise business leaders venturing into the territory of rapid change keep a close eye on fear and frustration levels in order to remain in a 'healthy state'. To do so, they implement early warning systems to quickly pick up deteriorations in quality, so that they can take fast corrective action.

Vision for the future
Changing the way we change

12

> *He who understands love, is not equal to he who loves,*
> *and he who loves is not equal to he who delights in loving.*
>
> **CONFUCIUS**

The stakes for businesses could not be higher. Now, more than ever, organizations need to address a fundamental challenge that will increasingly determine whether or not they prosper – or even survive. Change will no longer be about the success of individual projects or programmes; instead it will predominantly be about whether organizations as a whole have the capability to successfully manage change on a daily basis. In short, the competence to manage continual change will need to be woven into the very fabric of the way that organizations do business.

Towards the agile organization

Far-sighted executives have already recognized the critical importance of not only addressing geopolitical and macroeconomic risks, but also managing other disruptive forces such as digital technologies, dramatic changes in customer behaviours and threats from new and highly innovative global competitors. Indeed, with greater unpredictability in the business environment, agility has become a prized capability. For organizations, this means having the nimbleness to execute on new business strategies, to introduce products in new and emerging markets, to restructure to better satisfy customer needs, and so on.

There is, however, considerable debate about the combination of capabilities that go into building an agile organization. To be sure, many factors need to be considered: a company's market position and its business portfolio, products, services and technologies mix; how it structures and organizes its operating model; the role of its human capital strategies; and so on. Whatever combinations of these elements that an organization prioritizes – what needs to be built, what needs to stay and what needs to go – they all involve making changes. As such, it is not surprising that our research shows that organizations that attain the highest levels of performance are those that truly thrive on change. Such organizations are faster and more responsive to unpredictable events in the business environment, and that agility comes from a strong core competence of managing change.

The goal now is to implement change in a more holistic way, building change capability into the heart of the organization, making it easier for people to achieve and sustain high performance levels over the long run. In the past, big-ticket change initiatives were treated as separate and discrete programmes with a beginning, a middle and an end. The focus was on change being well managed in each initiative. Going forward, the emphasis will be on creating a broader organizational ability to be adaptable and agile in all programmes, all of the time. Implementing an initiative means managing multiple, overlapping systems – such as rapidly fluctuating international financial markets, global supply chains and social media – in which various changes are taking place simultaneously. Well-managed change will simply be part of the way that organizations do business in the future. In other words, the focus will be on enterprise-wide capabilities for managing change, and when that core competence is attained the organization will be able to handle just about any change project or programme. And that, fundamentally, is what organizational agility is all about.

Change leaders at all levels

But how can enterprise-wide capabilities for managing change be achieved? We have seen throughout this book that the best approach is to master all of the drivers of change and the capability to unlock the most difficult problems in each of the nine capital cities. In addition, a deeper and more fundamental shift is now needed in that people must 'change the way they change'. In other words, widespread behavioural change is needed in order to make organizational agility sustainable in the longer term. This means that *all* individuals must accept personal responsibility and accountability for change, with direction being set from the top down. The Conference Board summarized that finding in its 2015 annual survey, in which CEOs of global corporations were asked to report on their most pressing business challenges. Their response was: 'organizations must focus on behavioural change to make change more sustainable and become agile. It is about helping people embrace and adopt change by building personal competencies... It is about installing personal responsibility and accountability for change at every level. The focus should be on developing change leaders at all levels, not just reactive change managers' (Mitchell *et al*, 2015).

Indeed, the goal is not to push change management methodology down to the rank and file but to achieve organizational self-sufficiency, in which all employees are enabled to personally manage change and deal with its effects. To that end, **the approach to managing change is shifting from one dominated by an external 'change expert', in which employees are consulted, to a process in which change practitioners help people to help themselves by building resilience and by taking personal responsibility for their actions.** In doing so, organizations are becoming better equipped with the capabilities to manage continual change indefinitely.

Of course, it would be very convenient if there were a nice, neat, linear relationship between what people do, how they respond to change and the impact of those actions on business outcomes, but we know that this is not the case. As such, more emphasis on the use of insight from sophisticated measurement systems and techniques will become the norm to help leaders and their teams at all levels to trace the cause-and-effect relationships between their individual and team behaviours and business outcomes. We have seen how good maps and the systems to track organizational travellers' progress enable multiple, complex and interrelated change variables, and the interactions between them, to be turned into insights and actionable results. This empowers leaders to take greater ownership and personal responsibility for the outcomes of their groups, in addition to fine-tuning any interventions to stay on course.

When it comes to 'changing the way we change', top leaders' attitudes and actions have a powerful effect on the work environment. One of the most important assets of an organization is a top management team that learns quickly by thinking and doing, fostering an open-minded culture. That culture, in turn, will support and sustain innovative ways of working, including organizational changes in structure, to gain the most from the benefits that new technologies can bring. Leaders, for their part, can accelerate innovation by encouraging experimentation and by reinforcing the message that setbacks along the way are not failures but a natural part of the learning process. The bottom line is that, for an organization to be truly agile, it must deftly manage trade-offs between cost-effective efficiency and the flexibility needed for innovations to occur.

Building the capacity to continually change

In the future, organizations that want to attain even higher levels of agility will need to become increasingly sophisticated about the ways in which they manage change. Insights provided from real-time change analytics accompanied by deeper skills and change capability hold the key to continually managing change indefinitely. From our research, we see that the leading-edge businesses will significantly improve their capacity to manage change in the coming years through the use of the following:

- 'change-smart' platforms;
- business support from change navigators;
- bottom-up teams;
- communities built around change.

Let's take a closer look at each of these important components.

'Change-smart' platforms

In the coming era, so-called 'change-smart' platforms could potentially make a huge difference in the way that organizations manage change. Such platforms will support decision-making, guide change navigation in real time so that people can immediately find the best course of action, and enable everyone to share information and learn from one another.

The use of 'smart' digital technologies can provide the means to manage and scale change in a way that organizations have never had access to before. For example, new technologies will allow real-time feedback with a simple user interface for people to interact with others and discuss results, making analytics accessible and usable. Much like interactive maps on a smartphone, this will change the way that people manage change. Change-smart platforms will enable individuals and teams to gain quick access to the information they need, when it is needed. Moreover, multiple views can be accessed as users interact with the data, enabling people to follow their line of inquiry and not be restricted to others' views of what they consider to be important. In addition, data visualization tools, such as the change map, will provide the capability to create, use and share information among many users simultaneously.

Change-smart platforms should enable leaders to dramatically speed up their response times. As data is collected across multiple projects and programmes across the organization, leaders will be able to 'visualize' the strengths of the drivers for which they are responsible – vision and direction, accountability, skills and staffing, and so on. With that knowledge, they can take rapid action before problems become major issues. For staff, the frustrating lag of months between completing a survey to receiving any feedback – which ultimately reinforces the message that management is out of touch – can be reduced dramatically. As soon as people click the submit button on a survey, for example, they can view video clips from executives clarifying the situation. Specific groups or individuals can also receive instant, tailored messages regarding suggested actions and, if required, information about whom to contact for support.

Applications running off a change-smart platform – including crowd-sourcing, online events, 30-day challenges and gaming software – can help tackle even the most difficult organizational problems. Such technology would enable systemic issues to be identified and then solved by anyone across the organization, encouraging people with different perspectives to have a say. In this way, more imagination and creativity can be brought to bear, offering new solutions while breaking down silo mentalities. Gamification and gaming software, for instance, can tap into people's competitive nature to tackle problems in novel ways. Also, simulation applications will enable leaders and teams to perform 'what if' scenario-planning, exploring potential pathways and identifying possible roadblocks and obstacles along the way.

Support from change navigators

Organizations can nurture the talents of 'change analytics teams' to provide fact-based decision support to business improvement programmes. Highly qualified data scientists would sit at the centre of change teams, collecting and analysing data and acting as internal consultants supporting the business in their decision-making. The roles of these new-era change navigators, who speak the language of business but also know the data science, could help bridge that gap. Their roles in working with and inside change analytics teams could include the following:

- collecting and maintaining datasets in many forms such as surveys, texts, social media, voice, images and video;
- using sophisticated analytics to establish a common language for managers to talk about change;
- tracking change programmes, showing the actions that lead to success and those that cause change to go off track;

- testing assumptions linking change measures back to financial outcomes and other key performance indicators (KPIs);

- sharing best practices among leaders and through change communities, debunking myths and highlighting the lessons learned.

Change analytics teams can be instrumental in reinforcing specific messages – for example, that a group needs to increase its accountability – by linking survey responses to actual KPIs and other business metrics. As data become available, automated algorithms running on the change-smart platform can send alerts to business leaders. This is similar to how electrical sensing devices pick up changes in environmental conditions and trigger alerts, only in this case the 'sensors' are picking up signals from human dimensions, such as fear levels reaching critical risk thresholds.

We are currently undertaking work that would allow us to predict the region where a group is positioned on the change map just by analysing the text of a sample of respondents in that group, using a mixture of measures of their psychological state and the situation in which they find themselves. Using text collected from a variety of sources – written survey responses, comments from a workshop and social media posts, for example – we can then position a group in a region, and start to make accurate statements about what those individuals might best do to improve their performance. In such ways, organizations will be able to track and manage change in more of a 'real-time' fashion.

Bottom-up teams

When teams know their position on the change map, they can access the collective wisdom of other travellers who have been in similar situations before, providing a much wider source of knowledge. When enabled by a change-smart platform, teams can quickly locate where they are, understand the issues they are facing, and see how other teams in that position have succeeded or failed in the past. They can then use that information to plan their own course, setting targets and priorities. The platform would also enable teams to track their progress along the way, confirming or not that the decisions they are making are good ones. During any journey, managers and leaders can be sought out for support, additional resources or advice, but if a team is moving steadily up the map it does not need to ask others if it is doing the right things. In other words, when it comes to finding the optimal path forward, teams' options would not be limited by what top management considers to be the best alternatives, especially if executives are completely out of touch with what is happening at other levels in the organization.

In addition, technology has removed boundaries that have traditionally controlled the flow of information across time zones, organizational levels and groups. Platforms for collaboration can help locate answers to be shared with others in the organization. Not only does this enable teams to broaden their knowledge, it also helps leaders and managers to gain visibility about what is actually going on. Leaders know some things but teams know more. Tapping into what a team knows, however, is not always easy. Fostering open and honest conversation can be difficult, especially in times of change, when fear and mistrust are prevalent. But because the issues and concerns are already generally known for groups positioned in any region on the change map, conversations can be facilitated more quickly and in a more open and straightforward manner in order to overcome barriers and get to the root causes of even the most difficult issues. It is one thing for team members in a fear-laden climate to risk speaking out in the presence of managers who hold the power of repercussions over them. It is quite another thing when managers and employees have in front of them, as objective evidence, the issues that confront them in a particular region.

Such transparency of information – the team's view of itself and its view of leaders, as well as the potential interventions – allows all parties to distance themselves dispassionately from the personal baggage of the evidence, and ask: 'Given what we see in front of us, what would reasonable people do, working together?' Focusing everyone's attention on the objective data in that way ultimately helps empower teams, providing them with the 'ammunition' they need to make their case for additional resources, stronger business leadership, better systems and processes, and so on.

Communities built around change

According to Mark Zuckerberg, the CEO of Facebook, there is no need to create communities – because they already exist. All that is needed is to put 'elegant organizations' around them (Jarvis, 2007). People talk regularly about the impact of change initiatives, and they seek answers and want to share information about what has worked and what has not worked. There is no stopping participation when communities are built around genuine interests and, with the advent of the internet, online communities can connect people easily over different time zones and cities. A problem in the past, though, has been the lack of a 'common language' to talk about change. The change map – with its 20 regions, including 9 capital cities, 10 drivers, different pathways between regions, and other aspects – can provide that common language for communities to discuss and engage in change.

Using that common language, people can more easily interact, share and learn. They can gather around maps and models developed from others' experience of change, exchanging valuable information about the dos and don'ts of implementing initiatives. After people have identified where they are on the change map, they generally want to know, 'Where do I go from here and how do I get there?' They have a choice to make, even if that decision is to stay within the same region. Through communities, people are encouraged to share information with those who are or have been under similar circumstances, and they can learn about what actions tend to lead to success – or failure. Digital technologies can help enhance such information exchanges. Leaders, their teams and others can upload user-generated content such as videos to an online platform to show, for example, how they managed to reduce fear and frustration to improve the performance of a particular group. Any individual can comment on or share that information with others, and those responses from members of the community can be used to bring best practices to the forefront.

It is important to note here that there is a huge advantage in a metaphor like a change map that shows people where they and their co-workers are located. When all teams along a business value chain can see where everyone else is, the business strategy becomes much like climbers roped together as they ascend a mountain. People know that if one person falls they are all at risk and therefore will be more inclined to actively help one another to succeed. That type of mentality helps support and sustain broader change communities, creating a greater sense of shared responsibility.

Towards a new era

We are now on the cusp of a new era, where we will need to expand our focus beyond the limitations of the organization as a standalone system and take into account its integration into the larger economic, social and environmental ecosystem. New forms of virtual businesses and networks are making organizational boundaries more fluid, and change is seen as a continual process of adaptation to constantly fluctuating external conditions. The result has been that organizations are now increasingly being challenged with managing change at a scale and speed never encountered before.

Some readers – faced with a dramatic step change in the scientific knowledge needed to successfully navigate change and the growing use of sophisticated technologies – may be asking themselves, 'Is there still a place for the knowledge I have accumulated, the experience I have gained and the change leadership skills I have developed?' The answer is unequivocally yes. We began this book by sharing what we sometimes jokingly referred to in our analysis and results as an 'excuse' to have difficult discussions about the real issues of organizational change. In the business world, the reality is that people generally need hard data in order to talk about softer and more intangible issues. Throughout our research, we never lost sight that our purpose was to accurately identify important issues and have the conversations required to better drive and manage change. This is still very much the case now and into the far future.

Over the past 15 years, the wisdom of travellers has been our source of knowledge, and the mantra 'Let the data do the talking' our inspiration for inquiry. Our hope is that this book will act as a catalyst in promoting discussion among all parties intimately connected with change inside modern organizations. We would like to see business leaders, teams, change practitioners and researchers working together to find new ways of operating, new paradigms of changing. We have set out along the path of insight-driven change. We believe we have traced the paths left behind by the change travellers who have gone before us. We extend an invitation to you, the broader audience, to help light up the way to the future.

REFERENCES

Bertrand, J and Robinson, P (1985) *Born to Win: A lifelong struggle to capture the America's Cup*, William Morrow, New York

Brynjolfsson, E and McAfee, A (2014) *The Second Machine Age: Work, progress, and prosperity in a time of brilliant technologies*, W.W. Norton & Company

Conner, DR (1993) *Managing at the Speed of Change: How resilient managers succeed and prosper where others fail*, Random House, New York

Covey, S (2008) *The Speed of Trust*, Free Press, New York

Dalmau, T (2014) [accessed 30 June 2015] Cycles and Levels of Organizational Life, *Dalmau Consulting* [Online] http://www.dalmau.com/wp-content/uploads/2014/02/Cycles-Paper1.pdf

Deci, E (1975) *Intrinsic Motivation*, Plenum Publishing Co, New York

Dweck, C (2006) *Mindset: The new psychology of success*, Random House, New York

Frost, CF (1996) *Changing Forever: The well-kept secret of America's leading companies*, Michigan State University Press, East Lansing, Michigan

Gates, B (1995) *The Road Ahead*, Viking Penguin, New York

Hillary, E (1955) *High Adventure: The true story of the first ascent of Everest*, Dutton, New York

Hurley, RF (2006) The decision to trust, *Harvard Business Review*, **84** (9), September, pp 55–62

Jarvis, J (2007) [accessed 30 June 2015] Media Owners: Ask not what Facebook can do for you, *The Guardian* [Online] http://www.theguardian.com/media/2007/jun/11/mondaymediasection.news

Kerpner, J (2004) When the Killer Whale Came Panicked Herrings in Fishnet, *Aftonbladet*, 8 January

Kposowa, AJ and D'Auria, S (2010) Association of temporal factors and suicides in the United States, 2000–2004, *Social Psychiatry Epidemiology*, **45**, pp 433–45

Krakauer, J (1997) *Into Thin Air: A personal account of the Mt. Everest disaster*, Villard, New York

Kübler-Ross, E (1973) *On Death and Dying*, Routledge, New York

McFadden, RD (2008) Sir Edmund Hillary, a Pioneering Conqueror of Everest, Dies at 88, *The New York Times* (Online edition), 10 January

Mitchell, C, Ray, RL and van Ark, B (2015) Creating Opportunity out of Adversity – Building Innovative, People-Driven Organizations, The Conference Board CEO Challenge 2015

Murray, W (2011) *Military Adaptation in War: With fear of change*, Cambridge University Press, Cambridge

Pink, D (2009) *Drive: The surprising truth about what motivates us*, Riverhead Books, New York

Reedy, H (2012) *Maori At War: Ngarimu VC battle for PT209 March 1943*, Kindle Edition

Richmond, FL and Schepman, S (2005) Fifty years of employee motivation surveys: three from the final half of the twentieth century, *Journal of Organizational Culture, Communications and Conflict*, **9** (2) July

The Global Agenda: Competing in a Digital World, CEO Briefing 2014, Accenture & The Economist Intelligence Unit

Weick, K (1979) *Social Psychology of Organizing*, Random House, New York

Yoshikawa, E (1981) *Musashi*, trans. Charles S Terry, Harper, New York

Zenger, J and Folkman, J (2014) Your employees want the negative feedback you hate to give, *Harvard Business Review*, 15 January

INDEX

Note: *italics* indicate a Figure or Table in the text.